The Nagas

Groups of men sitting beneath eaves. Chang, Tuensang village. 1936. CFH.

(Cover) Naga posed with a collection of objects. 1875. RGW.

Hill Peoples of Northeast India

The Nagas

Society, Culture and the Colonial Encounter

Julian Jacobs

with Alan Macfarlane, Sarah Harrison and Anita Herle

Thames and Hudson

Sema youths kick fighting in front of carved Y-posts.
1913-23. JHH.

First published in Great Britain in 1990 by
Thames and Hudson Ltd, London

First published in hardcover in the United States of America in 1990 by
Thames and Hudson Inc., 500 Fifth Avenue, New York, New York 10110

First paperback edition 1998

British Library Cataloguing-in-Publication Data
A catalogue record for this book is available from the British Library

ISBN 0-500-97471-3
Library of Congress Catalog Card Number 90-70288

Printed in Thailand

Key to field photographs

Where no institution is given, the photographs are from private collections.

CFH : Christoph von Fürer-Haimendorf

CP : Collection of Sir Charles Pawsey, Centre for South Asian Studies, Cambridge

CS : C.R. Stonor, Pitt Rivers Museum Archive, Oxford

HNL : Hseng Noung Lintner

JA : Joyce Angami

JHH : J.H. Hutton, Pitt Rivers Museum Archive, Oxford

JPM, PR : J.P.Mills, Pitt Rivers Museum Archive, Oxford

JPM, SOAS: J.P. Mills, School of Oriental and African Studies Archive

SK : Sunil Khilnani

RGW : R.G. Woodthorpe, Pitt Rivers Museum Archive, Oxford

UGB : Ursula Graham Bower (Betts), Pitt Rivers Museum Archive, Oxford

WGA : W.G. Archer

Key to Colour Plates

All photographs by Heini Schneebeli.

CUMAA : Cambridge University Museum of Archaeology and Anthropology

MOM : Museum of Mankind (The Trustees of the British Museum)

PC : Private Collection

PR : Pitt Rivers Museum, Oxford

The principal collectors whose objects figure in the museum collections include (with approximate dates of their period in the Naga Hills):

Henry Balfour (1922-3);

Capt. John Butler (1869-75);

Ursula Graham Bower (1937-46);

Christoph von Fürer-Haimendorf (1936-7);

J.H. Hutton (1909-35);

J.P. Mills (1916-38);

Sir Charles Pawsey (1920-48);

Col. R.G. Woodthorpe (1875-6).

Contents

Acknowledgments

This work, which attempts to combine historical and anthropological perspectives, is very much a collective effort by members of the Cambridge Experimental Videodisc Project on the Nagas. I wish to thank my colleagues Alan Macfarlane, Sarah Harrison and Anita Herle, for their advice and encouragement over the several years in which the Naga videodisc, museum exhibition and book have come to fruition.

The Project is indebted to the many individuals and institutions who have made textual and visual materials available to us, or who have willingly shared their knowledge and experience of the subject, and to others who have helped with research and data preparation: Mildred Archer; the late Ursula Graham Bower; Lily Das; Niu Lungalong; Ben Gellner; Janet Hall; Barbara and Julian Harding; Vibha Joshi; Pamela Mills; Schuyler Jones, Ruth Barnes, Bob Rivers, Helene la Rue, Elizabeth Edwards and staff at the Pitt Rivers Museum, Oxford; David Phillipson, Paul Sant Cassia and staff at the University Museum of Archaeology and Anthropology, Cambridge; Lionel Carter and staff at the Centre for South Asian Studies, University of Cambridge; Dr. Brian Durrans and staff at the Museum of Mankind, London; Dr. Deborah Swallow and staff at the Victoria and Albert Museum, London; staff at the Library and Archive, School of Oriental and African Studies, London; staff at the Royal Geographical Society, London; staff at the India Office Library and Records, London. I wish to acknowledge the thinking of Andrew Gray and Andrew West, whose unpublished work on the Nagas has been of particular help in the writing of this book.

Our biggest debt is to Professor Christoph von Fürer-Haimendorf, whose fieldwork materials and pioneering photographs have been extensively drawn upon in this book.

Sections of the book in an early form were read by Professor Rodney Needham, Andrew Gray, Andrew West and Dr. Leo Howe. I am grateful for their comments. Remaining errors of fact or interpretation are of course mine. To Cherry Bryant I am grateful for a thorough reading of the entire text. My thanks also to our publisher and fellow Naga enthusiast, Hansjörg Mayer, and to Heini Schneebeli for his photography of museum artefacts.

The Project gratefully acknowledges funding from the Economic and Social Research Council; the Leverhulme Trust; the Nuffield Foundation; the Crowther-Benyon Fund, University of Cambridge; the Wyse Fund, Trinity College, Cambridge; and King's College, Cambridge.

Julian Jacobs
Cambridge, December 1989

Head-receiving dance.
Man wearing a huge hat decorated with hornbill beaks and feathers, horns and goat's hair tassels. Konyak, Wakching village. 1936. CFH.

CHINA

THE NAGA TRIBES

c1931

I N D I A

Nagaland

BURMA

Konyak

Phom

ASSAM

Ao

Chang

Lhota

Sema

Kalyo- Kengyu

NAGA HILLS DISTRICT

UNADMINISTERED

AREA

BURMA

NORTH CACHAR

W. Rengma

HILLS DISTRICT

Yimchungr

Sangtam

Angami

E. Rengma

Kabui

10 miles

Zemi

Tangkhul

MANIPUR

8

Chapter 1

Introduction

'The King Worm went down to the bottom of the water and made worm casts until he had made all the earth, and the crow patted it flat and smooth, but by the time he came to do the hills he was too tired to flatten them properly, and that is why the plains are smooth and the hills are steep and full of cliffs.' [1]

In the mythology of the Zemi Nagas, the hills and the plains are recognised as opposed but complementary. The geographical distinctiveness of the hills and plains is matched by the cultural distinctiveness of their respective populations. The Nagas are quintessentially a hill people. Today numbering over one million, the Nagas are spread throughout the Indian states of Nagaland, Arunachal Pradesh and Manipur, and parts of Burma. The majority of them live in Nagaland, and it is with them that this book is mainly concerned. [2]

The people of the Hills and of the Plains or Valleys are radically different but have always been interconnected. The 'tribal' Nagas share little in terms of politics, economics, religion or culture with the Plains kingdoms of Burma or India. Yet there has always been some form of relationship between them, and the Hill groups nearest the Plains traditionally functioned as a buffer, mediating between the remoter Hill groups and the Valley kingdoms, in terms of political alliance and trade relations. In addition, there is a strong memory among the Konyak Nagas of the semi-legendary Ahom (Assamese) king who married a Naga woman from what today is the village of Wanching; at least up to 1936 this village continued to receive an annual tribute from the Hindu village in the plains to which the Naga woman went. [3] Indeed, some have argued that the majority group in the Hindu Plains kingdom of Manipur, the Meithei, are in fact themselves originally a Hill community who overran the valley and settled there. Their king, on his installation, traditionally wore a costume very like that of the neighbouring Nagas. [4]

Some items of Naga material culture indicate a long history of contact between Plains and Hills. The 'elephant cloth', for instance, resplendent with complex animal designs, worn by the southern Nagas of Manipur, has its origin in the wish of the ruler of Manipur in the mid-seventeenth to present his Naga allies with a special cloth. [5]

The British interest in the Naga Hills, from the 1830s on, represented another stage in the history of Hills-Plains relations. This book portrays Naga society as it was in the colonial era - or at least as it was perceived by European observers - and in particular in the last two or three decades before Indian Independence in 1947.

(top) Young Zemi man. Hangrum village. 1941-42. UGB.
(middle) Man blowing horn. Konyak, Hungphoi village. 1936. CFH.
(bottom) Young woman wearing a Manipur cloth. Tangkhul, Chingjaroi Khulen village. 1937-46. UGB.

9

Man wearing 'elephant' cloth from Manipur. Eastern Angami. 1947. WGA.

The decision to describe a former era was largely prompted by the fact that a considerable body of ethnographic material from this period, much of it hitherto unexploited, was available to the research team of which the present author was part. [6] By contrast, few Europeans or Indians have been able to visit or study at all widely in Nagaland for the last twenty-five years. The post-colonial era is therefore not described in detail in this account. [7]

The historical inter-relationship of the Nagas and the British is central to this book in two ways. First, it is through European observers that our knowledge of Naga society has been formed. This account uses these sources to describe the characteristic features of social organisation, cosmology and material culture, and how these changed over time. A key consequence of this process of observation was the emergence in the literature of the various Naga 'tribes'. The implications of this way of looking at things are discussed in what follows.

Second, the British were of course not only present as observers, but also as rulers. This account therefore also looks at the changing political relations of the British and the Nagas, in the hope of shedding some light on one lesser-known example of the colonial encounter.

In what follows, the 'anthropological present' is used as a convention to the describe the past. The past tense is used, however, where particular stress needs to be placed on the historical nature of the subject-matter.

A note on the early history of the Nagas [8]

Ancient Sanskritic books speak of the Kiratas, a golden-skinned people of the sub-Himalayan region. Although this suggests that a people akin to the Nagas were present in the region perhaps 2000 years ago, our knowledge of the early history of the Nagas is necessarily sketchy. In the first decades of this century, the ancient history of the region was a major subject of study within the context of the search for a universal history of mankind, its origins, evolution, migrations and so forth. In the more sociologically-minded present, such conjectural history is less favoured, but there remains a certain fascination in the question of origins.

Physically, the Nagas are predominantly Mongoloid. That is to say, they have the straight black hair, black eyes, epicanthic eye-fold and other features of the huge spread of Mongoloid peoples, who now inhabit areas as diverse as China and Amazonia. The general expansion of the Mongoloid peoples throughout South East Asia (including to North East India), may have begun as much as 10 or 12000 years ago, possibly from a region of North China. This movement has continued into recent historic times.

In much of South East Asia the Mongoloid peoples appear to have supplanted earlier aboriginal populations, generally characterized as Australoid or Negrito. This may well have happened also in the Naga Hills. Certain non-Mongoloid physical characteristics are still regularly seen in the Naga population, especially small size and frizzy hair. In addition, Naga stories refer to encounters with populations with such characteristics. The Mongoloid populations brought with them neolithic traits (horticulture, stone axes, pottery), but it is possible that the Australoid populations also developed early horticultural skills.

This general outline has long been associated with a theory of origins based on the nature of stone tools. [9] Throughout South East Asia (here including the islands and mainland, but not China) there are two principal language groups, the Austroasiatic and the Austronesian (sometimes called the Malayo-Polynesian). The historic spread of peoples speaking these two languages is often measured according to the incidence of particular stone axe-heads: a shoulderd or tanged tool (that is, with an elongated butt, to allow more efficient hafting,) associated with the Austroasiatic-speaking peoples, and a facetted, polished quadrangular adze (that is, with a rectangular cross-section), associated with the Austronesian peoples. The Austronesian influence is generally thought to be the more recent, perhaps from around the middle of the second millenium B.C., from a point of origin either in island South East Asia or China.

Both tools have been found in the Naga Hills. [10] It may therefore be that the shouldered tool is evidence of an Austroasiatic-speaking population (possibly, though not necessarily, the Negrito population referred to earlier) and the quadrangular tool evidence of a more recent Mongoloid, Austronesian-speaking population. Some tools found in the Naga Hills with a shouldered butt and quadrangular section, suggest a mixed culture that developed either in the Naga Hills or brought there from outside.

The Austroasiatic and Austronesian groups are also of relevance because it may be that one or both is connected to the widespread occurrence of what some have called a 'megalithic culture', found throughout island South East Asia (the 'Indonesian' culture area). Its characteristics are the erection of large stone monuments and forked wooden posts, both to commemmorate the dead and as part of status-enhancing Feasts of Merit, and a set of beliefs about ritual prohibition or taboo and about a powerful soul-substance or virtue residing in the human head. According to Fürer-Haimendorf, 'The megalithic complex found in Assam and in many other parts of Southeastern Asia appeared thus not as an accidental aggregation of various culture elements, but as a well co-ordinated system of customs and beliefs, a philosophy of life and nature'. [11]

Page 12.

(top) Chingmak's second wife, with face tattoo, wearing necklace of large shells. Chang, Chingmei village. 1936. CFH.
(bottom) Headman of Jessami village. Angami. 1939. UGB PR.

Page 13.

(top) Village elder. Tangkhul, Chingjaroi Khulen village. 1939. UGB.
(bottom) *Ang's* wife wearing typical Ao necklace. Ao, Longmisa village. 1948. CS.

(top) A pair of male and female monoliths. Angami. 1913-1923. JHH.
(bottom) Y-posts. Ao, Ungri village. 1936. CFH.

In addition, in terms of culture and social organisation, a great number of parallels can be suggested between Indonesian. Oceanic societies and certain of the Nagas, though not en bloc. In technology this would include the Indonesian (backstrap) loom, the vertical double-cylinder bellows, and making fire with a flexible thong; in economy, both slash-and-burn and terraced cultivation; in funerary customs, platform exposure of corpses and the storage of skulls in stone jars; in social organisation, the young people's dormitories; and in miscellaneous practices, such diverse traits as tattooing, head-taking, betel-chewing and a body ornament called, and resembling, 'enemy's teeth' found amongst people in the Philippines, Melanesia and Burma. [12]

Thus on the basis of archaeological and ethnographical reports, the theory of Austroasiatic and/or Austronesian influence may be tenable. But it is much harder to identify routes. There are perhaps two possibilities. Sea-faring peoples in out-rigger canoes might have brought this influence from island S.E. Asia to mainland S.E. Asia and the Bay of Bengal, and hence overland to the Naga Hills. Alternatively, it may be that the route was more directly overland from a postulated source area in southern China.

However, the Nagas speak neither Austroasiatic nor Austronesian. Rather they speak as many as thirty diverse and sometimes mutually incomprehensible tonal languages [13] that all belong to a large language family called Sino-Tibetan, and within that family to the sub-family Tibeto-Burman. This latter group also includes the neighbouring hill peoples such as the Garo and the Kachin. In general this must point towards an origin in the north, that is, to South-West China and Tibet. This does not undermine the theory of a South-East Asian cultural affiliation. The Tibeto-Burman populations quite possibly constitute movements into the Naga Hills coming after the Austroasiatic or Austronesian influences. Many commentators have noted the links between the Nagas and other hill peoples speaking Tibeto-Burman languages. Hutton notes parallels, for example, between the Sema and the Garo in language and in the erection of Y-shaped posts, and between the Sema and the Kacharis in the name of the Creator-god. [14]

In the more recent past, there has also been migration from the North-east, including the ancestors of the present Tai-speaking Shans and Ahoms of Burma. The latter invaded Assam in fairly recent historical time (the 13th Century). There are of course, still many Nagas on the Burmese side of the India-Burma border.

Lastly, and continuing into the 20th Century, there has been migration from the south, of Kuki-Chin peoples, who appear to have been driven south down the Chindhwin River under pressure from the Kachin leaving south China, and who then turned back to the north once they had reached the Bay of Bengal, and who

entered the Chittagong Hills and then the Naga Hills from this route. The peoples we now describe as Lushai, Lakher Chin and Kuki perhaps arrived in this way, as did some of the southernmost Nagas, such as the Sema, who have retained an expansionist polity, driving out other Nagas such as the Rengma, and adopting their customs, as they moved northwards. [15]

Naga origin stories have two aspects. One aspect is essentially mythological, and describes the supernatural origin of mankind from a stone or (in the case of the Konyaks, for example) a pumpkin or a giant bird. The other aspect describes in detail actual movements of people in the Naga Hills. As one might expect, these stories suggest movement from all directions. Like the Ilongot of the Philippines, the Nagas seem to be able to recall historical movements in considerable detail, both within the Naga Hills and from beyond, though of course there are no doubt elements of myth included in such stories too. The Konyaks derive their origin from both the south and the north; the Sangtam from the Chindwin valley to the south-east; the Aos in part at least from the north-west; the Angamis variously to the west, south-west and south-east; and the Rengmas to the south. [16] Such movements relate to a period up to and including the last few hundred years.

It would therefore seem that the only conclusion is that drawn by Hutton, that the present sociological make-up of the Nagas is 'mixed' and so is their pre-historic origin, there being no unique origin for any of the tribes separately or for the Nagas as a whole.

As an example of this one might take the case of the Ao Nagas. The Aos erect not only Y-posts but also, uniquely among the Nagas, round-topped wooden posts, apparently related to the stone pillars of the non-Naga Kacharis at their capital Dimapur in the 16th Century, which suggests a northern influence; they possess (again uniquely among the Nagas) a single-piston bellows that is found far to the east in the Mekong valley among the Miao-speaking peoples whose origins are thought to be in South-east China. They possess a large number of traits that connect with the Austronesians of Oceania, including a throwing game not found amongst other Naga tribes but reported in Fiji; they use the euphemism of 'plantain tree' to indicate a human victim, as in Fiji. Their origin myths indicate that they have moved from an area to the east of their present location, and in the course of their migrations encountered a number of already-existing peoples, probably within the relatively recent past. [17]

However, a caveat must be entered at this point. It is easy, but probably unhelpful, to imply that social or linguistic influences are a matter of the physical intrusive migration of discrete social groups or entire populations at a particular point in time, carrying a package of social or economic traits.

Rather, it is possible to envisage widespread cultural horizons and traditions sharing parallel developments, with contact and borrowing resulting in a gradual process of change. Migrations there may have been, but this does not require the identification of a single source of origin from which occurred the physical transportation of traits from one area to another. An area characterized by migatory slash-and-burn cultivation will after all necessarily bring neighbouring peoples into contact with each other, facilitating a process of contact and borrowing. No single people are the ancestors of the Nagas, nor did the Naga amalgamation of customs and beliefs arrive en bloc. The present arrangement has most probably been created by the interaction of the Naga groups in their present location: interaction with other Nagas, with non-Nagas, with their environment.

Leach, in considering a similar question of origins for the Kachin in Burma, severely criticises the relevance for sociology of any speculation about pre-history: 'Kachin society as we know it today is a society organised to cope with the ecological situation that exists in the Kachin Hills. Kachin culture and Kachin political organisation, as systems, must be regarded as having been developed in situ where we now find them.' Despite borrowings, Kachin society is a 'local complex'; [18] the same is no doubt true of the Nagas.

Page 14.

(top left) Young woman in festival dress. Konyak. 1937. CFH. (centre left) Youth with the face tattoo of a head-taker. Konyak. 1937. CFH.

(bottom left) Warrior's hat decorated with flat transparent horns and a chin strap of teeth. Kalyo-Kengyu. 1936. CFH.

(centre) Man and his wife. Sangtam. 1947. WGA.

(top right) Old man with carved wooden head pendant indicating head-taker's status. Konyak. 1937. CFH.

(centre right) Young Konyak with blackened teeth. 1937. CFH.

(bottom right) Old man with tasselled ear ornaments. Konyak, Oting village. 1936. CFH.

Page 15.

(top left) Old man wearing a hat made of wild cat fur decorated with feathers. Konyak. CFH.

(centre) Girl dressed for Spring Festival dance. Konyak. 1937. CFH.

(top right) Boy with a spear and decorated shield wearing a hat with three hornbill feathers. Konyak. 1937. CFH.

(bottom left) Girl wearing large shell discs around her neck. Chang. 1936. CFH.

(bottom right) Young boy wearing a necklace decorated with coins. Konyak. 1937. CFH.

Kabui Nagas. c.1873-1875. RGW.

Chapter 2

The Observers and the Observed

From the early days of contact with the Nagas in the 1830s, Europeans struggled to make sense of the ethnographic chaos they perceived around them: hundreds, if not thousands, of small villages seemed to be somewhat similar to each other but also very different, by no means always sharing the same customs, political system, art or even language. The gradual extension of British control of the area was therefore accompanied by a number of tools which helped create a classificatory system according to which the diversity of facts could be arranged. Photography, map-making, the collecting of objects, anthropological and anthropometrical research, all contributed both to knowledge and to a subtle form of control: indeed, some would argue that these were one and the same thing. [1]

Administrators and ethnographers shared a common interest in classifying things in a certain way. 'If we aim at equitable administration of subject races,' suggested the museum curator and Naga scholar Henry Balfour in 1923, 'the chief essential is close investigation of their indigenous culture.' [2] One of the effects of this kind of classificatory investigation was the emergence in the literature by the late 19th century of separate 'tribes', whereas earlier mid-century writers had understood Naga villages to identify themselves on an individual basis, and had therefore dealt with them in this way. [3]

In a sense, therefore, we can say that the British over a period of time 'created' the Naga tribes as relatively fixed groups each with a distinctive kind of social organisation and language. Material culture was also a crucial determinant of 'tribal' affiliation. One of the earliest classifications of the Nagas, by Col. R.G. Woodthorpe in 1881, sought to distinguish the Angamis from all the other tribes on the grounds of the presence or absence of the male 'kilt' as a basic item of dress. In time, a sort of circular process developed: objects once collected were assigned to a particular tribe, for which they in turn functioned as identifying badges.

It was Woodthorpe who provided a classic visual representation of the Nagas in his painting of about 1880. [4] Centre stage sits Captain Butler; next to him are Mr Brown, with a camera, Woodthorpe with a sketch pad, and Indian soldiers. Around them are gat' red representatives of some of the diverse Naga tribes, ea'   red in typical costume. The picture combines the realism of the figures with a representation of a desired set of relations in the colonial system: exoticism tempered by the order and harmony of the Raj.

(top) Namkiabuing, Ursula Graham Bower's chief assistant, with her movie camera. 1941-42. UGB.
(bottom) Tangkhul men posed for a photograph in front of a screen. c. 1890. C.A. Gourlay, Centre for South Asian Studies, Cambridge.

(top left) J.P. Mills with freed slave child. 1936. CFH.
(centre left) Anthropometrical measurement was given considerable emphasis by earlier generations of anthropologists. 1937. CFH.
(bottom left) Veranda of the District Commissioner's house in Mokokchung. 1913-23. JHH.

Collection of Naga objects laid out for display, destined for museums in Europe. 1936. CFH.

(top right) Human skulls decorated with horns from Yacham village. Ao. 1918-23. JHH.
(bottom right) Skulls taken from Yungya, a Konyak village, hung on a line behind the District Commissioner's house. 1918-1923. JHH.

19

(top) Haimendorf drinking from a bamboo vessel, with Nagas on the way to Wangla village. 1937. CFH.

(bottom) Women dancing with Mildred Archer at a Feast of Merit. Ao, Ungma village. 1947. WGA.

For a number of reasons, the term 'tribe' is problematical. It certainly cannot be used in the technical sense that has emerged from the classic studies of tribes in Africa, where the tribe can be defined as the largest group within which compensation is paid for homicide (rather than resort to force), and in which machinery exists for reconciliation. For, with the exception of the Lhota Nagas, the Nagas practised head-taking within the 'tribes'. 'Tribe' also often implies some kind of overarching political organisation, which again is not the case with the Nagas, although it is true that the Tangkhul Nagas had tribal councils or *longs*, which sought to settle disputes between Tangkhul villages, and which in the last resort would oversee an ordeal by pitched battle between the contesting parties. [5] On the whole, however, manifestations of 'tribal' structure are not frequently found, and organisation above the level of the village is only a matter of temporary alliances: there is no system of balanced segments which are normally autonomous but which combine together, 'automatically' as it were, at a higher level against a third party. [6]

Furthermore, few if any of the tribal names appear to be indigenous. 'Naga' itself is a name used by the people of the plains, rather than by the people of the hills themselves. 'Konyak' as a name may well derive from the Chang word for 'man', and many other commonly-used 'tribal' names seem to stem from use by outsiders (whether Plains people or other Hill groups). The 'Lahupa', considered by some a sub-division of the Tangkhul Nagas, appear to have been named thus (not by themselves) after their distinctive red-seeded headgear. [7]

In the more general sense of tribes as culture groups, the complexity of linguistic, cultural, kinship and political patterns, means that there is no answer to the question, How many Naga tribes are there? One early British military explorer in 1879 suggested 18; 17 years later, a survey listed nine. In 1921, Hutton listed 14; as did Elwin in 1961 (though not the same ones); in the 1970s Horam gave 30 and Yonuo 38. [8] Both these last include some groups living in Burma, and a number of groups who would probably not have counted themselves as Nagas fifty years ago, but who for various reasons find it appropriate or advantageous to do so today.

Later, we will outline a different way of thinking about the Nagas, that is, as a single society, comprising certain core principles which can be, and were, combined and emphasised differently. Thus different groups may emphasise the village, the age-grade system, or the clan system, though each will always be present to some extent, and movement from one combination to another was very likely.

Here, however, we could perhaps consider the colonial encounter from the other point of view. What did the Nagas make of the intrusion of the British into their world ?

The answer is elusive, because the Nagas have no written records of their own. But it seems that to begin with they took the British to be very much like the Valley kingdoms of Assam, to the west, and Manipur, to the south. To take the case of the former, some of the Nagas had had political and commercial relations with the Ahom kings for a long time. The Nagas were granted lands in the valleys, fought in the Ahom armies and sheltered Ahom princes fleeing from court conflicts. The Nagas nearest the plains ('bori') acted as a buffer between the Nagas of the interior ('abori') and the valley population. In mythology, the Nagas consider themselves siblings of the Valley people.

The British realised that 'The Naga territory was never considered an integral portion of the sovereignty of Assam',[9] and British officers of the 1840s arrived with formal 'treaties' addressed to the Naga 'Rajas' in the hope of securing peaceful relations. Some of these were, to the satisfaction of the British at least, signed by both parties.[10]

But the Naga interpretation of such treaties was different from that of the British. As Major Jenkins noted in 1841, 'The Assamese...consider the offerings of the Nagas as dues; but the hill tribes, I have no doubt, looked on the presents they received in the same light, and viewed the matter as a mere interchange of presents'.[11] In pursuing this way of thinking when the British arrived, any treaties would only be tactical, and probably temporary, alliances that might be useful for traditional political purposes. In 1847 Major Butler recalled his meeting with the chief of Mozoma, who expressed incomprehension that troops offered to him to guard his village in exchange for his promise not to continue raiding, could not be used by him in an immediate revenge attack on the neighbouring village of Khonoma.[12]

The difference was that the British were, ultimately, far more willing to try to enforce peace and secure their economic interests (namely, the valley tea estates) against Naga raiding, than the Assamese had been. Hence a long stop-start process of pacification and administration began. The boundary of the 'administered area' was pushed further and further back into the hills, though British policy oscillated between favouring annexation on the one hand and complete non-intervention on the other. The Nagas resisted this expansion, resulting in ten punitive expeditions between 1835-51. This culminated, albeit after an attempt at complete non-intervention, 1851-78, in an uprising in 1879 in which 6000 Angami Nagas laid siege to Kohima, the new British military base in the Hills. In retaliation, the village of Khonoma was subjected to very severe reprisals the following year. In some ways 1879-80 marked the end of the military phase of colonial rule.[13]

(top) Gaonbura and other headmen entertaining W. G. Archer at Helipong village. Chang. 1947. WGA.
(middle) Ursula Graham Bower at Laisong village. Zemi. 1941-46. UGB.
(bottom) The anthropologist Kauffmann photographing young men against a white cloth. Konyak, Longkhai village. 1937. CFH.

(top) Man wearing characteristic Tangkhul head-dress, *luhupa*. Tangkhul, Somra Tract. J. Shakespear, School of Oriental and African Studies Archive. (bottom) *Morung.* c.1900. W.H. Furness 3rd, published in 'Customs of the World'.

Page 23.
Two men, and a boy with a painted face, wearing dance dress. Zemi, Lakema village. 1918-45. JPM SOAS.

Relatively peaceful administration followed this. British policy was explicitly characterised as a 'civilizing' mission. This was to be achieved through trade and administration. In 1888, the Government noted that 'Each household still, excluding almost the sole article of salt, produces what suffices it for its needs. The multiplication of mutual wants, on which progress in civilization depends, is a process which has hardly yet had a beginning among the Naga tribes'. [14] This sanguine view of the benefits of trade was complemented by a comparable attitude to the house tax, levied in return for administration and services. The Government view of this was phrased in paternalistic language and undoubtedly was seen as a measure of control appropriate in conditions where order was no longer threatened by armed opposition. Captain Butler, the Deputy Commissioner in 1870, noted, 'I know of nothing which has so great an influence or which acts so quickly in civilizing barbarous savages as the infliction (or rather blessing I should say) of a fair and moderate taxation'. [15]

It should be said that the Government's paternalistic assumptions about 'civilization' were not shared by all. J.P. Mills, writing as the District Commissioner in the 1931 Census, concluded that the expansion of trade, contact with Plains people, administration (including education) and missionization had had almost entirely adverse effects on Naga society and culture. On the other hand, this view would no doubt itself be seen as paternalistic in the eyes of modern Nagas since it seemed to imply a preference for deliberate under-development, as if a way of life admired by outsiders could be indefinitely and artificially protected from all 'modern' influences. [16]

From the Naga perspective, the imposition of taxation had dramatic consequences, and was recognised as a turning point in their history. [17] Paying the tax in cash forced households to look to the market economy and brought each household at least in theory under the direct control of a centralized authority for the first time. Payment in times of hardship was a considerable burden and a Naga rebellion in the 1930s included a house tax boycott. [18] In addition the Hills were made an Excluded Area, intentionally protected from the influence of the rest of India.

In the administered areas the British prohibited head-taking raids, and sought to mitigate it in the more remote tribal area: a contradictory policy which always left some groups divided on either side of the line. Military pacification remained the policy in the remoter areas which did not readily accept the colonial Pax Britannica. As late as 1946, one villager explained his attitude to punitive expeditions thus: 'A column - what is the use of that? It comes and burns a village. Then it goes away. And we simply sit and laugh'. [19] The administration sought to work through indigenous people, appointing individuals as *gaonburas*

(government-appointed chiefs) and Assamese-speaking *dobashis* (interpreters). Although these were usually men, some women gaonburas were also appointed. As in the Kachin area of neighbouring Burma, the British preferred to work through chiefs, and favoured those communities organised in a hierarchical manner, as opposed to those organised in a more egalitarian - or as they saw it, anarchic - way. [20]

The earliest accounts seem often to include ambivalent attitudes towards the Nagas. On the one hand there is evident a paternalistic attitude of superiority, coupled with condemnation of supposedly 'savage' habits. Woodthorpe begins one paragraph with the statement that the Angamis are 'cheerful, frank, hospitable, brave' and in the next characterizes the same people as 'bloodthirsty, treacherous, revengeful'. [21]

But there is a secondary, romantic sub-theme, revealed in John Owen's account of 1844 of the building of a new village: 'Such a scene is very romantic and reminds one in some degree of a gipsy camp'. [22] This is an attitude built on a fascination with the discovery of a society that seemed wholly opposite to that of Europe. Once safely defeated, the Naga as exotic alter-ego could prevail over the primitive Naga, as a stereotype. To some extent, both these colonial attitudes can still be found today.

From the 1870s, a tradition of descriptive ethnography began, first with the 'soldier-ethnographers' such as Butler and Woodthorpe, and later with the 'administrator-ethnographers', such as J.H. Hutton and J.P. Mills, resulting in the comprehensive tribal monographs of the 1920s and 1930s. Hutton went on to become Professor of Anthropology at Cambridge, and Mills a Reader in Social Anthropology at the School of Oriental and African Studies, London.

A body of knowledge emerged, through publications, photography and the collecting of objects, which parallelled and buttressed the development of the colonial administration. To take the case of the collecting of objects, there seems to be a movement from the ad hoc collection of weapons and obviously 'exotic' ornaments in the earlier phase of military pacification, to the systematic collection of all items of material culture in the period of indirect administration. As in similar developments elsewhere in the colonial world, two points can be made. First, indirect rule that is, government largely working alongside and through indigenous institutions – implied a certain relation of paternalistic respect and understanding. The collection of the totality of Naga material culture, in a deliberately 'scientific' idiom, was parallel to the need to gather information about every detail of society, economy and culture, providing a basis of knowledge through which indirect rule could be implemented. Any and every aspect of life became of intrinsic interest; this extended to the collection of

(top) Animist or traditional believer alongside Christian minister in modern dress. Ao, Yongyimsen village. 1936. CFH.
(bottom) Men wearing the Angami black kilt decorated with lines of cowrie shells. The man on the right wears a badge on his chest which indicates he is a government servant. Kohima village. 1918-45. JPM SOAS.

(left) Angami Nagas. c.1873-1875. RGW.
(top right) Head-taking dance. Konyak, Tanhai village. 1936. CFH.
(bottom right) Man holding skull decorated with horns and large fibrous tassels. Konyak, Wakching village. 1937. CFH.

the totality of objects. Second, however, this process of collection can be seen as a metaphor of the relationship between observers and observed. The observers possessed such collections and drew particular conclusions about the nature of Naga society from them as they ordered the pieces around. They could therefore stand as elucidators of Naga culture to the Nagas. The collectors thereby reinforced their role as rulers, through their supposed unique understanding of the totality of Naga society, while the Nagas themselves were considered ignorant of their own society in its broadest, rather than particular, aspects. [23]

Benevolent in intention, both ethnography and administration therefore served a controlling function over the peoples of the Hills. The exhaustive detail of the resulting research and writing, however, only seemed to highlight a basic question: were the Nagas one people or many tribes?

Morung. Konyak, Tamlu village. 1946. CS.

(top) *Morung* carvings of two human figures. Konyak, Chingphoi village. 1947. WGA.
(bottom) Carving inside Lingba *morung* of elephant and human figures. Konyak, Kongan village. 1936. CFH.

Chapter 3

The *Morung*

The *morung*, or youth's dormitory, is typically a huge building which physically dominates a Naga village, resplendent with carvings representing hornbills, tigers, mithan (bison) and human heads and sometimes with projecting barge-boards resembling wings or horns. Sociologically it is a key institution of Naga society, though its importance varies between the different groups.

A Naga village is typically divided into two or more geographical areas called *khels*, and in each *khel* there are one or more *morungs*. Where the emphasis is very much on the *khel* or *morung*, as amongst the Angami Nagas, a *khel* may in effect become a sub-village in itself, each *khel* pallisading itself with stone walls against the other *khels*. Usually, however, the two (or more) *khels* would cooperate on the ritual, economic or political occasions where village unity was vital.

Each *khel* and its *morung* will contain members of one or more clans. The *morung* fulfils various functions. It is a sleeping place for the young unmarried men and in former raiding days it served as a guard-house for the warriors. It is in some senses a school, since young people learn about social practices and belief from their elders. Often individuals retain a life-long connection with the *morung*, even after they have started their own households, and will identify themselves by the *morung* rather than by the *khel*. Although typically it is a male institution, in some communities a counterpart exists for girls too.

Membership of a *morung* may determine choice of marriage partner, for it is usually forbidden to marry within the *morung*, and reciprocal relations are therefore built up with other *morungs*, from whom a marriage partner is chosen. Such reciprocal relations would also involve helping with rebuilding the *morung*. The area around the *morung* is a social centre for the *khel*, and also a centre for important rituals, especially where it is strongly associated with a log-gong, a huge gong fashioned out of a single tree trunk. In days of head-taking, a captured head would be brought to the *morung* or its log-gong, where the necessary rituals would then be performed. *Morungs* are often more or less autonomous and are managed by a council of *morung* elders, even conducting their own political relations with other villages' morungs. This might include the *morung* (not the village) receiving tribute from subjugated villages nearby. The elders would adjudicate disputes, determine the choice of fields to cultivate, and proclaim village ritual days. These morung elders would then meet together to form a village council.

The *morung* as an institution is most developed among the Ao Nagas, where it is characteristically a huge building, over 50 feet

(top) The *Ang* of Chintang village sitting on low wooden chief's stool with hornbill head carvings at one end. Konyak. 1936. CFH.
(bottom) Chinkak, the *Ang* of Wakching, making a model of an *Ang's* stool. Konyak. 1936. CFH.

(left) Log dragging for rebuilding the Thepong *morung*. Konyak, Wakching village. 1936. CFH.
(bottom left and right) Rebuilding the house of the Ang of the Thepong *morung*. Konyak, Wakching village. 1937. CFH.

long, 30 feet high, and richly carved. Every three years, a group of boys about 12 years old is initiated into a *morung*. This marks the transition from childhood to adolescence and the boys remain in that age-group until they die. Outside the *morungs* in Chuchu-Yimlang, large bamboo X-shaped crosses are erected when a new age-group is being initiated, emphasising the transition from one state to another. [1] In the past this initiation could be a frightening affair, involving tests of courage and instilling in the boys a sense of the seriousness of *morung* membership. Much of the initiation involves actions plainly symbolic of head-taking: in the Konyak case this includes throwing miniature spears into a tree just outside the village. [2] Every subsequent three years they take on the role and responsibilities of a new age-grade, starting as the menial 'unripe gang', and then moving through the many grades of war leaders and councillors. Admission to a *morung* is important in terms of economic cooperation, for the boys cease to work their families' land, and instead work the land of their fellow *morung*-members. The age-groups are also found for girls, but tend to have less functional significance.

But the importance of the *morung* varies from group to group. In some groups, such as the Angamis, the *morung* is an unimpressive building and membership of it is of minor significance. Why should this be so ? The case of the Konyak Nagas may point to an answer.

The Konyaks are divided into two categories, the Thenkoh, who are relatively democratic and where power is held by a council of elders, and the Thendu, who are autocratic, and are ruled by powerful sacred chiefs *(angs)*.

Thenkoh	Thendu
each *morung* makes foreign policy	*ang* makes foreign policy for village
morung the largest building	*ang's* house the largest building
morung elders rule jointly with chief	*ang* is paramount ruler of village

It is clear that a strong *morung*, that is age-group, system is in some way counterposed to a strong chief system. An ideology favouring rule by paramount chiefs over a whole village, means that the *morungs* are weaker. But this does not mean that the Thendu and the Thenkoh are different groups, only that the emphasis on one principle rather than the other, shifts. Over time, this has indeed happened, as will be described below.

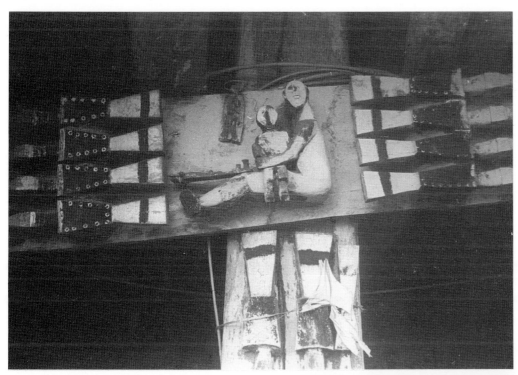

Morung carvings. (top left) Large human figure and a row of heads, both human and mithan. Ao, Yongyimsen village. 1936. CFH.
(top centre left) Two warriors and hornbills inside the Aukheang *morung.* Konyak, Wakching village. 1947. WGA.
(bottom left) Hornbills and tigers on *morung* posts. Ao, Chantongia village. 1947. WGA.
(bottom centre left) Tigers and leopards. Ao, Chuchu Yimlong village. 1947. WGA.
(top centre right) Mother and child surrounded by hornbills inside Pala *morung.* Konyak, Wakching village. 1947. WGA.
(top right) Monkey holding a human head in the Pala Konyak, Wanching village. 1947. WGA.
(bottom right) Warrior and hornbills in Long-wok *morung.* Konyak, Shiong village. 1947. WGA.

Circular stone sitting-platform, *tehuba*, situated in front of the house of the
descendant of the village founder, *kemovo*. Both irrigated and dry terraces can
be seen in the background. Angami, Khonoma village. 1918-45. JPM SOAS.

Chapter 4

Environment and Economy

The use of the land underlies all other aspects of Naga society.
That is to say, not only must the land be worked to produce basic
subsistence food for the people, but the ladder of social prestige can
only be climbed by individuals accumulating sufficient surplus to
afford the lavish sacrifices and feasts involved. Wealth is also
sought in order to make a good marriage or a political alliance.

The Nagas are farmers and practise two kinds of agriculture,
both obviously well adapted to the difficult hilly terrain. The most
common is slash-and-burn or swidden agriculture, and the main
crop is dry rice, though Job's tears, millet, taro, maize, ginger,
chillis, cotton and other plants are grown.

The Nagas call this kind of agriculture *jhuming* or *jooming*.
An early observer noted some of its characteristics: 'There seems
hardly a flat stretch of land anywhere, all is hill and valley, and
thus the system of cultivation is mainly by what is called jooming,
where forest is felled and the site used for two years only, when, in
consequence of the growth of rank weeds, fresh forest is again
joomed, and a system of permanent culture on one spot is
impossible.'[1]

With good rainfall and fertile soil this system can provide an
annual surplus of rice, but it depends on having plenty of land and
on leaving some trees standing, since the soil quickly becomes
infertile, and new sites have to be chosen. After being worked for
two years, each site needs up to ten fallow years. The principal
tools used are the hoe, digging-stick, sickle, rake, winnowing fan
and the all-purpose *dao*, which serves as a cutting and chopping
tool. Carrying the crops back from the fields to the village is done
in large conical bamboo baskets. The Aos remember a Golden Age
when all you had to do was call the rice in the fields and it would
come flying back to the granaries.[2] But people noticed that the
rice tended to end up in rich men's granaries, so poorer villagers
began to use baskets to carry the rice, and since then rich and poor
have had to labour up the hill slopes with baskets full of rice. These
may weigh up to the body-weight of the carrier.

The second kind of agriculture is terraced wet-rice cultivation,
in which terraces (sometimes called *panikhets*) are cut into the
hill slopes and the water supply is carefully controlled through a
system of canals and pipes. This system was admired by one early
observer: 'December 25th (1873). Today the peculiar terrace
cultivation of these tribes is observed in perfection. The labour
incurred in first making these terraces must be very great, and the
skill manifested in irrigating them would do credit to a trained
engineer.'[3]

(top) Fields cultivated by slash-and-burn, *jhum*, method. Eastern
Angami, Pfutsero village. 1946. CS.
(middle and bottom) Girls weeding protected from sun and rain by
bamboo shields. Konyak, Wakching village. 1937. CFH.

(top left) Boys hoeing. Konyak, Wakching village. 1937. CFH.
(top right) Loosening the soil with hoes while rice seeds are broadcast. Konyak, Wakching. 1937. CFH.
(bottom left) Group of young men and women planting rice in a flooded terraced field. Angami, Yorobami village. 1936. CFH.
(bottom right) Girls with carrying baskets. Angami. 1936. CFH.

Page 35.
(top) Harvesting. Konyak, Wakching village. 1936. CFH.
(middle) People from Wakching village going to the market at Santok with mats to trade. Konyak. 1937. CFH.
(bottom) Young men carrying bundles of palm leaves. Konyak, Wakching village. 1936. CFH.

This system is confined mainly to parts of the Angami Naga country, and to the Tangkhuls and Eastern Rengmas, who have both adopted the system of their Angami neighbours. The Konyaks far to the north have a sort of terraced system but only use it for taro; and elsewhere there has been a lot of resistance to Government schemes promoting terraced cultivation, even though it needs somewhat less labour-time than *jhuming*. Why is this ? In the first place, terracing demands high initial capital investment; there is also said to be more danger of destruction from pests. [4] But there is a more fundamental reason. Terracing seems to be one possible response to population pressure, which is likely to surface as a problem since the demand for surplus can only initially be met by increasing the number of workers. In Nagaland, though not necessarily elsewhere (and certainly not in valley terraced cultivation generally in South East Asia), terracing seems to be associated with the egalitarian principle of social organisation, that is, equally-ranked clans. Age-groups are not required in any large-scale weeding operations, and the system does not favour chiefs, whose concentration of land ownership cannot meet the demand for increased production, unless there is plenty of spare land into which to expand. Rather, terracing allows individuals to compete on a fairly equal footing to produce the surpluses which will give them high status.

Land ownership is varied. To remain with the Aos, the village of Waromung had in 1961 four different kinds of land ownership. Most households owned and worked family land, and some leased land from other families. A smaller number of households worked land owned by the clan or the village. Most households owned two or more plots in the village. As has been mentioned, the age-group *morung* system is particularly important for the Ao, but the *morung* does not actually own land, apart from some land on which grow the logs and bamboos used to build the *morung.* Some land is owned by religious officials. Most land is therefore owned by families or lineages, and even clan land tends to be worked in practice by particular families. In some groups (for instance the Sangtams), family plots are marked out with stone boundaries. The village as a whole, however, through its elders, decides the rotation through which new areas of land will be worked.

Other systems are found in the other groups. Among the Lhota, the *morungs* do own rice land. Among the Sema, there is a concentration of land in the hands of the powerful secular chiefs, who bind their followers (*mughemi*) to them in an almost feudal manner by gifts of land, which could be confiscated if the dependent deserted the chief's service. Every male in the area ruled by the chief is obliged to work in the chief's fields for some days every year, usually for only nominal payment. This system is not stable. It is bound to run into trouble where land is short and a

(top) Demonstrating a cross-bow. Konyak, Namsang village. 1937. CFH.
(middle) Last sheaves with offerings to spirit of harvest. Sema, Alapfumi village. 1917-23. JHH.
(bottom) Man inspecting spoor while hunting. Yimpang village. 1947. CS.

chief is unable to found or rule other villages as colonies. The chief's land may therefore become fragmented between his sons and the chief's power (through the allocation of land) will be diminished.

Most Naga communities build permanent villages, often with large-scale defences, buildings and monuments, though of course there would often be processes of dispersion and division. An exception appears to be the Zemi, who practised a form of cycle migration, apparently in response to land shortage. Three or four villages were therefore occupied in a cycle, each for two or more generations, and a deserted village was therefore nonetheless strongly identified as belonging to a particular group who would one day return to it. This system was not understood by the British, who at the turn of the century began distributing the apparently deserted areas to incoming Kuki farmers. [5]

Although the Nagas are primarily farmers, other forms of economic production are important. The collection of wild jungle plants is an important complement to domesticated plants, and might be particularly important in times of crop failure. Wild yams and other tubers and roots are dug up with a digging stick or hoe.

Nagas hunt several species of wild game animals, including barking deer, serow, elephant, wild boar and tiger - though the latter is hunted as a predator rather than as food, and its death is surrounded with ritual restrictions (*gennas*) in most groups. Before the advent of guns, the main methods of hunting were with spears, hunting dogs and pit-fall traps; smaller animals and birds were caught with palm-fibre spring traps. The cross-bow was restricted to only a few groups, though it was a powerful weapon.

Fishing is also important. Thorn-lined fish traps are constructed so that fish can swim in but not out. In another method, often referred to as fish 'poisoning', the sap of a creeper is washed into a damned-up river, causing the fish to float to the surface. (This is something of a misnomer, since the sap de-oxygenates, rather than poisons, the water.)

Most of these economic activities are distinguished as to gender, though this is a general tendency rather than a set of strict rules. Agricultural work, set out here in chronological order, is almost always divided as follows:

clearing jungle : mostly male
tilling soil : mostly male
demarcation of plots and construction of field work-house : mostly male
sowing : mostly female
path clearing : mostly male
weeding : mostly female
reaping : male or female
threshing : mostly male
winnowing : mostly female
clearing fields for next year's sowing : mostly female

(top left) Fishing in a dammed pool with a casting net. Zemi. 1941-42. UGB.
(bottom left) Fish poisoning. The men upstream are beating the poison creeper and the water is white with the suds from the juice. The boys are searching the shallows to catch the stupefied fish. Zemi. 1940. UGB.
(top right) Men fishing in the Dikhu river. 1936. CFH.
(centre right) Fish poisoning expedition. Konyak, Wakching village. 1936. CFH
(bottom right) Weir with fish traps. 1941-42. UGB.

(top) Imitation pig offered to evil spirits. Ao, Ungma village. JPM SOAS.
(middle) Sacrifice to regain the soul of a sick person. Konyak, near Wanching village. 1922. JPM PR.
(bottom) Separate offerings of rice flour on banana leaves for the fourteen major spirits during the *Heramui* ceremony. Zemi, Hangrum village. 1941-42. UGB.

It should be added that the richer a man, the more likely he is to engage labourers to do his work for him, and to rely on the efforts of his wife or wives. Women in any case do the bulk of agricultural work. The significance of this will be considered below.

Agricultural activities are permeated with rituals, though there are three stages which are particularly stressed with important rituals: the initial jungle clearance and the burning of the felled trees; sowing; and reaping. These rituals typically take the form of an offering of a sacrifical animal, the observance of a genna period of general abstinence from work, sex and other everyday activities, and feasting and dancing. The rituals, which are variously led by the head of household or the village ritual leaders, reveal much about Naga society. Clear analogies between sex and agriculture are repeatedly made.

As an example, the Lhota Nagas require an old woman to act as a ritual First Sower. Before the actual sowing by the man and his wife begins, the First Sower goes down to the fields and leaves a small offering of leaves and rice. What is the significance of this? First, the old woman is the same old woman who played an important part in the marriage ceremony of the couple, placing a leaf on the ears of the bride and groom: a link is being symbolized between marriage (as the basis of human fertility) and sowing (the basis of agricultural fertility), and both require the mediation of an old woman, the *ponyiratsen*, who is distinguished by being no longer fertile. The interplay between fertility and non-fertility is further seen in the fact that the Lhota couple abstain from sex the night before the fields are sown. A similar system is seen in the Eastern Angami, where the First Sower is an old, chaste, man, and the First Reaper is an old, chaste, woman. [6]

One other important feature of the Naga economy may be mentioned. Although each village was usually more or less self-sufficient, trade was also important. This was of two kinds. There was trade between the Nagas and the people of the Plains, and between the different Naga groups. Salt, for instance, appears to have been traded in a circular way. The Konyaks traded salt from their salt wells to the Plains, and this salt was then brought back into the Hills by the Aos, who might then sell it on to other Naga groups. The Hills provided the plains with wild cotton, chillies, ginger, ivory, palm-leaf mats, gourds and betel (*pan*) leaves; the Plains provided, in addition to salt, dried fish, cowrie shells, brass wire and metal sheets, and some ornaments produced particularly for the Naga market. By the mid-nineteenth century, gunpowder was also a valued commodity imported from the Plains. [7] Certain Plains objects had a particularly well-established destination. After about 1910, enamel plates were traded up to the Ao village of Mokokchung, from where they were traded to the

Yimchungr villages who cut the plates into crescent shape used on their highly distinctive helmets. [8] China plates were used in similar ways from about the same time. [9]

There was considerable specialisation: Khonoma, for instance, had more or less a monopoly in cowrie shells for the whole of the Naga area, obtaining these from Calcutta. It appears that with improvements in security and communication under British administration, the opportunities for trade increased significantly. The Assam Administration Report for 1886-67 noted that the gross value of Western Angami imports had increased by over 50 per cent in the previous four years. Included in this was an increase of nearly four times in the value of beads and ornaments imported, 'purchased for trade with the Eastern Angamis, from whom fowls, pigs, and dried fish are received in exchange'. Angami traders then traded beads widely, including into Burma, along old trade routes. The increased opportunities to trade in traditional ornaments, such as ivory armlets and woven baldrics, meant that more ornaments were probably worn by more people, than in pre-colonial times. Ivory armlets, for instance, once only available when Nagas killed elephants themselves, became worn far more widely in the twentieth century, as Naga traders obtained ivory from the Plains and as far away as Calcutta. [10]

The Lhota imported the cattle from the Plains which were so vital for sacrifices and ceremonial feasts, selling these on to the Aos and others. The Kalyo-Kengyu to the east were the producers of the basic conical red-and-gold cane hats which were traded to the Aos, Konyaks, Phom, Chang and others. The Chang village Longtang specialized in the spears decorated with short red hair trimming, which were traded across a wide area of Chang and Ao villages.[11] Before the advent of the British and the rupee, most goods would have been exchanged by barter. A man wanting to buy a mithan for a feast, would probably have to pay for it in rice. There were some items, however, which more resembled 'money'-type objects. Brass discs, wooden or metal spear-shaped objects called *chabili* and shell- or bone-strings served the function of widely recognised objects of value. In the early part of this century at least, a large conch shell was generally reckoned to be worth one cow. [12]

The Konyak village of Wakching has clearly been at the centre of Naga trading relations for a long period of time. Known by its earlier name, Jaktoong, it was one of the 'bori' villages sited on the passes leading from the Hills to the Plains, giving it an intermediary role both in terms of trade and in protection for the Plains population from the interior tribes. [13]

In 1936, Wakching was involved in a number of trading activities. It was the local centre for iron tools, producing *daos* and chisels for at least twelve villages without their own smiths. In

(top) Granary built on stilts. Konyak, Oting village. 1936. CFH.
(middle) Threshing and reaping. Lhota, Sanis village. 1948. CS.
(bottom) Paying land rent in rice after the harvest. Zemi, Laisong village. 1941-42. UGB.

39

return it received salt from those Konyak villages with their own brine wells, such as Mon. These villages created wells by sinking a hollow tree stump below the water table and drawing up the salty water, which was boiled in earthenware pots. In 1936 Fürer-Haimendorf noted, 'In Chinyang's youth Wakching still bought its salt from Chi and Mon. It was traded in stick form, as long and thick as a man's lower arm and for two such sticks Wakching gave one *dao*.' [14] The salt was then used not only in cooking, but also in political exchanges. The Thepong morung in Wakching received husked rice from its tributary village Chongwe, and made a gift of salt in return (though by this date the political relation of subordination was symbolic). [15]

Trade was undertaken by women as well as men. In a diary entry for 1936, von Fürer-Haimendorf noted, 'On our way home we passed a woman with two big mats. She was from Wakching and had walked all alone to Chongwe to trade salt for mats and chilli peppers. The mats are then sold to Assam.' [16]

By the 1930s the Nagas had become involved in economic activities quite outside the traditional patterns of Naga trade. Naga men in particular worked on the railway, as load-carriers, in the coal mines at Borjan and as seasonal labourers on the tea plantations in the Plains. Increasing contact with Plains immigrants also created new trading opportunities. Addiction to opium, which affected a large number of villagers particularly in the northern communities, seems to have been largely a result of increased contact with foreigners. The Government sought to control the trade through granting licenses to traders and through allocating 'passes' allowing set amounts of the drug to known addicts. The evidence is that this policy did not work. Plains traders sold the drug illegally to Nagas, and some Nagas took up the trade illicitly within Nagaland. [17]

Sagazumi village. The horns on the houses show status gained through Feasting. Angami. 1936. CFH.

(left) Grain being turned with a rake while it is drying. Angami, Sagazumi village. 1936. CFH.
(top right) Children pounding rice. Eastern Angami, Cheswezumi village. 1948-48. WGA.
(centre right) Girls pounding rice. Sema, Litsimi village. 1947. WGA.
(bottom right) Girls winnowing. Konyak, Longkhai village. 1937. CFH.

Man beating a huge log gong. Kalyo-Kengyu, Yakao village. 1936. CFH.

Chapter 5

Technology

By and large Naga technology involves simple materials and tools, and until the mid-nineteenth century Nagas could be considered essentially a neolithic people. It is true that they work in metal, but this does not include mining or smelting, the metal being bought in sheet or scrap form before it is worked. Most production is the concern of the household group, which produces for its own needs. But some goods are the specialised concern of particular individuals, producing not only for the rest of the village but for a whole area.

The process of fire-making is usually done, for both everyday and for ceremonial purposes, by the 'fire-stick' method. A stick is split half-way down and a small stone inserted to keep it open. A notch is cut in the underside of the split end, in which a thong of bamboo fibre can be placed. Tinder is placed around the end of the stick. When the bamboo thong is drawn rapidly to and fro, the friction lights the tinder. The other main way of making fire is by striking a flint stone with a piece of iron. The origins of these vital processes are recorded in the Ao Naga story of the ancient enmity of Fire and Water. Fire fled from Water and took refuge in bamboos and stones. The grasshopper saw this and told the monkey where Fire was hiding. The monkey then made fire with a fire-stick and bamboo thong. But man was watching and stole the fire. The monkey still needed his fur to keep warm, but man lost his fur because he could make fire with the materials in which Fire once hid. [1]

The technologies which are common to all households are basketry, the simpler forms of carving, and spinning and weaving. More specialised arts are pottery, metalwork and ceremonial wood-carving. As in agriculture, there tends to be a gender division of labour, but it is not uniform between the groups.

Basketry: male
Spinning and weaving: female
Wood-carving: male
Pottery: Sema, Ao - exclusively female (up to the firing stage);
       Tangkhul, Eastern Angami - male
Metalwork: male
Work in bone, ivory, shell: male and female

Basketry is of vital importance, since solidly-constructed baskets are necessary for both the transport and storage of grain and other crops. Other items produced are hats and mats. The split bamboo canes are sometimes dyed (red is a characteristic colour) and are then worked, sometimes using a bone tool, in a variety of chequer, twill and wicker patterns. Often the work is extremely fine, and wicker drinking vessels are water-tight.

Basket making. Chang. (top) 1948. WGA. (bottom) 1936. CFH.

Page 44-45.
(left) Winding cotton thread. Kabui, Oinamlong village. 1937. UGB.
(top centre left) Seeding cotton. Sema. 1918-45. JPM SOAS.
(bottom centre left) Spinning cotton. Sema. 1918-45. JPM SOAS.
(top centre right) Making skeins of thread. Rengma, Tseminyu village. 1947. WGA.
(bottom centre right) Weaving with backstrap loom. Konyak, Longkhai village. 1937. CFH.
(top right) Sewing together woven strips. Kabui, Kokadan village. 1939. UGB.
(middle right) Weaving young man's gala cloth, *mpak-pai*. 1941-42. UGB.
(bottom right) Design created by supplementary wefts being placed using a porcupine quill. Kabui, Kokadan village. 1939. UGB.

The production of textiles is the preserve of women. Cotton (which is the main fibre, though nettle fibre is also known) is seeded by rolling a rounded stick over it on a flat stone, or by using a seeding machine of the type imported from the plains. It is then rolled into a sausage-shape suitable for spinning. This is spun onto a spindle, weighted with a stone spindle-whorl and twirled against the spinner's thigh. Weaving is always done by the 'backstrap' tension loom method (sometimes called 'Indonesian'), in which the fabric is kept taut by being tied to a tree or wall at one end and around the weaver's back at the other. While the cloth is being woven, small patches of embroidery can be added in, sometimes using dogs' hair; this is done with a porcupine quill needle. Dyeing is done with a number of natural plant dyes, though bazaar dyes became common by the 1920s.

Although textile work is the work of women, Ao men make one important contribution, in the painting of a white band found in the cloth known as 'tsungkotepsu'. The painting of figures of mithan or heads on this cloth indicates the owner's social status, and it is done by applying with a pointed bamboo, a waxy pigment made from tree sap, rice beer and ashes. Although the cloth is widespread in the Ao area (and beyond), the painting of these bands is the preserve of the men of Lungsa village. The Rengma are the only other group to make such painted cloths. It was perhaps because they symbolised both lavish feast-giving and head-taking, that the Baptist missionaries sought to suppress these cloths completely.

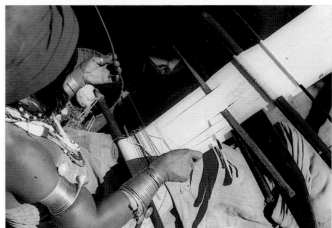

Woodcarving produces a variety of objects for functional and ritual purposes. The tools are simple: the *dao*, hand-drill, adze and chisel. Functional objects such as husking tables or dishes, and small ornaments, might be carved by any man. On the other hand grand-scale carving of house-posts, grave effigies, gates and log-gongs, are more likely to be done by specialists or at least on special occasions. When a village gate is carved, for instance, it is a time of special rituals or *gennas*. One observer noted that the carving of a gate in 1947 was very much a 'collective act', up to 20 men working on the carving without obviously having a leader. [2] In some cases, however, a particular man's skill is obviously pre-eminent: in the 1930s the Ang of Longkhai and his half-brother were reckoned to be particularly fine carvers.

(left) Warrior figures carved by the *Ang* of Longkhai village and his brother. Konyak. 1937. CFH.
(right) Carving a new village gate for the Tsotonoma *khel*. Angami, Kohima village. 1947. WGA.

(top) Carvings of men with heads and mithan horns on gates at Pfutsero village. Eastern Angami. 1947. WGA.
(bottom left) Carved Y-post with stylised heads. Angami, Ungoma village. 1936. CFH.

(bottom centre) Soul figure at Tofima village with characteristic large nose. Angami. 1925-28. JHH.
(bottom right) Wooden figures of the leading inhabitants of Mongsemdi village and their wives. Ao. 1913-1923. JHH.

The potter's wheel is unknown, and therefore all objects are made by the processes of modelling or coiling. Pots tend to be of a basic design, without varnishing or handles and rarely with ornamentation. The tabu on men making potttery seems only to apply to cooking pots, since men are allowed to make pottery pipe-bowls. [3] There is considerable specialization: the only Rengma village that produces pots is Tseminyu, and there is a pot-making season which dictates when pots can be made. Making pots after the sowing of millet would harm the crops.

(left) Women making large pots. Konyak, Longkhai village. 1937. CFH. (centre and right) Stages in making pottery vessels. Tangkhul, Nungbi Khunou village. 1939. UGB.

Metalworking is also specialized - indeed it is ritually prohibited in some villages. There are two kinds of metalwork. First, pieces of iron, tin or sheet brass (typically spade- or hoe-blades from the Plains tea-estates, and old *daos*) are bought by blacksmiths and are reworked through repeated heating and hammering. Tempering is achieved through immersion in a solution of pickles or chillies. The Konyaks and Kalyo-Kengyus are held to be the masters at this sort of work. Brass bracelets are also made in this way. The second kind of metalwork is casting, using the lost-wax process. Brass pieces are melted down and poured into stone moulds lined with pig fat. The Aos, Konyaks and Kalyo-Kengyus work in this way, producing armlets and other ornaments to which ornamentation is sometimes added with a punch or a chisel.

As has been mentioned, craft production is surrounded by ritual restrictions. A common theme seems to be the idea of manufactures as periods of creative force. Like sex and agriculture, these creative forces are capable of good and bad consequences, and must therefore be controlled. Thus we find that craft production is restricted at crucial periods in the agricultural year. At the time of the first sprouting of the rice, the Konyaks are forbidden to carve and the Rengmas to do metalwork. [4]

Village blacksmith forging a spear-head. Zemi, Laisong village. 1940. UGB.
(right) Wangpo making a brass bracelet using a clay mould. Konyak, Wakching village. 1937. CFH.

House with carved mithan heads, house horns, and Y-posts all of which indicate that the owner had given many Feasts of Merit. Tangkhul, Chingjaroi village. 1913-1923. JHH.

Boys preparing for the *Oulingbu* or Spring Festival, decorating their faces
and bodies with white chalk and putting flowers in their ears. Konyak,
Wakching village. 1937. CFH.

(top) Three children eating off a leaf plate. Konyak, Wakching village. 1937. CFH.
(bottom) Woman with children. Sema, Longsa village. 1947. WGA.

Chapter 6

Social Organisation

Naga social organisation is made up of cross-cutting group ties. That is, the individual and the household are in very few senses autonomous, but are integrated into the society, by being members of larger functional units: lineages, clans, age-groups, classes, *morungs* and villages. The individual experiences these ties sometimes as complementary and sometimes in tension with each other. It is quite typical, for instance, for two *morungs* each to have members of two or more clans.

Allegiance to the *morung* and clan might not always pull in the same direction. Among the Konyak, for instance, on the whole, membership of the clan overrode *morung* membership. [1] But in Wakching village in the mid-1930s, the members of the Bala *morung* made themselves so detested that the other *morungs* desired to expel them and destroy their *morung*. This might have led to the spilling of fellow clan-members' blood, which was altogether forbidden. So the other *morungs* invited the neighbouring *Ang* of Chi to do this work for them. Here, the loyalty to the *morung* overrode the ties to the clan; on the other hand, afterwards the Bala people found refuge with their fellow-clansmen, belonging to the other *morungs*, in the village.

One way to look at the interplay of social groups in operation is to examine the individual's life-cycle and the routine of daily life.

Children are usually born in the parents' house, the mother being helped in the delivery by female relatives. During the pregnancy the woman is especially careful not to eat particular tabu animals, but otherwise her life is much as normal. Therefore, it is not uncommon for the mother to feel labour pains when she has started work in the fields, and she may therefore give birth there: the Rengma Nagas among others say that this is in fact an auspicious birth, perhaps because it is part of the analogy between human and agricultural fertility. The Lyengmai Nagas (neighbours of the Zemis) put up a small stone monument on the path leading to the fields, to every child born in this way. When the birth takes place at home, the father remains in an outer room during the delivery, though it may fall to him to cut the umbilical cord and to bury the placenta.

A child is born into a household, but also into a clan. This is made clear early on, for the child receives its name from a number of possible clan names. In many cases this means that it takes its name from the name of one of its deceased ancestors on its father's side; but names may also be given which suggest desired or fortunate qualities in the child. On the second day after birth, an Ao child has its ear pierced and a tuft of hair cut off by the father:

(top left) Woman washing under a bamboo pipe. Sema. 1913-23. JHH.

(top right) Shankok demonstrating old method or trimming hair against the sharp edge of a *dao*. Konyak, Wakching village. 1937. CFH.

(bottom) Old woman with children. Konyak, Hungphoi village. 1937. CFH.

(top) Leggings of split cane made on boy's legs in preparation for the Spring Festival dance. Konyak, Wakching village. 1937. CFH.

(bottom) The girl on the right wears the head fillet which signifies that she is betrothed. Northern Sangtam, Mangaki village. 1918-45. JPM SOAS.

this is the formal recognition by the father that the child is his and is therefore a member of his clan. In the Zemi Naga community, a baby is also claimed by one or other of the *morungs* of the *khel*, as well as by a clan: shortly after birth the old men or women of different *morungs* 'compete' to be the first to tie a thread around the baby's wrist, signifying his or her life-long *morung* membership. [2] In both cases, however, the child from the start grows up knowing that it is a member of one or more kinds of groups.

The 'social paternity' of a child is on the whole more important than 'biological paternity'. That is to say, the legal paternity of a child counts for more than who exactly the natural father is. The child belongs to the clan of the man who is married to the mother, even if it is understood that he was not the natural father; on divorce, the child once weaned would be raised by the father's family, the mother having no more connection with the child once she has been paid a compensatory 'milk price'. [3] Marriage is usually signified in stages, but what counts is not so much the exchange of gifts (the 'engagement') but the entry of the woman some time later into the man's house (in the Konyak case it is at this point that girls complete their women's knee tattoos). If on the other hand the mother is not married, the child belongs to the clan of the man who paid a brass plate to the mother's father, in recognition of his paternity. It is very rare, if not unknown, for a child to be illegitimate, in the sense of having neither kind of paternal recognition.

As a slight digression, it may be added here that the Nagas do not appear to identify their clans very strongly with any sort of 'totemic' origin. It is true that some clans are named after animals or plants, and that these then become tabu as food for the clan. The hornbill appears to have a special relationship to the Konyak Ang clans, and it may not be carved by other clans. [4] Similarly, the Ao Wozükamr clan say that a woman called Lungkhungla was sitting weaving one day, when a feather from a hornbill flying by landed in her lap; she tucked it into her waistband, and eventually became pregnant by it; now the Wozükamr may not eat or even touch a dead hornbill. But such stories seem to be random, and do not add up to a system. An equal number of origin stories name the clans after places of origin, or after particular ancestors: the Angami clan Thevoma seem to be named after a human ancestor, Thevo, which is also the word for pig. This clan is, as it were, the clan of Mr. Hogg. [5]

Very often clans claim to have counterparts in villages outside their own community ('tribe'). There are two ways to look at this. Given the history of migration and interchange of population, it is quite possible that clans do have common ancestors which allow quite distant clans to claim a special affinity. On the other hand, by definition a clan is a kinship group which maintains, but cannot in detail trace, an alleged common ancestor. Clan connections can thus logically be manipulated to reveal a desired relationship between lineages, perhaps for political reasons: strict genealogical truth is not quite the same thing. [6]

To return to the question of life-cycle, children are expected to help with basic household and agricultural tasks. From an early age they are incorporated into work gangs. These are sometimes largely composed of clan members, but are often an entirely separate grouping, containing members of several clans. Even in the more autocratic communities, the gangs are organised democratically, and even a chief's son would expect to do his share of work. They are a key feature of agricultural production: few families could complete their yearly farming tasks without hiring the work gangs. Before marriage, work gangs are usually mixed; after marriage men and women make up separate gangs.

Children's toys include tops and 'bullroarers' (which produce a humming sound when whirled round on a string). Ao boys play at mock tiger and elephant hunts, and girls have an elaborate seed-throwing game. Most of their playmates will be members of the same *morung*. In some communities, a boy at age six will start sleeping with his father on the male side of the house; [7] in communities where the *morung* is an important institution, at some age between six and twelve children will stop sleeping in their parents' houses, and will start to sleep in the *morung*, learning the skills and responsibilities of adults, and there will be some form of initiation into the *morung*, or into the category of 'adult man woman'. In the case of the Zemi Nagas, for instance, such adult status for girls, is signified by starting to let the hair grow - up to this point, girls had their heads shaven. Even before this, children will start to realise that their membership of a clan is very important: it will influence how they speak to people, what food they are forbidden to eat, who they can and cannot marry, even who their likely enemies are.

Essentially the clan functions as a unit of collective responsibility. The Konyaks speak of the clan as a pyramid of 'houses'. All the 'small houses' (junior lineages) recognize descent from the 'great house' (the senior lineage, which represents the clan). Together all the clan houses are responsible for the debts, fines, obligations and proper behaviour of their members. This corporateness would especially be seen at a clan ceremonial feast. Each small house would subscribe some food to its parent house, which in turn would supply its share to the most senior house.

Children, like adults, show their status through ornaments. Thus, an Ao boy at three months starts to wear a goat's hair earring, which is only discarded when he is admitted to the

(top) Sema sports, awoli-sheshe. 1917-23. JHH.
(bottom) High jump. Sema. 1913-23. JHH.

(top and middle) Boys playing with a ball. Konyak, Wakching village. 1937. CFH.
(bottom) Boys playing with tops. Konyak, Oting village. 1936. CFH.

morung; at puberty Rengma girls wear particular skirts and ornaments indicating their unmarried status, and their heads are shaved until marriage. Their dress may also indicate the status of their fathers and grandfathers. Eastern Angami girls don a particular type of dress at puberty which is then worn for the rest of their adult lives. [8]

Soon after puberty, boys and girls from different *morungs* or clans may begin to meet, and in most groups (the Sema are an exception to this) young people are wholly free to make love. But it is not puberty as such which marks the young person as an adult, so much as the social initiation which takes place at about this time. Among the Konyak, adulthood is indicated by the initiation into the *morung*, which is followed (for the boys) by a head-taking expedition. Wisely, the heads of the youths themselves are not put at risk, and a mere setting-foot in enemy territory is considered adequate. In the past some Naga communities would obtain and kill a slave for this purpose.

At this stage the boy and girl may exchange customary love-tokens or small gifts (the boy giving bamboo combs or ear-plugs and receiving an embroidered loin cloth). [9] Subsequently, the girl may ask the boy to work with her in her father's fields the next day, where they might share food from the same dish (something forbidden to members of the same *morung*). These relationships are often not very serious, but it is likely that marriage negotiations will eventually result from one such liaison. In earlier writing, these relations were condemned as institutionalized 'promiscuity', but this misses the point. The liaisons followed a set pattern of gift-giving and formulaic question response between the young people. [10]

Young women marry at between 15 and 20; young men between 20 and 25. The marriage partner must (ideally) be from outside the clan or *morung*: these are 'exogamous groups', and marriages often take place between particular clans or *morungs* which have built up a reciprocal relationship. There is a preference for marriage with women who come into the category of 'mother's brother's daughter' (that is, your cross-cousin on your mother's side). Why should this be? The Nagas are patrilineal, that is, descent and inheritance go through males. A man's mother's brother's daughter is therefore a fairly close relation, but not too close - she is not from the same lineage as himself (which would be a forbidden marriage). The woman need not be a 'real' cross-cousin, but might in fact be one of many women of the mother's clan who are classified in this way. A girl, on the other hand, will see it as a situation in which she is likely to marry a man in the category of 'father's sister's son'. This marriage rule is only a preference; some significant variations are considered below. [11]

In the Rengma myth, the first man tricked his brother the tiger, resulting in their permanent hostility. Before parting, the tiger warned man to keep clear of him, but also had three pieces of brotherly advice. Two of these concerned agricultural practices, and the third was, 'Never marry a woman of your own clan'. [12] Agriculture and marriage are indeed fundamentals of Naga society, and although individuals are not forced to marry, marriage should be thought of as a relationship between the main units of society, rather than as a relationship between individuals.

In the Konyak village of Wakching, for instance, men and women of the Bala and Thepong *morungs* often inter-marry. As in all Naga groups, the man pays a 'brideprice' of, say, ten pigs, to the family of the woman. But he receives gifts in return, and gift exchange continues between the two groups for the whole of their lives, and beyond. When the man goes hunting, he shares his bag with his wife's parents. His wife's brothers give him presents of rice and rice-beer at feasts, and he reciprocates. The woman never ceases to belong to her own clan, and a husband who mistreats his wife will find her clan brothers lining up behind her. When his wife dies, he must give her family a field; but his children will receive gifts from their mother's brothers. In other cases a man will do bride-service, working for his father-in-law for some years; often the bride-price will be paid in instalments over a long period of time. The Rengma illustrate the fact of group relationships being established in the custom of the groom's family presenting a spearhead to the bride's family - a gift of a spear is a universal Naga symbol of tribute between groups. The general rule seems to be: the more stratified the group (i.e. the more unequal the distribution of wealth between lineages, and hence the more unequal the value of its women), the higher will be the bride-price, and the more uncommon divorce will be.

Marriage payments involve exchanges of objects of material and ceremonial value. This is not always clear in accounts which stress the fact that cash (rupees) is handed over. In fact, the cash is precisely divided up into specific kinds of payments from the husband's family to the bride's relatives, of symbolic as well as material value. In the case of Lhota bride-price, there are eleven exchanges, whether of rice or cash, each meaning something quite different: the first payment, for instance, *chuka*, is paid by the husband to the woman's mother's brother or father after the first eating and drinking together of the two families, and the third payment, *nzuiman*, is the price of 'not working in his father-in-law's house'. [13]

Marriage means the setting-up of a new household unit, though in some groups, such as the Yimchungr, the married couple may continue to live in the father's house. [14] The exteriors of Naga houses vary considerably from group to group, and depending on

Family sitting around the fire in Shankok's house. Konyak, Wakching village. 1937. CFH.

Page 58.
Wedding at Laisong village. Zemi. 1941-42. UGB.
(top) Arrival of the bridal party from a neighbouring village.
(middle) Procession approaching the groom's house. Cloths which the bride has woven for her trousseau are displayed on poles.
(bottom) Bride pouring rice beer for a guest at her wedding.

Page 60.
(top left) Wooden beds for young bachelors inside a *morung*. Kalyo-Kengyu, Nokluk village. 1937-45. CP.
(top right) High bamboo platform erected at the back of a house both to work and sit on. Konyak, Yungya village 1918-45. JPM SOAS.
(bottom left) Pigs scavenging below platform at back of house. Konyak, Oting village. 1936. CFH.
(bottom right) Sitting platform. Angami, Sagazumi village. 1936. CFH.

Page 61.
(top) Houses with platforms. Ao, Ungma village. 1946. CS.
(bottom) Huge vats for rice beer. Eastern Angami, Cheswezumi village. 1947. WGA.

the wealth and status of the owner. But the interior would typically have a small front room containing the pounding table, spears and baskets; a main living and sleeping room, raised slightly on poles, containing the hearth and the beds, with baskets, shelves and dried foods suspended from the ceiling; and at the back an open 'sitting-out' platform. Here rice is spread out to dry before pounding, women weave, children play, and entertaining is done.

The husband-and-wife unit forms the basis of economic activity, but the typical Naga variations occur even within this simple statement. In some Chang villages at harvest time the husband and wife go down to the field: 'One of them reaps the ears, the other pulls off the grains by hand into a basket and throws the empty ears to the ground. It is not defined who does one and who the other'. [15] In other Chang villages, this stage is done by the man and his work-gang.

The wealth of the domestic unit will be affected by the inheritance laws of each group. Generally, in practice each brother receives a similar amount in property from the father, but the Angamis leave most of the property to the youngest son, while the Thenkoh Konyaks prefer to leave all the property to the eldest. Moveable property can be inherited by sons and daughters, and no fixed rules apply.

Marriage is also vital for the social advancement of the individual male, for most of the ceremonial feasts that confer status depend on a man having a wife. The new household is both a new economic unit and ritual unit, for the head of the household and his wife become in effect a ritual unit responsible for the daily and yearly rituals which promote the health of the family and the family's crops.

In time the new household will have children of its own, and these in turn will have to be married off. The parents in a hierarchical group such as the Sema will try and use their daughters (and the daughters of their dependants, for whom they provide wives) to secure the highest possible bride-price, and will insist on their marrying within the chiefly clans, which are more or less an aristocratic class. Equally, chiefs will want many sons in order to expand the area of their political influence. As the couple grow older, their status changes. If a man is fortunate, he may complete all the Feasts of Merit and end up with the high social status of head-taker and feast-giver; or he may move through all the *morung* grades, and become a *niengba* (elder), sitting on the *morung* and village council of elders.

At death, bodies are treated in diverse ways. The Angamis bury their corpses, sometimes in stone-lined graves; the Lhota do likewise, though sometimes using a canoe-shaped coffin; the Konyak practice platform exposure of the corpse, though first removing the head, which is placed in a pot or stone cist. It is then

(top left) Men carrying corpse. Konyak, Wakching village. 1937. CFH.
(centre left) Corpse platform with all of a man's possessions beside it. Kalyo-Kengyu, Panso village. 1936. CFH.
(bottom left) Memorial to an elephant hunter. Lhota, Yekhum village. 1922. JPM PR.
(top right) Chief's grave with representations of *daos* and hoes painted on the wood posts. Sangtam, Chimongre village. 1918-23. JHH.
(bottom right) Man's grave with wooden carving of mithan heads, bears, and tigers which the deceased claimed to have killed. Tangkhul, Chingjaroi Khulen village. 1939. UGB.

(left) Men's graves with the deceased's shield, spear, ornaments, eating and drinking utensils and the skulls of sacrificial cattle slaughtered at the funeral feast.
top: Eastern Angami, Lozaphiyemi village. 1918-45. JPM SOAS.
bottom: Angami, Jotsoma village. 1947. WGA.
(top right) Rainbow grave of Kikanuksini. Ao, Mongsenyimti village. 1947. WGA.
(bottom right) Soul effigies and grave goods are placed under a pipal tree in which corpse platforms are placed for exposure. Konyak, Totok village. 1918-45. JPM SOAS.

(top) Stone grave effigies. Eastern Angami, Chizami village. WGA.
(bottom) Wooden grave effigy of Vetzore Angami. Angami, Ketsapomi village. 1947. WGA.

fed over the subsequent years, particularly at the times of agricultural festivals. [16] After the next harvest, the skull, which is painted with a geometric design, is turned to face outwards. This is significant, because there is often some ritual which links the death with the harvest, making a connection between taking fertility out of the earth (the harvest) and returning it (the deceased). The corpse is often buried with implements of the sort he or she will need in the next world, or with a dog or chicken. Chinyang, a Konyak Naga, told Fürer-Haimendorf in 1937 that he wished his impressive ceremonial hat on his death to be placed on the frame of his corpse platform, so that everyone would know (from the decorations) that the deceased was a head-taker, and because he would need his helmet for fighting future battles in the next world. [17] Often some sort of edifice is erected at or near the site, indicating the status of the deceased. This is described in more detail below.

It is clear that changes in burial practice could occur within a relatively short period of time. Chang villages which in 1922 practised platform exposure had by 1936 changed to burial underground. This may have been the result of external influence such as missions. Further aspects of death are considered below, in the section on fertility.

Thus far we have established that certain groups exist within the village, which are of importance for the individual. These are basically ascribed: the individual is born into a lineage, clan, work-gang, *morung*, class and village. The importance of any of these particular groupings, varies from one Naga community to another. There are, of course, opportunities for individual social advancement in warfare and feast-giving, which will be dealt with later. The question of relevance here, however, is the key sociological one. How can diverse types of groups exist and the Nagas still be one society? Can the Angami Nagas, noted as 'democratic' as long ago as 1847, be part of the same society as the class-divided Thendu Konyaks, whose leaders were described at the same time as 'Rajahs'?

The answer is that Naga society is one society, an aggregate of communities who share a set of structures or principles in common, but who emphasize them differently. [18] It can be shown as a diagram thus, using certain of the Naga communities as examples; other groups can be placed as more or less strongly identified with one or other principle. In the diagram, the autocratic-democratic spectrum is shown left to right.

Structural Principle	residence	age	kinship
Dominant unit of society	the village	the *morung* village council	the clan
Found, for example, in	Sema Thendu Konyak	Ao Thenkoh Konyak	Angami

64

(top) Woman's grave. Angami, Jotsoma village. 1947. WGA.
(bottom) Slain tiger. Yimpang village. 1946. CS.

The point being made is that these principles, because they are emphasized differently, give each community a quite different appearance. The emphasis can, and does, change, for reasons that will be touched on later, in the sections on chiefship and Feasts of Merit. However, the possibility of chiefship remains in the democratic communities, and conversely the village council of elders is present and can be significant among the autocratic communities. [19]

The ornaments and particularly the cloths of the Nagas reflect a concern for minute identification of social organisation and social status. The designs and colours of cloths symbolize ascribed status such as village, clan, and *morung* membership, and achieved or prestige status arising from head-taking and feasting exploits.

Perhaps the most developed system of cloth design as indication of status, is found amongst the Aos, who have a wide variety of significant colours and designs, each meaning something very specific. An interesting feature of this is that the emphasis on the clan seems particularly prominent. That is, although the *morung* (as explained above) and the principle of age are the key features of Ao society, this is cross-cut by the emphasis on clan (or at least lineage) membership. The Ao cloth *aosu*, for instance, is worn by a man who has done the mithan sacrifice at least once, but is also worn by his sons, his daughters, and his sons' sons - that is, his lineage descendants. [20] Other groups who also celebrate the mithan sacrifice, such as the Lhota, do not necessarily allow clan members to take advantage of this descent-based contact with fertility. This may be because in the not very distant past, the Lhota did have a more developed kind of chiefship than at present, and in such a society chiefs would want to restrict the ability of other individuals to establish competing powerful lineages based on the principle of heredity.

Thus far we have considered some of the key social units found in varying degrees among the Naga communities. Another kind of grouping, however, seems to exist, though it is sometimes elusive and often does not seem very important. Many observers have noted that the Nagas have aspects of 'dual organisation' or a 'dyadic principle'. That is, it appears that at various social levels, the Nagas distinguish one thing (it might be a social group, or a belief about an animal) by its opposite or antithesis. Some examples will make this clearer.

The Angami lay particular stress on clans, as we have seen. They also group the clans into two broad divisions, called *'kelhu'*. The two ancestors of the Angamis (thought to have been brothers or cousins) founded these two *kelhu*, Kepezoma and Kepefuma. Recently, it appears that many villages are made up of clans belonging only to one *kelhu* or the other. But in the past, or in theory, these *kelhu* were the exogamous groups (that is, the group

within which marriage was not permitted) in each village, thus resembling a 'moiety' marriage system. The two *kelhu* distinguish themselves linguistically by using different terms for 'mother' and 'father'. As an added complication, in practice one of the two *kelhu* has itself divided into two sub-divisions of equal status, so that a three-phratry system in fact appears to obtain. [21]

The Eastern Angamis repeat the idea of the two brother-founders of the tribe, in their village role of *tevo* (or *thevo*), or sacred descendant of the founder. The tevo is from the original founder's clan, but there is always an assistant, descended from the co-founder's clan. The early observer Major Butler, when describing the 'two chiefs' of each village, hereditary but with only 'nominal' authority, was probably describing the Tevo and his assistant. [22] The Zemi Nagas also have, at least in theory, a dual system based on two exogamous divisions, the Nriami and the Neomi. [23]

Other dualistic features can be found. But it would seem that division into three rather than two, is equally common. The Aos recognise two fundamental language-groups (Mongsen and Chongli), which then assign their clans between three theoretically exogamous phratries. The Lhota clans are also found in a three-phratry system. [24]

Effigy of a warrior, Devore Angami. Eastern Angami, Nerhema village. 1947. WGA.

Men in full dress dancing at the annual ceremony after sowing, the *Moatsu*.
Ao, Ungma village. 1918-45. JPM SOAS.

Chapter 7

Chiefs and Democrats

As has been mentioned above, some Naga communities are organised very strongly around the principle of the village as a unit, ruled over by an autocratic chief. Let us look at what this means in more detail.

'Villages of the Thendu group, which were ruled by powerful chiefs, invariably faced the outside world as united communities,' wrote Christoph von Fürer-Haimendorf of the Konyak Nagas as they were in 1936. [1] Their chiefs, or Great *Angs*, were not, however, only political leaders; their persons were also sacred, and so they were dominant in secular and ritual senses. They were a special vehicle for an indefinable quality we will call 'fertility', which they channelled to their communities. They married strictly within other Great *Ang* clans, and children of their secondary commoner wives were not members of their chiefly lineage, but had the rank only of small *Ang*. Their *morungs*, coffins and stools uniquely featured carved hornbill heads: the Konyaks say that 'the hornbill is Ang of the birds'. [2] They expected deference from the villagers as well as part of their crops and labour; they could exercise sexual rights over the women of commoner (*Ben*) clans. Their houses were the largest in the village, outshining the *morungs* in wealth of carvings; they were entitled to the first share of meat, typically the leg, at feasts. They and their close clansmen were entitled to particular ornaments: in Longkhai, for instance, the wives of Great *Angs* were entitled to carry a specially carved spear. [2] *Ang* and *Ben* also had different funerary practices. In the Thendu village of Wangla, the heads of *Ang* corpses were placed in stone pots, while those of *Ben* corpses were placed in clay pots. [4]

The situation of a chief was not, however, altogether secure. At a ritual level, if a village did not prosper, the *Ang* might be held to blame, just as he was also held responsible for the village's prosperity. If his crops failed he would be unable to give the feasts that symbolized, and to some extent brought about, his power. [5] Equally, if land was unavailable for expanding his domain, his power could be questioned. In 1936 the Great *Ang* of Mon received tribute from several neighbouring villages (or rather particular morungs); but elsewhere *Angs* had to become accustomed to receiving a token tribute from villages they were no longer powerful enough to dominate. Quarrels between rival *Ang* lineages, or between two *Ang* sons, over succession to the position of *Ang*, could also lead to a diminution of an *Ang's* power.

Supposing such a change, or rebellion, did occur, the villagers might well start to move towards a more egalitarian system, and this is what in fact is found in the Konyak area. More or less side by

side with the autocratic Thendu villages, are the egalitarian Thenkoh villages. They recognise the same classes of commoners, intermediate and *Ang* clans, but the distinctions are mostly only of importance in matters such as the non-sharing of food from the same plate. In the Thenkoh group the *morungs* are the biggest buildings in the village, and the government of the village is by a council of elders. In this council the *Ang* is only one member, sharing authority with leaders of each of the *morungs* (*niengbas*). The council is responsible for settling inter-*morung* disputes and for determining, through reading omens, which fields the village should cultivate each year; the *niengbas* also announce the *gennas* designed to protect the fertility of the crops. Each *morung* is free to make its own alliances with neighbouring *morungs* and villages.

Thendu and Thenkoh seem to distinguish themselves very obviously. Thus, Thendu men tattoo their faces as a sign of head-taking and wear their hair long, while Thenkoh men do not face-tattoo and keep their hair short. There are also obvious differences in dialect and kinship terminology: in Longkhai (Thendu) husband and wife call each other by their personal names, while in Wakching (Thenkoh) they call each other 'mother of / father of so-and-so'. Nevertheless 'Thendu' and 'Thenkoh' should not be thought of as separate groups or societies, despite these differences. They are, rather, the same society with a different stress on the importance of the hereditary principle of chiefship. Thendu and Thenkoh are two potential transformations of one kind of society, and it appears that over time villages changed from one to the other. It is not clear how long the time-scale concerned might be. In 1936 Wakching (then known as Jaktoong) was a Thenkoh village, and the evidence suggests that it was also Thenkoh a century before, when an observer noted that it had more than one chief. By contrast, Wanching (then known as Tabloong) at that time appeared to be ruled by a single powerful chief, whereas by 1936 it too had Thenkoh characteristics. [6] Both Thenkoh and Thendu categories, however, recognize the existence of noble and commoner clans, of unequal status, even if the distinction in Thenkoh villages is of minor practical importance. Even within Thenkoh villages, the relative importance of chiefs clearly varies.

In this respect Tamlu is an interesting case in point. Tamlu is a Konyak village, but with a very obvious degree of Ao influence in its language and social structure. It follows Ao rather than Konyak marriage patterns, several of its clans are from Ao villages, and it is known that it did not have chiefs at all until three generations before 1936. At this point, for unknown reasons, it received an *Ang* from Wanching, since when there has been an *Ang* clan, as in other Konyak villages. [7]

The Konyak people of Kongan village also insist that they did

Page 68.
Headman of Yimtsong-Awenrr village drinking from a horn and wearing a hat with a hornbill decoration. Yimchungr. 1947. WGA.

Page 69.
(top) Sha-long, the *Ang* of Zu-nyu with face tattoo. Konyak, Wakching. 1936. Photo. CFH.
(bottom) Warrior wearing a hat decorated with hornbill beaks and boar's tusks. Konyak, Wakching village. 1937. CFH.

Page 70.
(top) Headman with his daughter. Chang, Chingmiren village. 1947. WGA.
(bottom) Man from Ponyo village wearing a turban, with tattoos on his chest, arms and chin. 1936. CFH.

Page 71.
(top left) *Ang's* wife holding a two-pronged spear as a sign of her status. Konyak, Longkhai village. 1936. CFH.
(top right) Descendants of Sakhai, a famous Sema warrior. JHH.
(bottom) Chief of Chingmei village dances at the ceremonies that follow the conclusion of a successful raid. He wears full ceremonial dress and, as he dances, he strikes his shield with his *dao* to tally the number of captured enemy heads. Chang. 1918-45. JPM SOAS.

not originally have *Angs* at all; their acquisition of two *Ang* clans from Wakching village happened within the recent historical past, and thus here too the society has adopted an aristocratic ideology. [8]

In 1934, the Deputy Commissioner was called to Wanching, to help settle a succession dispute. Different factions favoured either retaining the village's own small *Ang*, or inviting into the village a Great *Ang* of the village of Chi, who would bring with him an autocratic rule unfamiliar to Wanching people. The villagers listened to what the Deputy Commissioner had to say (he recommended inviting in the Great *Ang* of Chi, but imposing restrictions on his rule), and made the opposite decision. [9] In this case such a debate seems to make the Thendu/Thenkoh models almost the objects of conscious choice. This suggests that though the outward signs of difference between democratic and chiefly models are marked, fundamentally the two categories may not be far apart. A change of emphasis rather than a change of nature may be at issue.

The same process may well be going on in the southern part of the Naga country. Anthropologists have come to think of the Angami and their neighbours the Sema as distinct 'tribes'. It has long been held that the Angami are the most egalitarian of all the groups. 'Their government' wrote Major Butler in 1855, 'is decidedly democratic; for, although each village community has a nominal head or chief, it is evident their chiefs have no absolute power over the people.' [10] The Sema, on the other hand, have powerful secular chiefs, distinguished in their appearance by ornaments such as the large cotton-wool ear-pads. [11]

There is evidence that Sema chiefs can run into the same sort of problems as their Thendu counterparts; and on the other hand there is evidence that the Angami may at one time have stressed the chiefly principle, even though it is now largely absent. They have a ritual specialist or *tevo* who embodies and symbolizes the unity of the village for ritual, but not political, purposes; and they have clan chiefs who may be considered as de facto war leaders. Among the Lhota we know that the formerly powerful hereditary clan chiefs have almost disappeared altogether and a more egalitarian government by clan and *morung* elders is found. Perhaps this is the direction in which the Angamis too have moved. If this is the case, the Thendu/Thenkoh distinction may also be relevant to the Sema/Angami area.

At this point the anthropologically-minded may be reminded of a significant academic debate concerning oscillation between two pole positions of democracy and hierarchy in a neighbouring Hill people in Burma. Since this is of relevance to the Naga case, but is a somewhat technical debate, it is dealt with in the following Note which general readers may prefer to skip.

(top) Konyak warrior wearing a hat decorated with hornbill feathers. 1936. CFH.
(bottom) *Angs* from Chi and Sheangha villages at Shiong. Konyak. 1936. CFH.

A Note on the Nagas, the Kachin and the oscillation model

At this point it is as well to make explicit reference to the major theoretical system that underlies ideas of structural oscillation, as developed by Edmund Leach for the neighbouring Kachin of Burma. In the classic *Political Systems of Highland Burma*, Leach outlines an oscillation (that is, a cyclical rather than a unilineal direction of change) within the single Kachin society with its generalized culture: a hierarchical/aristocratic model is termed *'gumsa'* and an egalitarian/democratic model *'gumlao'*. There is a prima facie similarity with the Konyak Thendu and Thenkoh, and Leach himself records his supposition that Kachin and Naga hill areas share a similar kind of organisation. Kachin and Konyak Naga share a basic class structure. The Kachin recognise four classes: chiefly, aristocrat, commoner and slave. These correspond to the Konyak Great *Ang*, Small *Ang*, Intermediate, and Commoner (*Ben*). [12]

To take the Kachin *gumlao* or egalitarian model first, *gumlao* ideology denies legitimacy to the ranking of lineages. In doing so, it has evolved a mechanism which counteracts the otherwise inevitable tendency to hierarchization that accompanies the asymmetrical Kachin marriage rule. According to this rule, lineages X and Y cannot stand as both wife-givers and wife-takers to each other. Rather, X give wives to Y, who give wives to Z. In this system, wife-givers are reckoned superior to wife-receivers; but this potentiality for hierarchy is restrained in the *gumlao* case because the lineages marry in a circle: X marries Y, marries Z, marries X. Strict equality is not easily maintained in the long run, but equality is strongly asserted at least at the ideological level.

There are some parallels here with the Thenkoh Konyaks. In Wakching village in 1937, Fürer-Haimendorf recorded the details of 310 first marriages [13]. No Great *Ang* clan existed, and the ranking of the aristocratic, intermediate and commoner clans was of minor importance (and as has been said, was insignificant for most purposes in daily life). But although there was a relatively classless ideology, the marriage rule was different from the Kachin and there was no evidence of marrying in a circle. Unlike the Kachin, the Nagas do not prohibit marriage with the Father's Sister's Daughter. It is admittedly less common than Mother's Brother's Daughter marriage, but if it occurs at all, it precludes the possibility of asymmetrical relations being the norm. Thus in Wakching in 1937, there was complete inter-marriageability between clans, who might be both wife-givers and wife-receivers to each other. The clans of the Bala and Thepong *morungs* are traditional marriage partners. Of 15 actual clan unions between the two *morungs* in 1936, 10 involved inter-marriage. Clans within a class did not use marriage to express a relationship of superiority. Between classes, women moved up or down between intermediate and commoner clans. Between the Oukheang and Balang *morungs*, *Ang* and *Ben* clans also inter-married.

In the Kachin *gumsa* case, by contrast, hierarchy is pronounced. The potentiality within generalized exchange for relations of superiority/inferiority between lineages, is fully realized. The relationship between two lineages is always asymmetrical: the expression of political ranking between lineages within each class derives from the marriage system, where a basic rule obtains: the wife-giving lineage X is superior (*mayu*) to the wife-receivers Y who are inferior (*dama*). This is not necessarily a totally one-sided relationship. It exists within the idiom of kinship and is thus to some degree equal. Although Y owes X allegiance, X and Y exchange gifts, and X is obliged to offer protection. According to Leach this system is inherently unstable. The senior lineage may feel excessively burdened by these kinship obligations, and will seek to transform them into a purely political relationship of domination/subordination, unrestrained by the kinship requirements of reciprocity. The spur to this may be the ideological influence of the neighbouring autocratic Shan princes of the valleys, but the main motor force remains internal – the obligations inherent in the kinship system, which come into tension with the material desire to accumulate surplus on the part of the wealthier lineages. If this happens, it may cause the inferior lineages to revolt. The revolt does not merely produce a fission into smaller-scale replicas, but produces an oscillation towards another model altogether – the democratic *gumlao* described above. [14]

There are clearly some parallels with the Thendu Konyak case, it being assumed here that the Kachin lineage and the Naga clan are roughly comparable. In the Thendu village of Oting, for example, there are clans divided into the classes listed above. As primary marriages, the Great *Angs* marry only within their own class, among neighbouring villages. If Great *Ang* women do not marry Great *Ang* men, they marry down, into an inferior class, which creates a relationship of superiority favouring the wife-givers, as in the *gumsa* model. Within the other classes, however, the *gumsa* preference for marrying within the class is not found. There is a well-developed rule for commoner men to marry aristocrat women, [15] and this cross-class marriage is the norm, and not the exception as in the *gumsa* case. The parallel is also not sustained in the case of the 'intermediate' clan men who generally marry down, accepting wives from commoner clans.

In the village of Nianu, [16] we find that there is a preference for marrying within the class as first choice marriages, but when this is broken, it is the men who marry down, and not the women: small *Ang* men marry intermediate clan women of their own village;

intermediate men marry commoner women. [17] In another Thendu village, Chingphoi, the record shows that two *Ang* clans and one commoner clan inter-marry, women move in marriage up and down the class hierarchy, and lineages stand as both wife-givers and wife-receivers to each other. [18]

In other words, in the case of Thendu Konyaks, the *'mayu-dama'*-type relationship only clearly obtains in the case of the Great *Ang* class, where it is certainly an ideological preference. Therefore there are clear differences in the kinship system between Kachin and Naga. There exists, nevertheless, a possible motor for oscillation which may be applicable to both the Nagas and the Kachin: the desire for surplus.

In both the Kachin and Naga cases, the desire for surplus appears to be inherently in tension with the ideology of egalitarianism. Equality is in practice hard to maintain. If an individual or lineage produces a surplus, two related consequences may occur.

First, the lineage is able to attract wives (particularly wives of other surplus-creating lineages), increase the labour power of the lineage, and increase the available surplus for Feasting. Second, the surplus is converted in Feasts into prestige and rank and the acquisition of higher brideprice through the marriage of lineage women. In this way the possibility exists for a breakdown of strict equality, though wealth is primarily converted into high ritual status rather than great material wealth.

In the case of the hierarchical Kachin *gumsa* and Naga Thendu Konyak categories, a tension may exist once surplus is gained. This has its roots in the competing claims of kinship and political dominance. Where the idiom of kinship entails a certain recognition of equality, the interests of power entail a negation of that equality. The dominance of the Thendu *Angs* is, in the end, based on their unequal ownership of land and their monopoly of Feasting. An *Ang* class which exacts too much from its followers, or which runs out of available land, cannot maintain its position. Its sacred status as directly linked to the ancestors and spirits will be undermined. Other chiefs may emerge, or a reaction towards the more democratic model may emerge.

Therefore, in summary, it may be the case that oscillation is found in both the Konyak and Kachin cases, though they do not share a common marriage rule. Its cause is a complex inter-relationship between material factors such as the desire for surplus and land shortage on the one hand, and the effects of a competitive cosmological system, which acts as a powerful incentive to produce, on the other.

To deal with the material basis first, the argument posits economic crisis arising out of land shortage. That is, the demand for surplus when it is at its peak, coincides with the point at which land is most in short supply, since increasing surplus can only be achieved by increasing population. Various structural transformations might emerge in this case. [19] First, expansion would involve the colonization or the seizure of land from others, and this process seems to be most associated with a strengthening of the principle of chieftainship, in which chiefs control a number of villages and exact tribute (as, for example, is characteristic of the Sema Nagas). Second, a kind of adaptation might occur, in which an autocratic system, coming under increased strain through land shortage and unable to continue accumulating surplus, finds the chiefly principle weakening, and instead a more equal system based on the organising principle of age, emerges (as, for instance, among the Ao). A third possibility might emerge if this age-grade system cannot cope with diminishing surpluses. Intensification or involution in this case might lead to a change in the agricultural method, and wet-rice terracing might supplant slash-and-burn agriculture. In this circumstance, the principle of the clan seems to be dominant. Age-set organisation is less necessary than in slash-and-burn tasks, and leadership is achieved through a sort of Big Man individualism.

On the other hand, the cosmological system, which encourages a quest for fertility-maximizing, through feasting and other exploits, is equally a causative factor in catalyzing or promoting changes in social organisation. [20] The system is considered in the chapters below.

It should be noted, however, in considering the 'pole positions', that most Naga communities fall solidly between the two, containing elements of democratic and hierarchical organisation. In most communities it is Feasting which offers all males equally a chance to gain status and to take on some leadership specialization (that is to say, village priests or council members are likely to be renowned Feast-givers). Indeed it has been argued that in the Naga case, unlike the Kachin, the presence or absence of chiefs is largely irrelevant to the basic features of Naga social organisation, in which not chiefly birth but Feasting (or other exploits) is the key to leadership for all males equally. This situation obtains in the case of the Chin, who share many aspects of Naga society and belief. [21]

Even if the oscillation model is accepted, however, it is not the only way in which villages change. There is plenty of evidence that simple fission occurs, in which a part of a village splits off, forming a smaller replica of its parent, and not organized according to wholly opposite structural principles. Many villages are able to describe this process happening within the recent past; in other cases, particular *khels* are known to be so antagonistic towards each other, fortifying themselves against each other rather than against the the outside world, that fission appears to be imminent. [22] Equally, rebellion need not imply structural change.

In one instance, the village of Chen killed their *Ang* and most of his family, after persistent deceit on his part. Soon after, however, they desired to reinstate the chiefly system, and asked the son of the deceased *Ang* to return, albeit with restrictions on his rights at sacrifices. [23]

(top) Woman with a shaved head which indicates her slave status. Konyak, Lunglam village. 1918-45. JPM SOAS.
(bottom) View of Longsa village showing layout of houses grouped in wards or *khels*.   Ao. 1918-45. JPM SOAS.

Y-posts carved with mithan heads and *aghuhu* or enemy's teeth. Sema.
1913-23. JHH.

Sacrificing an ox. Konyak, Namsang village. 1937. CFH.

Chapter 8

Feasts of Merit

Early writers noted that Feast-giving was an important part of Naga life. One account written in 1873 gives some idea of the practice: '(Stones) each represent a certain amount of wealth expended, for on setting them up a great Feast is given to many men by some individual who thus perpetuates his own memory. After Feasting & drinking 'moti' for 3 or 4 days, all proceed & drag in the stone & set it up...' [1] Such accounts correctly noted that the Feasts were intended to enhance the prestige of the Feast-giver, and that some large-scale collective act – such as dragging a huge stone into the village – was often the culmination. But what exactly is going on here ?

Feasts of Merit are optional Feasts performed by an individual. They are distinct from life-cycle and from agricultural-cycle Feasts, though all of these share the notion of *genna* (generally, a rite, but with strong notions of tabu or prohibition) and sacrifice. The Feasts are ranked in importance and scale, each stage carrying rights to new kinds of personal adornment and house decoration, and prohibitions in terms of permitted foods. Each stage burdens the Feast giver with ever greater expense in terms of slaughtered cattle and vats of rice beer. The final *gennas* in the series, which not all men will attain, may involve not only the stone-dragging mentioned above, but also the sacrifice of a mithan, the erection of Y-shaped posts, or the adding of carved house-horns. Theoretically, a man who finishes all the Feasts of Merit would then start again at the first, but this has probably never happened; rather, the final Feast is repeated, if the individual can afford to do it twice. In some communities, women have a parallel set of Feasts they undertake. [2]

These ceremonies both mark and create distinctions in social status. The Feast converts material wealth (the cattle and rice for rice-beer) into social rank. A man who has enough wealth to give a Feast would at the same time obviously be a man possessing 'fertility': his wealth is a sign of this. The Feast is therefore a recognition of his ritual status, and a mechanism for spreading his 'fertility' among his fellow villagers. In this respect two things are noticeable. First, the Feasts of Merit tend to take place at the same time as significant agricultural-cycle rituals (such as at the Angami Terhengi harvest-home festival); and second, the posts that are erected are said to be basically sexual in shape. The Sema forked Y-posts are symbols of the female sex, and the Angami erect two stones together – a male and a female. It is through their planting in the earth that the Feast-giver transmits his fertility into the common land of the village. An interplay between the ideas

relating to fertility, human sexuality and agricultural fertility, is being made.

Not all the groups stress the Feasts of Merit equally. In fact, given the information of the previous sections on social structures and chiefship, it ought to be predictable which groups would tend to favour these ceremonies: the groups at the egalitarian end of the spectrum. This is because the Feasts allow all men the opportunity to advance in social status. This individualistic competitiveness is quite at odds with the emphasis on ascribed status in the autocratic communities. We therefore find that among the Thendu Konyak, the Feasts, culminating in the dragging in of a new log-gong and the erection of a carved post in front of the house, are not open to all males, but have become monopolized by men of the Great *Ang* clans, who use it to enhance their power. The hierarchical Sema do celebrate Feasts of Merit, but the celebrants do not acquire status that would undermine the class basis of chiefly rule.

The unit of celebration in the Feasts of Merit is also predictable, given the spectrum of Naga social structure. Among the relatively egalitarian Lhotas, for example, the first *genna* involves a Feast for the individual's clan members; the second and third a Feast for the clans of the husbands of the women of the sacrificer's clan (i.e. certain other village clans); and the final *genna* a Feast for the whole village. [3] In other words, the Feasts expand out, starting from the primary stressed social structure, the clan. For the Sema, the stressed structure is the village, and thus the first *genna* is for the man's own village, and the last is for a neighbouring village.

The celebration of particular Feasts of Merit is vividly commemorated not only in the stones and posts erected, but also in the cloths worn by the celebrant – and indeed (in the case of an Ao Naga man) also by his wife, daughter, son and grandson. In 1947 one observer noted the details of status thus: 'A number of Lothas (Lhotas) have performed social *gennas* and wear corresponding cloaks. Nzuthang for example has done the Wozuya *genna* and was wearing a dark blue cloth with five pale blue bands in the centre and three pale blue lines at the top and bottom. Phandemo, who had gone considerably further and dragged a stone five times, wears a similar cloth but with four pale blue lines instead of three.' [4] The cloths do not merely mark status, but also, simply by the fact of constantly being seen, promote competitiveness.

Why should this be important ? Although not immediately apparent from the outside, two important functions are operating. First, the need for lavish outlay on cattle, pigs and rice-beer is an incentive to production, and ensures that poorer members of the clan and village are feasted when they cannot themselves afford to kill pigs or cattle. Equally, in conditions where storage of perishable foodstuffs is limited, the Feast ensures that food is not

(top left) Log dragging for the rebuilding of the
Thepong *morung*. Konyak, Wakching. 1936. CFH.
(top right) Women and children helping to drag log.
Konyak, Wakching village. 1936. CFH.

Dragging a gravestone. Zemi, Laisong village. 1941.
UGB.

wasted. And second, the Feast of Merit allows individuals to make symbolic statements about their power. Power ultimately is based on land. Even among the Angami some men own more land (and therefore wealth) than others, and this is the only basis of power. But rather than say, 'I am powerful because I own a lot of land,' the individual instead proclaims his contact with the mysterious 'fertility', which has allowed him to accumulate enough wealth to Feast his fellow-villagers.

It is possible to see the Angami or Lhota system of Feasts of Merit as maintaining a sort of balance. On the one hand, the system promotes the urge to accumulate, but on the other hand constrains too much accumulation by demanding that this wealth is redistributed in return for high ritual and social status. But is this really a balance ?

It might be argued, rather, that this system is inherently unstable and that it promotes a certain tension in the society. That is, individuals try to maximize their stock of, or contact with, 'fertility', particularly through Feasts: the result is wealth and hence power. [5] But 'fertility' is a slippery concept. There is no obvious way of controlling, measuring, or limiting it. The individual may be able to keep more of his wealth than he distributes, thus possibly starting down the road to a more hierarchical society. In the other direction, the ideology of 'fertility-maximization' could allow (especially in cases where the actual power of the chiefs was declining, such as when there was a shortage of land) non-chiefly individuals to claim that they, and not their chief, have a greater access to it.

Two points can be made in conclusion. First, Feasting and fertility maximization constitute a basis for Naga unity. Whatever the political structures in particular communities, in all cases greater or lesser importance is given to these related concepts. Second, the question of causality is again raised, and it remains very hard to answer. Is it the case that these beliefs are secondary to simple secular pressures for wealth and power as described earlier, which are the main determinant of particular kinds of political organisation ? Or is it possible that these cosmological beliefs can themselves also influence or cause social change through their capacity to stimulate competitive practices ?

If the latter is the case, it can be argued that Feasting and other fertility-maximizing activities provide the motivation for the production of wealth and confer high ritual status. Competition for such status, which is theoretically open to all individuals, results in particular patterns of social organisation. The pole positions in Naga political organisation show the results of this process. Among the Angami Nagas the intense open competition to maximize fertility result in a 'Big Man' system. Individual Feasting and warfare achievements alone confer high status, irrespective of

ancestry. It could also result in some villages in a Feasting inflation which equalized all individuals because none of them could any longer afford the Feasts. [6] By contrast, among the Konyaks, chiefs seek to monopolize fertility maximization and to deny commoners the right to participate in Feasting activities.

(top) Bull mithan. Sangtam, Changtorr village. 1947. CS.
(bottom) Men cutting up meat for a feast. Zemi, Laisong village. 1941. UGB.

(top) Dancing around Y-posts with mithan heads tied to them at a Feast of Merit. Sangtam, Phirre village. 1947. CS.
(bottom left) Elaborately carved Y-posts. Chang, Chingmei village. 1936. CFH.
(bottom right) Y-post. Sema, Litami village. 1947. WGA.

Humtso village street with groups of stones which have been set up in the
course of Feasts of Merit. Lhoto. 1918-45. JPM SOAS.

Chapter 9

The Ritual World

Ritual beliefs and practices permeate all of Naga social activity. This does not mean that the individual wanders around in a haze of mystical experience. Most of Naga life is eminently practical. Ritual, however, offers the possibility of understanding the world and of changing it.

Traditionally Nagas were described as animists; that is, they believed in the existence of spiritual beings inhabiting the natural world. In fact, this is only half true, because they also believed in gods. The spirits and gods have a particular relationship to the Naga concept of 'fertility'. This quality, already referred to above, is so important that it will be dealt with separately in the next chapter. But it should be said here that the gods and spirits are seen by the Nagas as not so much affecting society directly, but rather influencing for good or ill the natural cyclical flow of 'fertility'. Therefore, when the people offer a sacrifice to a god, it is usually to ask that he intervene beneficially in the matter of maximizing fertility – good crops, the heads of tigers or enemy warriors, healthy children. At the Feasts of Merit, the Sangtam say to their god Tsungrangre, 'Today we are offering you this mithan. May there be no rain today. May everything go well. May all our men and women flourish. Give us good crops.'[1]

There are three types of spirits in each Naga group: a High God or Gods, a god or spirit who lives in the sky, and earth spirits. Tsungrangre, the Sangtam god referred to above, for instance, is a little below the absentee High God, Makyupelara, but he is in charge of the world, and the sun and moon are among his incarnations.[2] The Ao High God, Lichaba or Lungkizungba, is thought to have created the world thus: 'Lichaba first created the plains and made it all smooth, then he made Nagaland but while doing so he started having stomach pains and rushed his job so that now all is hilly and torn up.'[3]

But although these types seem to be common, they have different functions, in terms of the extent to which they intervene actively in human society. Again, there is a predictable relationship with a particular social structure. The egalitarian Angamis, for instance, recognise a High God or Creator, Kepenopfu (who, uniquely among the Nagas, is essentially female). But this god is remote, vaguely identified, and does not act very strongly in everyday life. By contrast, there are many earth spirits or, *terhoma*: the spirits of evil, fruitfulness, game, the household, and so on. It is to these low-level spirits that the Angamis offer sacrifices. On the other hand, the hierarchical Konyak place a great deal of power in the hands of their High God, Gawang, who exerts

Parade of warriors from Chingmei village carrying shields and spears. Chang, Tuensang village. 1947. WGA.

Page 84-85.
Warriors from Chingmei village dancing at Tuensang. Chang. 1947. WGA.

a direct influence on earthly matters, and their sacred chiefs (angs) buttress their power through their special relationship with this powerful god.

The Lhota, in some sense intermediate between these two groups, give an important role to the sky spirits or *potsos*, who comprise one layer of several spirit worlds, extending from our earth upwards. The *potsos* visit the earth from time to time in order to advise the village shaman. In 1911 two sky *potsos* visisted the shaman of Illimyo village, bringing with them reeds (meaning sunny weather was ahead), part of a railway carriage (meaning elephants would give trouble), two loads of dark blue thread (meaning someone would die an accidental death), and a broom (meaning that wind would damage the crops). [4]

The Zemi also accord much importance to known spirits capable of exerting a malign influence on society. The *Heramui* ceremony, at which the fourteen great spirits are summoned and feasted, is performed outside the village perimeter, in case any error in the ritual leaves one of the spirits angry and vengeful within the village itself, and liable to cause illness amongst the villagers. [5]

The range of Naga gods and spirits, being thought of in fairly general terms, is generally open to outside influence, and there is evidently some borrowing between groups. There is also borrowing from non-Naga cultures. The pantheon of the Kabui Nagas living in or near the Hindu state of Manipur, for instance, includes the god 'Buicheniu', who is not of major importance, but is clearly a Naga transformation of the Hindu Vishnu. [6]

The essential part of Naga ritual practice is the sacrifice-*genna* pairing. The sacrifice comes first, and it may be of anything from an egg, leaf or rice, to a chicken or a mithan in the great Feast of Merit festivals. The object of the sacrifice may be the Creator God or a jungle spirit, as is appropriate to the situation. The *genna* follows it. In the *genna* period everything that is normally active becomes inactive: there is a prohibition on sex, work, certain foods, and travel. This period of *genna* may be up to several days, and transgressions are dealt with severely. What is the purpose of this restraint ?

Obviously, it is a dramatic way of indicating that something special is occurring, and the unit observing the *genna* (a man and wife at the time of childbirth or sowing; the whole village in the case of a major Feast of Merit) is brought into clear focus. But we can go beyond this by noticing that a key part of the *genna* is the prohibition on people crossing the boundary of the unit concerned: people may not, for instance, enter or leave the village. The purpose of the sacrifice-*genna* is to facilitate the proper flow of fertility in the relevant social group, but not outside it. The inactivity is a period of calm in which the group makes itself

receptive to fertility, to act as its vehicle, but only for the particular social group concerned.

The Nagas have complicated beliefs about the soul. It appears that all Naga communities say that human beings have two or more souls. These souls are separate from the ideas concerning fertility, though it must be said that the distinction is not always clear. Thus the Konyaks seem to identify one soul (out of three) as remaining in the skull, actively bringing prosperity. [7]

Despite variations from community to community, the Nagas think of souls in two general ways. There is a soul which is the soul of the person himself, who on dying an ordinary death, goes to the land of the dead. It is also this soul which may inhabit the body of a leopard or tiger. The other kind of soul is a more elusive entity, but it is liable to attack by spirits which can make the person ill, or it can wander away, which has the same effect. [8] When this happens a sacrifice is required.

All Naga communities believe in a close link between the living and the dead, who at one time inhabited the same world. [9] The land of the dead is variously thought of as in the sky or underground or on a far hill, and, on the whole, life there resembles life on earth. Enemies slain on this earth will again be fought in the land of the dead and there is no particular salvation held out for the poor and meek. But the land of the dead is not the only destination for the soul after death. The Yimchungr and others believe that one of the several souls is likely to return as an insect or other animal. [10]

The living and the dead are brought together in dreams, which are in many ways of great importance in ritual practice. Dreams can influence agricultural activities and close attention is given to unearthing their meaning. [11]

A unifying feature of Naga cosmology is the belief in a close connection between human beings and the large cats. Naga origin myths say that the spirit, man, and the tiger were the three sons of the same woman, [12] and it is common to find that a *genna* period for the killing of a tiger would be the same as that for a man. The most developed beliefs about were-tigers appear to be those of the Sema and Konyak Nagas. This may be because this phenomenon is a kind of possession, and possession is often found to be the only vehicle for individuals in closed or autocratic societies to express their individual aspirations. The Konyak sacred chief, powerful though he may be, cannot deny the legitimacy of his subjects' experiences of this kind, and Konyak women are therefore found in this role, occupying a public office of a sort not otherwise available to them. [13] In 1947 one Sangtam were-leopard talked about this relationship to W.G. Archer. 'My soul does not live in my body. It lives in the leopard. It is not in me now. It visits me in sleep. I meet it in dreams. Then I know what is has been doing....If

(top left) *Morung* carving showing a man holding leopard by the tail. Konyak, Anaki village. 1937. CFH.
(top right) Lemang the renowned were-tiger of Kongan village. Konyak, Tanhai village. 1936. CFH.
(middle) Figures representing 'Thepa' and 'Thevo' the founders of the village, made at the path clearing festival. Angami, Mezoma village. 1947. WGA.
(bottom) Crossed reeds on path to deter spirits of disease on path from Wakching village. Konyak. 1936. CFH.

anything happened to my leopard in the day, my soul would come and tell me. I would get the same wounds.'[14] Not all Nagas, however, accept these stories, and scepticism is readily expressed by some individuals.[15]

Other animals as well as the tiger have a close ritual relationship with man. The mithan, the semi-feral bison sacrificed at feasts, is closely connected to man. The Ao believe that every man has an alter-ego called a *tiya*, and that both man and the *tiya* have three souls; in each case one of the three souls is a mithan, so that the earthly man has a soul in a celestial mithan belonging to his *tiya*, and the *tiya* has a soul in an earthly mithan.[16]

The agricultural year is, as has been mentioned, marked by ritual practices. These may often be small-scale, but some of the ceremonies are village-wide and may go on for many days. An example of this is the Spring Festival, which marks the beginning of the new agricultural year in most Naga communities. In the Konyak villages the Spring Festival is the occasion for dances, feasting, drinking and sacrifices that go on for several days. Special platforms for dancing on are constructed outside the *Ang's* house. Individuals may paint their faces and will wear their most splendid ornaments, which may be those indicating their military prowess or may be precious clan heirloom objects. The dancing is organized according to *morung*, the members of each *morung* moving around the village and dancing in front of each of the other *morungs:* the rights to perform certain dances are jealously guarded by the *morungs*. During the Festival the village priest addresses the Konyak High God, Gawang, asking for fertility in the crops and among the people.[17] Other voices chant that the village will achieve victories over its neighbours,[18] and at this point in the year the captured enemy skulls stored in the *morung* are ritually fed with rice beer.

Ritual beliefs seek to explain the world, but also to allow some sort of control over it. A simple example of this is the Konyak belief concerning earthquakes. 'Earthquakes are caused when a village *Ang* dies and on his way into the land of the dead cuts through the strong creepers which obstruct his path. Then all the people call, 'Don't fall, don't fall, so that the earth may stay still'. The belief explains the phenomenon, but also prescribes a collective action which provides a remedy.[19]

A similar belief concerning eclipses of both the sun and moon, reveals a further important aspect of ritual: the symbolic re-enactment of significant social tensions. The Konyaks (and others) believe that eclipses are caused when an animal tries to devour the sun or moon, and carvings on house posts portray this event in Konyak villages. This animal is said by some to be a frog and by others a tiger or dog.[20] A remedy is available to counter this impending calamity. In Mon, 'When there is an eclipse and

Page 87.
(top left) Dancer. Oting village. 1936. CFH.
(top right) Girls dancing at the Spring Festival. Konyak, Chingphoi village. 1937. CFH.
(bottom) Head-receiving rituals. Konyak, Oting village. 1937. CFH.

Page 88.
(top and middle) Head-receiving dance. Konyak, Tamlu village. 1936. CFH.
(bottom) Decorating a shield with chalk in preparation for a head-takers' dance. Konyak, Wakching village. 1936. CFH.

Men and women dancing. Chang, Tuensang village. 1947. WGA.

Men dancing in ceremonial dress. Sangtam, Chongtore village. 1947. WGA.

(top) Men of the Tsotonoma khel wearing ceremonial dress while dragging in a new gate. Angami, Kohima village. 1947. WGA.
(bottom) Men dancing, some wearing necklets made from enamel plates. Yimchungr, Cheshorr village. 1947. WGA.

(top) Throwing darts at the *Hgangi* Festival. Zemi, Laisong village. 1941-42.
UGB.
(bottom) Young men and women dancing. Zemi, Laisong
village. 1941. UGB.

Dance with hornbill feathers. Zemi, Nenglo village. 1947. CS.

"the frog eats the sun", the Lukyem people shout, "Eat it all" and the *Ang* people shout and make a great noise, "Don't eat it, this is our sun".' [21] First of all, this belief connects with another Konyak belief, that once the moon was quite near the earth, but men and the animals pushed it away: [22] in the case of the eclipse the frog is threatening not only to push it away but to make it disappear altogether.

But it is of more importance to note which clans are involved. Mon is a Thendu village with a powerful Great *Ang*. The *Angs* are particularly identified with tiger. For instance, *Ang* clans are not allowed to eat tigers, though other clans can.[23] The Lukyem, in the quotation above, are, literally, the 'frog clan', and they are commoners. They are also a founding clan of the village, along with the *Ang* clan, and thus in a sense are complementary (as is also the case in Hungphoi), but they are also politically in a superior/inferior relationship (and indeed may be seen to represent the pole autocratic/egalitarian ideologies found in the Naga communities). An opposition is being elaborated on, between tiger/*Ang* and frog/commoner. In a symbolic contest at the time of eclipses, the frog and the tiger people take different sides, and (unsurprisingly) the tiger people (the *Angs*) win, since the frog does not manage to eat the moon/sun.

In the case of Mon, there is a particularly good 'fit' between the ritual belief and the political reality. Elsewhere in the Konyak area, there are variations on this basic idea. In some villages, no clans shout at all; in others the entire village shouts; and elsewhere it is *morungs* rather than clans which take sides for and against the frog. In wooden carvings, it is sometimes a frog which devours the moon, and sometimes a tiger, and sometimes the animal appears to be a mixed frog-tiger creature. The important point is that all these variations are transformations on a basic, underlying, shared set of beliefs.

Individuals generally conduct their own rituals in matters affecting their own household, such as taking omens before a hunt. For other ritual needs, most Naga communities have in addition ritual specialists of one sort or another. The Lhota Nagas have both a shaman (earlier writers might have used the term 'witch-doctor' or 'medicine-man') known as a *ratsen*, and also priests, called *puthi*. These two complementary roles are found in a number of Naga groups. The *ratsen* tends to be a non-hereditary position: an individual believes he or she has been called on by a god or spirit to be a shaman, or '*maiba*', to use the common Assamese term. For the Lhota, this kind of possession is usually manifested in fits. The shaman has no responsibility for village-wide rituals, but is called in by individuals for help with specific problems. The shaman is able to foretell the future, interpret dreams (in which the person's soul meets spirits or dead ancestors), and heal sickness. The latter

(top) Shaman in a trance. Lhota, Rephyim village. 1922. JPM PR.
(bottom left) Beating gongs at head-receiving ceremony. Konyak, Oting village. 1937. CFH.
(bottom right) The *Puthi* or ritual specialist of Lakhuti village. Lhota. 1922. JPM PR.

is often effected by a sacrifice and then the 'extraction' of a foreign body – a stone or piece of leaf – from the affected person.

In 1937, the shaman and were-tiger Shopong, from the Konyak village of Tanhai, described the curing process in this way to Fürer-Haimendorf.

First the relatives [of the sick person] give him some cooked rice. This he spreads out in his own house and then goes to bed. In the dream he will have, Hayang [the god] tells him whether the sick person can be cured or whether he will die. In the former case he also tells him where the pig for the sacrifice has to be killed, on the threshold, at the main post or in a corner of the sick person's house. In the latter case of death, Shopong declares that there is nothing further he can do and gives up all endeavours. If, however, Hayang gives him hope for the sick person's cure he goes into his house the next day and first of all strokes his whole body with *laim-mei* leaves and says, 'Hayang, cure him, cure him.' Then he kills the pig in the correct place and says, 'Hayang, eat, drive out the sickness, cure him.' Then the pig is singed, whereupon Shopong divides it, cuts off small pieces of the feet and of the heart and liver and mixes these with salt, ginger and sticky rice. (For himself he keeps a leg and parts of the belly.) This mixture he then spreads around in the house and says, 'Hayang, eat, drive out, cure.' Then he sits down to a meal with the relatives of the sick man and also receives one to three rupees for his services.' [24]

By contrast, the *puthi* is likely to be a hereditary post, or at least there will be particular clans from which *puthi* are generally chosen. The individual is likely to be a respected figure, who has performed many Feasts of Merit. But it is an onerous position. His mediation between the spirit world and the village leaves him vulnerable to bad as well as good forces; and he may have to endure burdensome restrictions, such as not being allowed to leave the village boundaries, lest ill befall him. A strong identification between the *puthi* and the village is clearly being made. Unlike the Lhota *ratsen*, the *puthi* is responsible for village-wide ceremonies, the most important of which, the Oyantsoa, is led by him on certain crucial occasions, such as the founding of a new village, the periodic renewal of the village, and when the head-tree (a symbol of the entire village) is damaged.

The Angamis ritual specialist, the *tevo*, can be seen to play a particularly important role in their community, even though on the surface his power seems to be very limited: he has no special rights to labour, and in the village council he carries no weight above and beyond that of a man of wealth. As already mentioned, the Angamis have no hereditary chiefs, but they do have a ritual leader called the *kemovo* (Western Angami) or *tevo* or *thevo* (Eastern Angami). The *tevo* wears a special white kilt, and also

(top) Man's grave surmounted by an elaborate structure, *nritang-peng*, resembling a *morung*. On this structure have been hung the spear and shield of the deceased and the symbols of the heads he took during his lifetime as well as other offerings to the spirit of the deceased. Lhota, Pangti village. 1918-45. JPM SOAS.

(bottom) Structure of wooden poles, *leo-tsui-bao-re*, made for the sowing ceremony, *Hele-bam*. These structures are designed to prevent pigs or rodents from eating the seed contained inside. Zemi. 1941-42. UGB.

head-taker's ornaments, though once installed he would never again go on raids; he and his wife observe extremely strict food and sex taboos for seven harvests after taking office; he eats first at Feasts of Merit, and blesses the Feast-giver. Most importantly, the *tevo* lives on the housesite of the original founder of the village, and if the village sets up a colony nearby, he (or a man of his clan) will have to perform the founding rites for the new village.

The *tevo* has no role in agricultural-cycle *gennas*; his ritual importance is as the descendant of the original founder of the village. This descent is what gives the *tevo* a most sacred character, as the embodiment of the village and its link with its founding ancestor. He is 'the mediator between the community and the supernatural world, the personification of the village in its relation to the magical forces pervading Nature and human life'. [25] Anything which affects him, for good or ill, therefore affects the whole village: this is why he and his wife are subject to such strict taboos.

From the sociological point of view, the *tevo* is also fulfilling a latent function. The chiefless Angami village is for almost all practical purposes a collection of self-contained wards or quarters (*khels*), each ward containing one dominant clan. In their internal and external matters these clans operate generally without reference to the other clans in the village. But the *tevo*, as descendant of the founder, is a symbol which makes visible the original unity of the village clans. His installation feast is attended by members of every clan, and he is entitled to attend every Feast of Merit given in any clan. Without this role, there would be precious little which would serve to unite the Angami village internally.

The *tevo* is only one way of symbolizing unity within a group or within the village. In other tribes, ritual practices focus on other objects or practices. The Tangkhul Nagas engage at the Spring Festival in a ceremonial tug-of-war, which pits the chief's clan against the commoner clans. In their competition the unity of the village is also emphasized. For the Sangtam, the log-gong is the symbol of the village, and in it resides the spirit of the god Tsungrangre, who protects the village and brings it prosperity. For this reason, heads taken in raids are offered to the gong before being placed at the head-tree. When a new tree is chosen to provide a gong, Tsungrangre is addressed: 'From now you are the head of our village. Give us many heads. May all the crops be good. Banish sickness. Aid us when we go for tigers and wild boars. May many tigers fall.' [26]

For the Lhota, the symbol of village unity is the 'head-tree' (*mingetung*), standing in the centre of the village. Heads taken in raids were hung at the tree, and the sacred stones (*oha*) are placed at its roots. The tree is a symbol of the unity of the village, and if it is

(top) Men of the Pala *morung* carrying a new log gong to a new drum shed. Konyak, Wakching village. 1948 WGA.
(middle and bottom) Log gongs in sheds. middle: W.H. Furness 3rd, published in 'Customs of the World'.
bottom: Ao, Khensa village. 1947. WGA.

Page 97.
(top left) Log gong in shed. Ao, Ungma village. 1947. WGA.
(top right) Beating the log gong with the head hanging in the basket at the end. Konyak, Kongan village. 1936. CFH.
(bottom left) Log gong and carvings inside Chingchongpang *morung*. Konyak, Wangla village. 1947. WGA.
(bottom right) Skull house of the Bilaishi khel showing carvings of men and animals with a log gong. Chang, Tuensang village. 1947. WGA.

(top) Luck stones *oha* which stand under the head-tree, *mingetung*, in Lungsa village. Lhota. 1918-45. JPM SOAS.
(bottom) Ritual sports. Jumping at the *hazoa* stone at the *Hgangi* Festival at the winter solstice. Zemi, Laisong village. 1941. UGB.

damaged even accidentally, a village-renewing ceremony (*oyantsoa*) must be held. [27] By contrast, the Aos have both a head-tree and sacred stones, but in both cases they are neglected and treated without reverence; instead, it is the huge log-gong, housed in or near the *morung* in each *khel*, which symbolizes not the village but the *morung*. All the members of the *morung* decide which tree shall be felled; the first cut is delivered by a representative of the senior clan in the *morung*, and the second blow is given by the next senior clan. [28] For the Zemi the ritual centre of the village is the *hazoa*, a tilted block of stone from which young men take off in a ritualized long-jump; it is at this stone that trophy heads are buried and where foundation ceremonies of the village take place. [29]

Predictably, the Angami focus attention on the gate leading to each *khel*. Sacred stones are placed by it; [30] great care is taken in carving it, and none but *khel* members may help drag it into the village, during which operation the *khel* observes a *genna* on all agricultural work. The rituals relating to the gate seem to stress the primacy of the *khel* as a unit, and thus, for instance, when the newly-sacralized gate is tied to the gate-post no outsiders should remain in the *khel*. But the installation of a new gate is also a time for renewing or establishing political pacts between *khels* and villages, so that units wider than the *khel* are also confirmed. [31]

The account of W.G. Archer, witnessing the dragging-in of a new gate in 1947 in one of the *khels* of the Angami village of Kohima, is unusually vivid:

The actual conduct of the gate from its place in the forest to its site in the wall is a gay triumphal march, and it will illustrate the ritual if I briefly describe what took place when the Tsotonoma *khel* of Kohima dragged in its new gate to the village on 23rd February 1947. The gate which had been roughly shaped lay by the roadside under a heap of thorns and bushes, a mile outside the village. The road glistened in the afternoon sun and from the hill-top, Kohima and all its village paths stood boldly out above the town. About 3 p.m. some blank bombs exploded and as I stood in the road below the gate I saw a long line of tiny figures, no larger than ants, hurrying down the paths. For a while the tin shacks in the bazaar engulfed them. Then they re-appeared, streaming up the road in a long winding line. As I looked they were still only an inch high, and the long procession itself only a line of broken colour – a gay yellow blending into pink and white. As the line came slowly nearer, shrill cries and rhythmic chanting and singing came up on the wind like the rich chords of a regimental band. Then the line came fully into view. The two 'first strikers' were walking at the head – one of them bearing a huge shield decorated with peacocks and chickens' feathers. After them

(left) Men of the Tsotonoma khel wearing ceremonial dress while dragging in a new gate. Angami, Kohima village. 1947. WGA.
(right) Carved village gates with warrior within mithan horns.
top: Angami, Khonoma village. 1936. CFH.
bottom: Angami, Jotsoma, Tseyama khel. 1947. WGA.

Page 100-101
Village gates.
(top left) Gate with warriors, stylised mithan and human heads erected by the Viyema khel in 1920. Angami, Jakhama village. 1947. WGA.
(bottom left) Gate of Puchatsuma khel. Angami, Kohima village. 1947. WGA.
(top centre) Entrance gate to the village decorated with painted carvings representing a warrior in full dress, mithan horns, and female breasts. Zemi, Nakama village. 1918-45. JPM SOAS.
(top right) Gate decorated with warriors and mithan horns, erected in 1943. Angami, Merema village. 1946-8. WGA.
(bottom centre) Painted village gate. Angami, Khonoma village. 1936. CFH.
(bottom right) Man standing beside village gate with carving of mithan horns. Angami, Thenizumi village. 1936. CFH.

came thirty warriors decorated in dangling braces of yellow fruits. Then came a long line of minor warriors with scarlet and white sashes on their chests, black kilts with lines of white cowries at their thighs, and huge balls of white cotton in their ears. After them strode young men in similar uniforms but with strands of cotton piled on their hair and huge circular headdresses fanning out above their heads. In the rear came swarms of children each resplendant in dazzling scarlet sashes. The whole procession must have covered over half a mile. When the head reached the gate site, the long line came slowly to a halt and the first striker approached the gate. He picked a little grass, then, standing at the foot, he sprinkled the blades on the ground and spoke to the huge piece of wood. He then pulled back a branch of thorns, others joined him, all the thorns and bushes were pulled away and the gate came fully into view. The surface was now carefully brushed with plants, the thick fibres of a forest creeper were attached to poles and the two sides were then linked to fibre ropes which stretched far down the hill. When all was ready, the leaders said 'We have besought Ukepenuophu for every good thing – abundant crops, many children, many cattle. She will grant them to us. Let us go'. Then the band was formed into two lines, each holding the long ropes, the strain was taken and the gate slid smoothly down the road like a vessel gliding on the slips. As the lines went slowly down, the tufted headdresses swayed and tossed like feathered blossom on a row of trees. When the lines reached the bazaar, the leader rushed and plunged ahead brandishing his shield, shaking his spear and cutting aireal capers over the ground. Younger warriors broke out behind him springing and leaping in the air, while shouts arose of 'No one can defeat us. We are the boldest warriors'. Then, finally the lines went up the hill, women from the *khel* stood round in bands gazing at the slow triumphal march. As the procession reached the wall, the fibres were stacked to one side and the warriors passed through the gateway and on to the village. When almost all were in, the gate itself came into view, a group of forty warriors heaved and strained at the ropes and gradually the huge frame mounted the slopes. About fifty yards below the wall, the party left the path and the gate was brought to rest on a patch of ground screened by tall bamboos. Here it was carefully covered with branches and left for the night. Later in the evening the whole *khel* shared a great feast. In its communal display, its dazzling brilliance of colour, its devoted service, the ceremony was a complete expression of religious homage.' [32]

Young men at Longphong village. Konyak. 1913-1923. JHH.

Chapter 10

Ornaments and Status Symbolism

At the great ritual occasions of Naga society, such as the Spring Festival, the Sekrengi *genna*, a Feast of Merit, the bringing-in of a head or a new log-gong, Naga men and women don ceremonial dress and ornaments. All is colour and motion. For the Nagas, ornaments are more than a matter of aesthetics. They help make statements about, and to define, the identity of individuals and groups. Indeed, their importance is such that ornaments are part of the definition of being truly human. It is only from a corpse that ornaments are removed. [1]

In this account a particular theory is put forward, which uses ornaments, as an item of material culture, to develop the idea that the Nagas are one society with a generalized culture that is capable of many specific 'transformations' (that is, the 'tribes').

This way of looking at ornaments – as a symbolic vocabulary – is not at all similar to earlier 'degeneration' theory, which conjectured 'origins' for particular ornaments in a supposed functional use. Thus, the Angami or Rengma 'tail' was held to be a non-functional ornament that derived from an originally functional panji-basket. [2] Earlier still, Col. Woodthorpe in the 19th century argued that ornaments were modern degenerated versions of weapons or armour. These ideas are impossible to prove, but are in any case beside the point. All societies have always used symbols: the interesting thing is to decipher what they mean, not how they may have originated.

It is also distinct from the idea that each tribe has its own 'package' of objects, which can be listed in a finite, even exhaustive, way, the tribe being by implication defined as the group which possesses this list of objects. [3]

In their material culture, the Nagas use many natural objects, but they constitute a finite list of possibilities (deriving from feathers, teeth, horns, shells, tusks, wood and so on). Over the Naga area as a whole there is considerable diversity, but the impression is given of 'variations on a theme', as the following diagrams suggest. The conclusion that is advanced here, is that these variations help to identify people and units to each other, but also contribute to changing the nature of these units, because merely by being displayed they encourage competition over an inherently intangible commodity, 'fertility'.

An initial point of importance must be stressed. Although there are some Naga ornaments which are of no particular significance and which can be worn by anyone as and when they like, most Naga ornaments have a particular meaning, and they are therefore 'powerful'. Not surprisingly, the right to wear them is strictly

(top) Mao dancers in full dress at Imphal, Manipur. 1938. UGB.
(bottom) Man in full ceremonial dress, wearing curved tail of human hair, *tsongotschap*, and carrying *dao* and spear. Lhota, Akuk village. 1918-45. JPM SOAS.

controlled. They seem to be a source of power in their own right, in the sense that they must be handled with care, as if their power were a double-edged quality that could be mishandled. The Lhota man who wears a head-taker's boar's tusk necklet or ivory armlet, is careful to buy them not directly, but through an intermediary, who will attract to himself any evil which may be contained in them; the Sema warrior may not wear the tusks of a boar he has himself killed, even if he is entitled to this ornament; the Angami man entitled to wear hornbill feathers may not do so in the period between sowing the millet and harvesting the rice. [4] If the idea is accepted that these ornaments are in some sense powerful, it comes as no surprise to find that the autocratic Konyaks readily pile these ornaments one on top of the other: the *Ang* of Seng-ha met Fürer-Haimendorf in 1936 wearing a magnificent cane hat containing a hornbill skull, hornbill feathers and boar's tusks. [5]

a) Objects used for identification within the group

Ao Naga men typically wear armlets made of a section of elephant tusk on their upper arms. But the right to wear them is not uniform, and they therefore serve to distinguish the various clans:

Chongli language-group	hereditary right to wear	earned right
clans of Pongen phratry	yes	
clans of Lungkam phratry	yes	
clans of Chami phratry	no	yes (must perform mithan sacrifice)
Mongsen language-group		
clans of first phratry	6 of 11 clans may wear two	
	1 of 11 clans may wear one	
clans of second phratry	4 of 7 clans may wear two	1 of 7 clans no right of any sort
clans of third phratry		1 of 11 clans yes (must perform mithan sacrifice)
		4 of 11 clans no right of any kind
Changki language-group		
8 clans	3 clans may wear two	1 clan yes (must perform mithan sacrifice)
		4 clans no right of any kind

Clearly this is a complex set of rights, but it is not accidental, and there are some points of interest that arise. First, the rights to wear this ornament are a microcosm of the general tension between hereditary and achieved status (i.e. hierarchy and egalitarianism) in Nagaland. Second, it is not surprising that the rights to wear these ornaments are subject to challenge, and one can imagine that over time a clan's rights to these ornaments will have changed, as its

(top) Two women and a baby, one wearing very large brass earrings and both wearing bead necklaces. Angami. 1936. CFH.
(bottom) Mao dancers in full dress at Imphal, Manipur. 1938. UGB.

Page 105.
(top left) Young Angami man wearing ceremonial headdress with hornbill feathers. The style is typical of the Mozema village group. 1913-23. JHH.
(top right) Young man with pith headdress. Angami, Mesolizumi village. 1917-23. JHH.
(bottom left) Mao dancers Imphal, Manipur. 1938. UGB.
(bottom right) Angamis of Khonoma and Mozemi villages. 1921. JHH.

status has risen and fallen. [6] In fact, the picture of rights above, as recorded in the 1920s, suggests a certain state of flux. The clans of the Chongli Lungkam phratry are usually considered to be the counterparts of the Mongsen second phratry (they may not intermarry). Yet the Mozur clan of the former has hereditary rights to this ornament, and the Mulir clan of the latter (its pair) is one of those which cannot win the right under any circumstances.

b) Objects used for identification between groups

It is rather more difficult, though logically so, to show how ornaments are used to make statements of identification between groups. We might take as an example the Angami and Sema, who are neighbours, but as we have seen represent the polar egalitarian and hierarchical ends of the Naga spectrum; moreover, the Angamis practise terraced agriculture and the Sema slash-and-burn. There are indeed ornaments which could serve to identify one group to the other.

| Angami | head-taker's ear rosette of hair and beetle-wing | men wear kilt with cowries, and leg cane-rings | women may not wear cowrie shells |
| Sema | head-taker's necklet of boar's tusks | men wear *lengta*, cowrie aprons, and no leg ornaments | (high status) women may wear cowrie shells |

But the above does not in fact prove very much, for there are many items of dress and ornament that the two groups share, and indeed, the significant differences are more within either group. Both use hornbill feathers in a fur head circlet to signify warrior status; both wear the ivory armlet (though the Sema wear one as commonly as two), also signifying military prowess; and both groups (as well as the Rengma, Ao and Lhota) wear the classic 'enemy's teeth' ornament. This dramatic ornament is a flat piece of wood, usually about one foot long, representing the head of an enemy, with cowries (or Job's tears seeds) for the teeth, red cane for the tongue, and a fringe of red hair for blood pouring out of the mouth; needless to say it is an ornament worn by a warrior. The Angamis wear it on the chest, and the Sema on the chest or on the back. The variations seem to be more important within the Angami group:

enemy's teeth	young men	warriors	Viswema and Eastern Angamis	Western Angamis
	worn horizontally	worn vertically	circular shape	rectangular shape

(top) Girl with hair knotted at back, a brass spiral head ornament, and red chilli pods as ear ornaments. Ao, Chungtia village. 1918-45. JPM SOAS.

(bottom) Rich man who has completed the full cycle of Feasts of Merit with fine ornaments. The painted band of his cloth is typically Ao. Chuchu-Yimlang village. 1936. CFH.

(top) Women dancing with *daos* at a Feast of Merit. Ao, Ungma village. 1947. WGA.
(bottom) Girls dancing. Sangtam, Chimongre village. 1947. WGA.

One can only conclude that the shared ornaments support the idea that the Sema and the Angami are particular transformation of the same social potentialities, rather than different societies. Their ornaments are drawn from a common pool, acting as a shared language, not only with each other, of course, but also with the other Naga communities.

c) The use of the same object in different collective functions

The hornbill is a particularly important bird for all the Naga groups. Its long tail-feathers are a part of ceremonial or ritual dress. In the diagram below, male ornaments are considered.

Angami:	one feather in headdress =	1 head taken
Ao:	one feather in headdress =	participation in raid
	or =	mithan sacrifice (daughter of mithan sacrificer also wears one feather)
	two feathers in headdress =	first spear in killing enemy
Kalyo-Kengyu:	two feathers in headdress =	warrior status, not necessarily actually head-taker [7]
Konyak:	two feathers in headdress =	warrior status; daughter of chief may wear feather headdress [8]
Lhota:	one feather in headdress =	taken a head or touched an enemy corpse [9]
Rengma – Western:	three feathers in headdress =	warrior status
– Eastern:	feathers in shield (never headdress) =	warrior status
Sangtam:	two feathers in headdress =	third of five Feasts of Merit
Sema:	three feathers in headdress =	warrior status

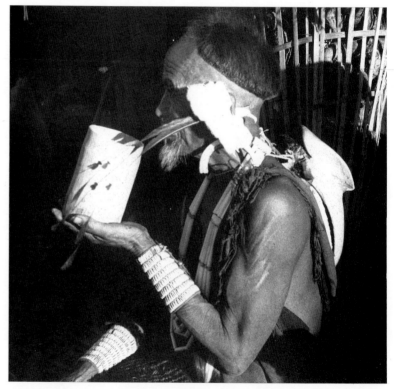

Man drinking from a bamboo cup. Lhota, Pangti village. 1946. CS.

There is clearly a basis of similarity in these cases. The hornbill feather is an element in a common language: it indicates high status of one sort or another. The same sort of diversity can be seen also in ornaments such as the boar's tusk, which is almost always the insignia of a warrior, but is worn variously as a necklet, on a helmet, through the ear lobe, and so on. It is often the case too that when women's ornaments are also considered, a pattern becomes evident.

Ao	kind of feather	worn by mate/ female	part of body	indicates	
	hornbill	m	on head	warrior/FoM	
	hornbill	f	on hair	FoM	[i.e. wife/daughter of mithan-sacrificer]
	drongo	m	in ear	warrior	
	drongo	f	in ear	FoM	" "

108

Host of a Feast of Merit with his wife and children. Ao, Ungma village. 1947.
WGA.

The pattern that seems to emerge is that a particular object often has a dominant meaning, and also a complementary meaning, so that here feathers indicate for men warrior status, and for women Feasts of Merit. A similar set of possibilities is seen in the case of cowrie shells, either worn as necklaces or sown onto cloths or aprons.

	male/ female	worn	pattern	indicates
Ao	m	necklace		mithan-sacrifice
	m	apron	zig-zag	warrior of many expeditions
	f	cloth	circles	daughter of head-taker who has burnt a village
W. Angami	m	kilt	4th line	highest warrior prowess
E. Angami	m	kilt	4th line	sexual prowess
Sema	m	belt	trefoil	drawn blood
	m	apron	circle	speared a corpse
	m	cloth	circles	great warrior (i.e. represent heads)
	f	dress	lines & trefoils	daughter of chief who has done mithan sacrifice
Rengma	m	apron	circles	killing a tiger
	f	cloth	circles & lines	wife/daughter of mithan-sacrificer (the circles are 'tigers' eyes')

It would be possible to give other examples of these kinds of variations. The points to be stressed, however, are really two. First, the insignia merely by being worn contribute to an individualistic striving after status, even though (as we have seen) this is restricted in the case of the more hierarchical communities. As in the case of the ivory armlets, even hereditary ornaments can be fought over. Warfare or feasting exploits are displayed in ornaments and encourage competitive emulation. In the 1930s the people of Chinkau offered peace terms to their rivals of the village Chi, which the latter rejected, since 'We have to get heads from somewhere as after all we want to dance and to wear ornaments'. [10]

Second, these ornaments constitute a sort of common language. What they mean depends on the limited set of possible contexts in which they are found, and there is a shared set of assumptions throughout Nagaland about what they mean. The ornaments therefore both reflect a particular Naga community's identity as it exists at any particular moment, and act as a means to change it, by encouraging individuals to strive for high status. Thus, it is a shared understanding in all the Naga tribes that the hornbill feather is a symbol of status, and the desire to wear the ornament promotes competitive emulation of status-enhancing exploits. But the particular meaning (head-taking or Feasting) and the particular arrangement (in the shield or on a hat) varies between the tribes.

(top) Old man wearing shallow crowned hat made by coiled process. Ao, Lungkam village. JPM SOAS
(bottom) Man wearing *dao* holder. Sangtam, Chongtore village. 1947. WGA.

Page 111.
(top left) Young men dressing up to be photographed using typing paper to simulate hornbill feathers. 1939. UGB.
(bottom left) Women wearing whole conch shells as bracelets. Konyak, Nokphong village. 1924-28. JHH.
(top right) Dancer with horned headdress. Kabui, Kokadan village. 1939. UGB.
(bottom right) Girl playing the role of a mother hornbill in a dance. Kabui, Kokadan village. 1939. UGB.

At this point it should be noted that at the time most of the information about ornaments was collected, in the 1930s, certain important changes had taken place as a result of British adminstration, in particular the prohibiton on feuding and the creation of better communications. First, the rights to certain ornaments denoting head-taking status could be gained not through actual military prowess, but through making an appropriate payment to the elders of the village. This probably meant a diminution of 'real' status differentials between individuals, with ornaments increasingly signifying age and wealth, rather than actual achievement. This tendency was accelerated by the increased amount of trade in traditional ornaments that arose as a result of peaceful administration and improved communications. [11]

As with any other ornament, tattooing serves to make statements about membership of groups and status within groups. The main method is to hammer the skin with a thorn implement and to rub a blue pigment into the cut. This is undoubtedly quite painful, and in addition can result in infection; but it is stoically and even willingly undergone because of the high value placed on the resulting patterns.

In some cultures, tattooing is a symbol of certain kinds of status that are not achieved by other means. This is not the case with the Nagas, where it would seem that tattooing, which is confined to certain eastern and northern groups, makes statements which in other communities are made with material ornaments. The Naga communities which practice tattooing are the Konyak, Ao, Chang, Sangtam, Kalyo Kengyu and Phom. These groups are geographically close, but do not obviously share any particular sociological features.

The most obvious distinction that tattoos can make, depends on a presence/absence opposition. The Thendu Konyak men tattoo their faces, but not their chests and arms, and the Thenkoh Konyak men do the opposite. [12] Because tattooing is permanent, the distinction enables a very strong statement of difference to be made between the two Konyak groups. In the case of the Sangtam, women have tattoos (on the calf and arm), and men not at all; for Konyak girls, the presence or absence of a tattoo on the back of the knee, signifies married or unmarried status. In all three cases, a distinction is being made by means of presence or absence (Thendu/Thenkoh, male/female, and married/unmarried). But these distinctions are made by other groups just as effectively (with, say, ornaments, or woven cloths), and tattooing should be seen simply as one more way to make these kinds of statements. Although apparently more 'permanent' than ornaments, there is evidence that over time changes in the use of tattoos do occur. Ao men, for instance, used to tattoo, but no longer do so.

(left and top) Girls dressing for the Spring Festival. Konyak, Longkhai village. 1937. CFH.
(bottom) Dressing the *Ang's* little daughter. Konyak, Longkhai village. 1937. CFH.

In addition to a presence/absence distinction, tattooing is also done so that variations in the pattern convey different messages about the wearer. In the case of Ao women, for example, both Mongsen and Chongli women are tattooed, and their chin tattoo is identical, but the pattern on their arms and legs clearly distinguishes them. [13]

It is perhaps not surprising that a culture much centred around the head, should have tattoos commonly found, for both men and women, on the throat, chin and around the eyes. But tattoos are found also on the chest, shoulder, back, stomach, leg, knee and calf. It is hard to discern any general rules in this. But it may be the case that a general distinction between men and women is established.

On the available evidence it would seem that female tattoos are geometric patterns which signify membership of a social unit or attainment of a life-cycle stage. Thus, for instance, the Ao women distinguish their membership of either the Mongsen or Chongli groups, as noted above, by variations in the lines and zig-zags of their tattoos; and it is the attainment of her first tattoos which gives the Ao girl the status of an adult, thus functioning as a sort of rite of passage. As in many rites of passage, the receiving of the tattoo is a time to emphasise the solidarity of women. The tattooing is done by an old woman, in the jungle, and men may not be present. [14]

By contrast, men's tattoos tend to be more representational, and concerned with signifying achieved status (particularly head-taking). In addition to some geometrical designs, typical of men are elongated tiger (or leopard) patterns, outlines of human figures, and a distinctive 'fleur-de-lys' or ostrich feather pattern. The latter, often referred to as the 'Chang head-taker's tattoo,' is a motif which reappears in a variety of contexts (on house posts, drinking vessels, and so on), and is said, by different observers, to be either based on a mithan head or ear or on the stripes on the head of a tiger. [15] Both, or either, may be true: in either case, men monopolize this symbol as part of their achievement of status in head-taking. The attainment of the tattoos is, as in the case of women, a kind of rite of passage.

(top) Tattooing a girl's legs. Konyak. 1936. CFH.
(bottom) Carvings of tattooed figures in a *morung*. Konyak, Chingphøi village. 1947. WGA.

Page 115.
(top left) Chest tattoo. Chang, Tuensang village. 1936. CFH.
(top right) Two young men with fresh tattoo marks on their checks indicating their recent achievement of head-taker's status. Konyak, Hungphoi village. 1937. CFH.
(bottom left and centre) Man from Ponyo village with tattoos on his chin, chest and back. 1936. CFH.
(bottom right) Man with eyes circled in white chalk. Head-receiving ceremony. Konyak, Wakching village. 1936. CFH.

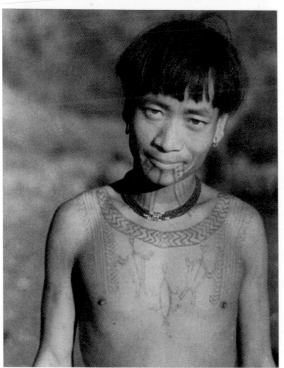
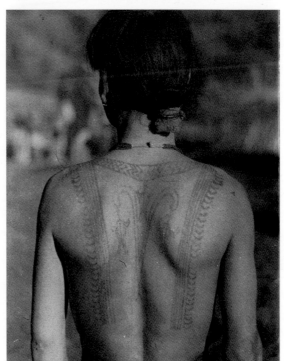

A rack of 151 skulls. Konyak, Yanha village. 1913-1923. JHH.

Chapter 11

Fertility

In a famous summary, Marx distinguished capitalism as a system in which money is transformed into commodities (goods) in order to make more money. Something similar is operating in Naga society in their concept of 'fertility'. It is a force or quality which can be transformed into goods (food and drink at Feasts) in order to produce more fertility. Possession of this quality affords high status.

But it remains an elusive concept. Others have used terms such as potency, life-force, prosperity, or the Ao Naga word *aren*. It is a little like *mana* in Polynesia: a quality inherent in the world, which can be channelled and increased, and which is in a sense 'contagious'. The individual who has it is able to spread it around his family and his village, where it is manifested in wealth (that is, the fertility of his crops). The belief in fertility is a central element in the cosmology which unites the diverse Naga communities. Agriculture, sex, death, Feasting and martial prowess are all united by the underlying concept of fertility, which is both gained by these activities, and is manifested in them.

In many ways, the beliefs about fertility are circular. A starting point is to be found in agriculture. If a man observes the correct ritual practices in the sowing and tending of the crops, he may end up with a good harvest and hence wealth. The Nagas say that this man is in contact with fertility: his wealth is the manifestation of this contact. The wealth allows him to hold a Feast of Merit, in which he Feasts family and villagers. The Feast of Merit does not therefore create high status, but it is, rather, a recognition or legitimation of his high status. From the outsiders' point of view, it is therefore 'naturalizing' a man's wealth, stating that the wealth is not the product of owning a lot of land or hiring many labourers, but is rather the product of the man's contact with the supernatural 'fertility'.

The last stage in the Feast of Merit cycle often involves dragging into the village a large megalith or stone. Lifting and dragging the huge boulder, which may weigh up to a ton and a half, requires the effort of the whole village, and it is no doubt a dramatic monument to the generosity of the Feast-giver. But it also fits in to the fertility cycle: 'The Feasts of Merit by which individuals acquire social status are likewise marked by ceremonies to promote fertility and magical rites for infecting the village as a whole with the fertility of the individual whose crops and cattle and affairs have so prospered that he is able to afford the Feast'. [1] The erection of a stone seems to achieve this end. Stones are often phallic in shape, or they are erected as a male and female pair. [2] They are dragged around the

Man holding head-trophy decorated with mithan horns and tassels of palmyra. The man wear a brass chest ornament and a hair pin with carvings of human figures, both of which signify that he himself has taken a head. 1918-45. Konyak, Kamahu village. JPM SOAS.

(top) Ponds which have been dug as part of the ritual, *matuira*, aimed at promoting the fertility of the crop. Zemi, Hajaichak village. 1918-45. JPM SOAS.
(middle) Fertility stones. Sangtam, Phelungrr village. 1937-1945. CP.
(bottom) The *Ang's* brother copying a *morung* carving of a copulating couple. Konyak, Longkhai village. 1937. CFH.

village and are then implanted in the earth. The Zemi Nagas build stone-lined ponds which are held to increase the fertility of the crops. [3]

These megaliths, and other large stone constructions, have long been a source of fascination, particularly for observers familiar with the stones of ancient European megalithic societies. It was obvious that the widespread occurrence of stone complexes throughout the hill and valley civilizations of South East Asia, suggested ancient links. The immediate lowland kingdoms close to the Nagas, such as the city of Dimapur, had stone phallic pillars apparently connected to those of the Angami. [4] An understanding of their meaning for the Nagas can be gained from considering the diverse contexts in which they are found.

In Angami villages, the youngest son sets up a stone to the memory of his father or his parents, and villagers erect stones in the middle of their rice-fields. The Angami stone-draggers stress the link between the social world and the influence of the spirits: 'I have not become rich through my own efforts, but because the spirits have blessed me. Our forefathers dragged stones , and I am going to see if I can't drag stones too.' [5]

The Konyak set up a stone in front of the *morung* on which the heads of enemies are exposed after a successful raid. The Lhota set up one stone in the first stone-pulling Feast of Merit, and two stones in the subsequent one. The Rengma Naga clans construct stone monuments to a Feast-giver and his wife. Although the contexts are different, they have in common the fertility complex: in each case the stone is acting as a vehicle for fertility. The Angami son seeks to channel the accumulated fertility of his parents into the earth, and specifically to communicate fertility to the rice fields; the Konyak uses the stones to channel the fertility of the heads to the *morung* unit; the Lhota communicates his abundant contact with fertility, through the stone, into the earth.

Just as it was argued above that the soul and fertility are separate though related belief-sets, it is probably the case that here the stones as channels of fertility are distinct from the stones as the physical abode of spirits. The latter is also a strongly-held belief, and is also revealed in the Naga 'luck stones', small black pebbles which are believed to be animate and capable of breeding. In a related set of beliefs, the Ao, Lhota and other Nagas trace their mythical origin to the six sacred stones at Lungterok. [6]

Given that the stones are vehicles of fertility, it is consistent that, as mentioned above, they are often sexual symbols, either resembling male and female genitals, or being described as a male and female pair. In this they resemble the large wooden forked posts found in many Naga communities, which appear to serve precisely the same function. In some communities, such as the Sema Nagas, the posts are wooden, rather than stone: 'It is by means of two wooden posts, one forked, the other straight, that this infection of prosperity is communicated to the village as a whole'. [7] Some authorities have sought to show that the wooden posts developed first, and the stone versions are more recent; but this is hardly provable, and it simply seems that what is done with stone in one case is done with wood elsewhere.

The association of fertility and sex is further brought out in certain communities, such as the Zemi, Rengma, Angami and Konyak, in which sex is held to be a positive force that gives the individual contact with fertility. In these communities the dormitories and *morungs* contain sexual carvings and in their costume particular ornaments declare that a man has had many lovers; unsurprisingly, women are not encouraged to display their amatory prowess to the world. The Konyaks erect small stones alongside the large megaliths which honour the dead as gravestones: the small stones indicate the number of lovers the deceased had. [8] The Zemi men wear particular feathers to signify the same [9] and the Eastern Rengma man arranges for an appropriate number of reeds after his death to be stuck in the ground next to his burial platform [10] It is also perhaps not fortuitous that in Konyak villages, lovers are expected to meet at night on the verandah of the granary. [11]

Some items of material culture reveal the link between sex and other practices which give high status. An Angami man, for instance, would aspire to wear three lines of cowrie shells on his kilt, to indicate success in warfare, and to add a fourth line to proclaim his sexual prowess.

Warfare, and particularly head-taking, were indeed central to the fertility complex. It is not an easy subject to comprehend. Nineteenth century writers saw it as a requirement for marriage (that is, youths needed to gain a head to be fully eligible marriage partners) and concentrated on its undoubtedly unchivalrous aspects – an unfortunately savage blot, in their view, on an otherwise splendidly warlike and virile character. Raiding by Naga warriors with a view to obtaining slaves who could be brought back to the village, and whose heads could later be taken, remained an intractable problem for Government officers in the eastern areas of the Hills, up to Independence. [12]

Naga warfare, like any other case of warfare, can be interpreted in diverse ways. In this chapter, head-taking will be examined in its ritual aspects, which are very pronounced. In this the Nagas can be seen to differ from their neighbours such as the Daflas, where violence is also institutionalized, but where there is no systematic social reward or prestige to be gained by it. [13] Different communities treated captured heads differently, but in all cases heads (or their substitutes or representative motifs) were a focal point of village life.

(top) House of Inato, chief of Lumitsami, with Y shaped genna posts and the chief's wife keening in the foreground. 1913-23. JHH.
(bottom) Skullrack in Michivam's house. One of the skulls was reputed to be of a British telegraph operator who escaped from Imphal during the attack on the Political Agent and other British in 1891. Tangkhul, Ukhrul village. 1937. UGB.

It is clear that head-taking as an activity took the form of a classic three-stage ritual. Among the Semas, for instance, the process began with the *agjucho* ritual, which inaugurated hostilities: an offering is made to spirit-containing stones which lie near the chief's house, and the warriors observe a *genna*, which takes them out of normal time and space and lifts them onto a ritually distinct level. The head-taking attack is then carried out, and if successful they return in a dangerous and holy state. They (and the heads) are re-incorporated into ordinary society by the *aghupfu* ritual. Before this is done, they are unclean, and a village which, for instance, was sowing, could not entertain them. [14] In the Zemi case, after the heads had been buried at the *hazoa* stone, the men were symbolically set apart from the rest of the community. They entered temporary huts where they wore only white cloths, with no black thread, ate food cooked only by men, and remained chaste for a period of time. [15]

It is also clear that the heads gained, played a central role in all kinds of Naga rituals. In 1946, W.G. Archer asked the Sangtam Nagas about their need for a head on every occasion when a log-gong was made and brought into the village:

'As soon as the drum is in position, a human head must somehow be got – as until a head is offered, the drum must not be beaten. If a stranger happens to pass by the village he is immediately beheaded – this is very rare – as all the neighbouring villagers are on the alert. The village therefore has sometimes to go far afield and sometimes it takes many months. When Sangsomo brought a new drum in 1917, they had to wait a year before they took a head from the Sema village of Komongsu (6 miles distant) and in doing so they themselves lost one man but not his head. When the news reached the village all the young men went down to the Tizu River with food and rice beer to meet the party and bring in the head and the corpse. They got back at midday. Young men (not yet warriors) touched the head with their *daos*, then they put the head in the hollow groove and everyone joined in beating the drum. Then the warriors who had shared in the killing gave animals for a village Feast and there was a general dance. That evening about 6p.m. they took the head from the drum and went to the *magutung* (head tree) – there the head taker cuts a bamboo in a special way ie slicing upwards. A hole is then bored in the head by an old man and the head is tied to the top of the bamboo. The bamboo then leant against the tree...' [16]

An incidental point of interest in the above passage is that the young men touched the head with their *daos*. This was adequate to earn them the status of warrior: it was not necessary to go on the

(top) Head decorated with horns and the eyes pierced with sticks brought back from Yimpang village. 1936. CFH.
(bottom) Pangsha skull displayed in Wakching village. Konyak. 1937. CFH.

(top) Hairpin worn in a knot at the back of the head used as a tally for the number of heads taken. Konyak, Wakching village. 1937. CFH.
(middle and bottom) Attaching long horns to skull retrieved from Pangsha, at Wakching village. 1937. CFH.

raid itself, but it was necessary to have physical contact with the head. The passage does, however, reveal that the Nagas considered it vital to gain heads. This can be linked up with the idea of fertility, both as cause and effect. On the one hand, the men who took a head demonstrated their potency: taking the head was a manifestation of their contact with fertility. On the other hand, taking the head brought them further in touch with fertility, and through them the village as a whole was able to share in the fertility.

A basic, perhaps obvious, point about head-taking can be made here. Taking a head is the ultimate transformative action. By killing another person, a man transforms life into death, and the accompanying rituals transform the biological (natural) fact of death into a social (cultural) object, that is, a skull. Other Naga processes are also to do with transforming nature into culture – the Feasts of Merit are a way of transforming natural wealth into cultural values (high status, ornaments and so on). The head-taker's ornaments may thus be seen as the symbols of the ultimate transformation. In this respect, an incident noted by J.H.Hutton in 1922 is of significance. In the Chang village of Hakchang, Hutton noted that 'Women whose blood relations on the male side have taken a head may cook the head, with chillis, to get the flesh off, and then assume the male tattoo – the double ostrich-feather tattoo worn by head-takers'. [17] This unique observation suggests that the head-taking tattoo is a symbol of nature-culture transformation: the woman, by cooking the head, is also contributing to the transformation, and thus (unusually) earns the right to wear the same tattoo as the man. In almost all other cases recorded, women do not play an active transforming role in the rituals whereby a head becomes a cultural object.

When asked, the Nagas themselves were very clear about why heads were important. 'Since head-taking was stopped, Wanching has got smaller. Formerly when illness swept through the village, we took a head, offered it and the sickness stopped. Nowadays we cannot offer heads and the sickness goes on and on. Man after man falls ill and dies, and there is nothing we can do. The fields too have gone off and we do not get the crops we did....' [18] In short when the village had heads, the people were healthier and the crops were better. Another Konyak put it thus: 'If we do not get a head every year, the crops will be bad, the pigs and cattle will not increase, our children will get ill'. The causal connection is stated here fairly explicitly. But, the informant goes on, 'We cannot say why this should be. It has always been like that.' [19] Anthropologists, however, have sought to provide a linking theory where the Nagas themselves do not.

The problem with this linking theory seems to be that there is confusion between the idea of fertility and the idea of the soul. The Nagas in effect say: heads → good crops.

(top and bottom right) Dangling skulls from Yimpang village collected for western museums. 1936. CFH. (bottom left) Phallic stone cists used by Wakching village for the skulls of their dead. Konyak. 1924-28. JHH.

(top left) Head tree. Chang, Tuensang village. 1947.
WGA.
(top right) Hand and foot of chief of Mongtikung
village hanging from a tree. Ao, Yacham village
1918-23. JHH.
(bottom) Skull trophies arranged on rows of wooden
shelves in a *morung*. Konyak, Chi village. 1918-45.
JPM SOAS.

Skull racks. Kalyo-Kengyu, Sanglao village. 1937-45. CP.

The anthropologists have sought to ask what causes this connection, and have suggested that

heads → soul substance → good crops,

that is, equating the 'soul' (or one of the several souls) with the 'fertility' idea, thus making the skull, as the receptacle of the soul, act as a sort of fertilizer, causing prosperity in the village and in its crops.[20] The problem is that the Nagas do not really make this link. Heads are good for crops; and there are a number of souls in the human body (including, possibly, one in the head). But they may or may not be causally connected in the manner suggested by J.P.Mills: 'A Naga who takes a head certainly wishes to bring home tangible proof of his valour; but he also wishes to add to the soul-force of his village by bringing home the head, in which it resides'.[21] It is suggested here that heads are indeed connected with an increase in fertility and well-being, but it is as well to be aware that in only a very few references do the Nagas themselves advance the idea that it is because the head contains the soul.

Indeed, on occasions the Nagas explicitly talk about the soul and the skull in a manner quite distinct from ideas about fertility. The Konyaks of Wanching separate the skull at death, place it in a stone cist and feed it, but this is discussed by them in terms of the soul, and not fertility: 'Every man has two souls. One goes to Yimpu [the land of the dead] the day he dies. The other lingers in the house. When the skull is brought in, washed, fed and taken to its pot, the second soul leaves the village and joins the first in Yimpu'[22]

A feature of note is that human heads are not uniquely privileged. The warrior who comes back with a tiger or leopard head is in precisely the same ritually dangerous state, and observes the same *genna* prohibitions (up to 30 days, in the case of the Sangtams), as the taker of a human head, and he is entitled to the same ornaments. This might support the idea that the soul which is common to man and the tiger (often thought of as brothers) is the active fertilizer of prosperity. On the other hand, where a warrior brings back only a foot or hand, rather than a skull, or where he is able merely to sink his spear into the corpse, he is deemed nevertheless to be rich in fertility, in which case the skull per se seems to be less important. The Eastern Angami warrior Huritsu of Chezubama took in his life-time three heads (all obtained, incidentally, while in British military service), but only brought back in each case the ear, which was considered perfectly adequate.[23] Moreover, if the Sangtam killed a mithan belonging to his enemy, the skull was brought back and offered to the log-gong in the same way as a human skull, even though there is no sibling relationship between the human being and the mithan.[24]

One other animal seems to be closely connected with head-taking – the monkey (in fact, usually the 'huluk' gibbon). In

Young man from Punkhung village demonstrating head-taking techniques. Konyak. 1936. CFH.

Page 126.
Sacrificing a steer in preparation for the Spring Festival. Konyak, Wakching village. 1937. CFH.

Page 127.
(top) Soul figures of the dead. Konyak, Mon village. 1923. JHH.
(middle) House of a man who has given a series of Feasts of Merit. The central post is carved with mithan horns and hornbill tails, the cross beam bears representations of women's breasts, and in the foreground stand a row of small stones which have been set up to commemorate the performance of the Feasts. Konyak, Akhegwo village. 1918-45. JPM SOAS.
(bottom) Skulls of deceased villagers placed in stone cists. Konyak, Wanching village. 1937. CFH.

Oting, a head-taker (or a man who Feasted the whole village at a head-taking festival) was entitled to wear a monkey skull on his basket. There is some evidence that the monkey is like the tiger in terms of its ancient links with mankind. Whereas the Konyaks say that man tricked the tiger to get food [25], the Aos say that man tricked the monkey to get fire. [26] Monkeys are even referred to as 'a low clan' by the Konyak [27], and when they are carved they very closely resemble human beings, sometimes even being carved with the Chang head-taker's chest tattoo. It was therefore logical for the British to try and persuade the Nagas that they should take monkey-heads rather than human ones; but the results were poor. Monkeys could stand as symbols for having taken a human head, but not as heads in their own right.

A more useful connection between heads and fertility is evident in the significance of an ornament such as the spectacular warrior's 'tail', a long projecting object worn at the small of the back, made of wood, with black hair hanging down from it. For the Angamis, this ornament was a mark of military prowess; but for the Rengmas it signified either completion of all the Feasts of Merit, or the head-taking genna. [28] An equivalence is being made between Feasting and head-taking, in the sense that both are means of acquiring fertility – and ideas about the soul in this context are clearly not a common denominator and are thus irrelevant. This equivalence seems, incidentally, to have become more common in the recent historical period. As head-taking was gradually suppressed, the right to head-takers' insignia has increasingly been granted instead for Feasting exploits. By 1946, for instance, the Chang were allowing head-takers' ornaments such as boars' tusks for Feast of Merit-givers.[29] This supports the idea that both are deemed to be equivalent in promoting fertility, but only one requires the 'soul substance' argument.

Lastly, it is appropriate to consider the key relationship between death and fertility. This is demonstrated, for example, in the funeral rituals of the village of Laruri, in the Kalyo Kengyu area. The corpse is smoked in the house to dry it, put into a canoe-shaped coffin and hung up under the eaves of the house. It remains there until the first day of the new year's sowing genna. Meanwhile little houses on stilts are built for the soul to inhabit, complete with miniature implements. On the first day of the sowing genna, all the bodies of people who died during the year are brought out of their coffins, the bones are separated and then put into a covered pot which is placed in the family's granary. The remains of the flesh and wrappings are put back into the coffin, which is then tipped over the side of a cliff; the little house is no longer given much attention. When the harvest is collected, a small portion is given to the miniature house, which is then neglected and the deceased is no more considered.

The general logic of this process is clear enough: social death, as opposed to biological death, is marked in stages between sowing and harvest. Human death is symbolically linked to agricultural birth. But in detail the process is not so obvious. We are again faced with the uncertain relation of beliefs about the soul, to beliefs about fertility. The observer of this ritual process clearly thought the soul was released when the bones were put in the pot, and then became free to fertilize the land, the bones in the granary acting as 'an additional inducement to the soul-matter to resolve itself into grain'. [30] But it is also said that the soul resides in the little houses [31]; and it is the bones (and not just the skull) which are kept in the granary. The other conclusion is that the soul is one thing and the fertility-inducing properties of the bones are another.

The erection of some sort of edifice, of stone, basketwork or wood, at or near the corpse seems to be common, and though there is much variation, there seems to be a link between the various practices.

It is appropriate at this point to consider one particular kind of Naga carving, that of the human figure. Such figures shed some light on the relationship between the soul and fertility in Naga culture. In the literature they are referred to variously as 'ancestor figures', 'effigies' and 'soul figures'.

Carved figures are made by only a few of the communities, and principally the Angami and the Konyak. This may be more than a matter of coincidence, for although the two communities at present occupy opposite geographic ends of Nagaland (and opposite ends of the political spectrum too), in dress and material culture there are striking similarities not shared by any of the tribes in between, including for males, the wearing of the hair long and tied up in a knot at the back, and the wearing of bunches of cane rings around the legs. In addition, a similarity can be seen between the large stone 'sitting-out' places on the graves of clan founders found in Angami villages, and the chief's stone seats and stone causeways found among the Konyak. [32]

In some Eastern Angami villages, tall wooden carvings are found, with pear-shaped faces and long vertical noses, square shoulders and long arms. Originally they would be dressed in warriors' costume, but in time this decays. They are said to be erected 'in the name of' a particularly successful warrior after (sometimes long after) his death [33], over the grave. Although they are not obviously a representation of the actual likeness of the deceased, they are identified by the Nagas as a realistic representation. [34] They are not merely a monument, however, for they are also carved when the village has gone through a period of misfortune, and it wants to gain some of the fertility of its deceased members: 'When calamity makes it necessary to invoke a dead warrior, the village subscribes rice-beer and two pigs, a member of the warrior's family cuts and carves a tree and after a general Feast the village youth drag the effigy onto its site.' [35]

In another Eastern Angami village, Chizema, stone effigies are also found on or near graves, indicating the number of heads taken or women seduced. [36] In Ketsapomi wooden effigies are erected either for head-takers or for Feast-givers [37]: the latter, however, may be a relatively new practice, compensating for the disadvantages of peace, since generally it seems that effigies are related to head-taking, and hence in many villages no new effigies were carved after about 1870. [38]

The Eastern Angami also erect effigies for women, whereas the other Angamis erect a diamond-shaped bamboo frame on which are stretched multi-coloured cotton threads. [39]

In the Konyak country, wooden carvings are erected for young men and women who have died, and also for adult men, and less commonly for married women. [40] In the Thendu group, effigies are restricted to members of the *Ang* class. [41] The effigies are not placed particularly near the graves, but rather in a shed belonging to each clan, or on the path, so that the villagers will see them as they go to and from the fields. The villagers do not particularly connect these figures with fertility: 'We put up the figures and dress them as they were in their lives. When their families see them their grief is a little less.' [42] The carvings for a man are often in pairs – one of the man himself, and one of a servant, to accompany him to the land of the dead. [43] The Konyak carvers say that their aim is a complete likeness, but this is made difficult because there are also conventions of form which mean most carvings look fairly similar.

There is, nevertheless, a submerged theme which may connect these carvings with the fertility complex. In the more remote Konyak villages of Yonghong and Angfang, the head of the deceased is not placed in a phallic stone cist [44] as in Wakching and Wanching, but is rather placed between the 'horns' projecting from the figure's head. [45] Some have argued that this is analogous to the placing of the skull in a stone cist. It could be that either the soul or the fertility (or both) of the deceased is channelled into the figure and then into the earth. [46] It may therefore connect with the idea that the Angami wooden figures act also as a vehicle for fertility, as suggested above.

Nevertheless, it must be borne in mind that this sort of argument is the theorizing of the anthropologist, and is sometimes directly contradicted by the people themselves: 'Chingai and Mauwang deny that there is any idea that the soul enters the figure – or that it affects the crops – they do not think of it that way,' noted W.G.Archer in 1947. [47] These Konyak Naga informants insist the carvings are simply memorials to the dead.

The human figure features very prominently in Naga art, in

house carvings, gates, trophy heads and in shell patterns on body cloths. But certain animals are also depicted with regularity. They include the same animals whose teeth, claws, feathers and beaks figure centrally in body decoration, notably the tiger, hornbill and the sacrificial mithan. These animals are strongly associated with different aspects of the belief in fertility. To take the case only of the hornbill, this association may be the fertility inherent in aristocratic clans (who have a strong association with the hornbill) or the fertility acquired through sexual or military prowess, or through Feasting (in these cases too the hornbill figures prominently). The prominence in Naga art of these animals suggests that they are powerful symbols of the belief in fertility, and are not merely passive representations. They are constantly seen and encourage emulation of the practices that indicate fertility and bestow high status.

The fundamental question that emerges, and has already been touched on above, remains hard to answer. Is it the case that the belief in fertility, and its representation in symbols, merely reflect particular social structures? Or is it that the competition for fertility (and hence high status) actually precipitates and catalyzes social change? If the latter is correct, it would seem that the shared cosmology of the Naga communities, which promotes dynamism rather than stability, could be the engine of the oscillation and variations observed.

Finally, in considering fertility, it is clear that fertility is a positive force, but equally it has a negative counterpart. Handled wrongly, the individual who seeks to enhance his contact with fertility will attract only negative, maleficent, forces. This is a common feature of ritual or sacred levels of experience, not only among the Nagas. Taking a head, for instance, can give a man contact with fertility; yet the successful Rengma warrior is ritually unclean for several days. His hands cannot be washed, he must eat with a special spoon and he cannot sleep in his own house until certain ceremonies of re-integration into normal life have occurred. The head he has taken is mollified, in the hope that the dead man's spirit will be more angered with his co-villagers who failed to protect him than with the men who in fact killed him. In some Chang and Sangtam villages, heads are taken but are specifically not hung in the *morung* because it was found that this damaged the crops. [48] There is, then, a certain danger inherent in contact with fertility.

This belief therefore amounts to a powerful explanatory system for all natural and social phenomena. Well-being can be explained by the proper handling of fertility, either directly or by the intercession of spirits and gods. Equally, misfortune is explained not as mere accident, but as the result of the presence of the negative aspect of fertility. This presence is manifested in

(top) Man dancing at Wakching with skull retrieved from Pangsha village. 1937. CFH.
(bottom) Young men in full dress engaged in ceremonial rice pounding. Angami, Kohima village. 1918-45. JPM SOAS.

particularly calamitous events, which are treated in a special manner because they are ritually powerful. The best example of this is the kind of death called *apotia*: deaths which we would think of as 'accidental', such as being killed by a wild beast, falling from a tree, drowning, or dying of an unusual disease or in childbirth. For the Ao Nagas, death in this manner is a disgrace for the family, the individual's property is destroyed and the house-site abandoned; burial is hurried and without ceremony and without the usual ornaments or provisions necessary in the next world. The relations of a man dying apotia in the jungle, on their return to the village go through a symbolic purification of walking through fire and then washing, and are kept in a sort of quarantine for some days. [49]

There is one way of avoiding this ritual and social calamity. If a man falls from a tree, but does not die straightaway, his co-villagers hastily offer a chicken as a sacrifice; if he dies after this, the death is not apotia. The logic of this is significant. Well-being is achieved by humans being 'in control' of the natural process of fertility; misfortune is the result of being 'out of control'. Both states are evidently contagious, for good or ill. If a man dies after a sacrifice, at least there has been some human agency involved, attempting to exert the usual control over fertility (albeit failing in this case).

Dying in warfare is the ultimate apotia death – the individual who is manifestly out of touch with fertility. In head-taking the stakes – glory or disaster – are high.

(top) Pig sent as a gift. Kalyo-Kengyu, Panso village. 1936. CFH.
(bottom left) Men being given a drink during warriors' dance. Kalyo-Kengyu, Panso village. 1936. CFH.
(bottom right) A woman of the Feast giver's household dispenses rice beer to the dancers at a Feast of Merit. Sangtam, Phirre village. 1947. CS.

Women and children taking part in the ceremonial tug-of-war during the annual ceremony after sowing, the *Moatsu*. Ao, Ungma village. 1918-45. JPM SOAS.

(top) Girls dressing for the Spring Festival. Konyak, Longkhai village. 1937. CFH.
(bottom) Boy with bird headdress, head-taking dance. Konyak, Tanhai village. 1936. CFH.

Chapter 12

The Relations of Male and Female as seen in Ritual

At first sight, it might seem that Naga society is extremely male-dominated. Males tend to monopolize ritual and political offices; [1] land passes between men; and the main ritual arenas – head-taking and Feasting – seem to centre around the exploits of men.

This is particularly so with head-taking, which is in many respects a male cult. Men are separated off from women, before, during and after a raid. Rengma warriors, for instance, returning after a raid, must sleep apart, and eat separately, from their wives for ten days. [2] Male obsession with, and dominance in, warfare, directed against outsiders, leads to an identification of men with the forest, as the buffer area between the group and its potentially hostile neighbours. Symbolically, this is expressed in the male near-monopoly of the products of the great forest animals: fur, feathers, claws, teeth and tusks of the forest animals and birds when used in ornaments, are largely a male preserve.

This is not to say that women do not participate in head-taking. Women usually play a certain role in the head-receiving rituals, the wife of an Angami warrior, for instance, feeding the skull with rice beer. [3] It is also, allegedly, women who encourage men to undertake head-taking, as a pre-requisite to marriage. But women are involved in a subsidiary way, as seen in two features. First, a man does not have to be married to participate in the cult; and second, head-taking by a man does not on the whole confer a right to ornaments for the woman, as it does automatically for the man. Head-taking is a cult which could, theoretically, continue without much involvement of women.

These two differences are significant when Feasts of Merit are considered, for although this too appears to be a ritual arena for men – in most of the communities women do not themselves give Feasts – in fact women play an important role and there is an emphasis on male-female interdependence or cooperation.

First, a man must be married in order to begin the series of Feasts. Being married is sometimes presented as being necessary merely because it is the woman who brews the beer which the man distributes to those attending the Feast; but it is clear that the woman's contribution goes deeper. In the case of Sangtam Feasts, for instance, the beer that she is charged with brewing is not mundane, everyday, rice beer, but has a sacramental quality: the rice is pounded in a ritual manner, and the rice is brewed on a new, ritually pure fire which is not allowed to go out during the Feast. [4]

Second, generally speaking a man's wife and some other female kin acquire rights to ornaments just as the man does. [5] Thus, while a man could gain status in the head-taking cult with minimal female involvement, men and women cooperate in the case of Feasts and share in the high ritual status acquired.

This is not accidental. The role of women in Feasting, and their right to ornaments as a result, may be thought of as a recognition first, of the female contribution to production, and second of women's relatively autonomous exploitation of their position in the kinship system. Whereas men dominate in economic areas of distribution (in Feasts) and exchange (in supervising marriages, and in trade), women are vital in production. In material terms, as already mentioned, women do the bulk of agricultural work, and therefore Feasting cannot happen at all without their labour. Furthermore, at another level, in Naga cosmology, there is much that suggests a close connection between the earth and the female principle: the first human beings, according to some myths, were born from a hole in the earth, and the earth and sky are sometimes contrasted as female and male. [6]

Moreover, women are in a potentially powerful position as a result of being, in the kinship system, between two groups of men. A married woman has ties to her clan of birth and also to her husband's clan. Her husband is dependent on her labour, to undertake the Feasting series, and this allows a certain degree of freedom of option, on her part, as to how much she identifies with her husband and his clan and how much with her clan of birth. A woman who chooses not to involve herself fully in her new clan may work less hard in the field, and produce less rice, thereby reducing her husband's ability to compete in the Feasting arena. Without her cooperation in production, the man is unable to gain status. He is unable to amass the necessary rice, or indeed the cotton, which the wife tends and then fashions into the cloths which portray his (and her) high status as Feast-givers. Here again the contrast with head-taking is seen. In the head-taking case, men appropriate jungle products as ornaments; in Feast-giving, the contribution of women in production is recognized, and men are dependent on women to produce the cloths that are acquired.

Other aspects of ritual belief seem to tally with this general division between male dominance in head-taking and male-female interdependence in feasting. This may not be altogether surprising, given that fertility is a concept that would always seem to necessitate male and female acting together. A nice illustration of this complementarity is seen, for instance, in the tug-of-war found in a number of Naga communities during agricultural feasts. In the Ao Moatsu festival, after the sowing, in addition to dancing, men and women form teams and pull a length of creeper; neither side 'wins', but rather both sides give and take in turn. [7]

(top left) Two girls spinning cotton with a spindle. Konyak, Longkhai village. 1937. CFH.
(bottom left) Girls pounding grain on an ornamented pounding table. Konyak, Longkhai village. 1936. CFH.
(top right) Girl drinking from a bamboo tube. Konyak, Longkhai village. 1937. CFH.
(bottom right) Women dressed in narrow cotton skirts fastened at one side which are characteristic of the Eastern Konyaks. They wear many bead necklaces and carry wood in plaited cane baskets by means of a carrying string across the forehead. Konyak, Lunglum village. 1918-45. JPM SOAS.

Men dancing with painted shields at the Spring Festival. Konyak, Wanching village. 1937. CFH.

Chapter 13

War and Feud

In a previous chapter it was argued that warfare has important ritual aspects: that killing an enemy brought the warrior and his village into contact with fertility. Although this would help explain the interest in taking heads, it would be wrong to suppose that this is the only reason why Naga society was traditionally characterized by institutionalised violence.

One of the puzzling things, at first sight, about Naga society was the apparent discrepancy between dispute-settlement within the group and between groups. Within the group – generally speaking the village – disputes were on the whole settled by talking; between groups there was quick recourse to fighting.

Within a village, protagonists would typically present their case before the village council of elders or the village chief. In the case of the Chongli Ao Nagas there was a progression of appeal upwards. The first unit attempting settlement was the minden. This was a grouping of men, and there may be two or three in each *khel,* each minden composed of men of different clans. If two people who belong to the same minden are in dispute, the minden will try to settle the matter. If the disputants are of different minden, the issue comes to the *khel* council of elders, and then to the village council: 'They either come to a finding and fix the penalty or instruct the parties to take oath and so leave the decision to Providence.'[1] Should the oath not prove conclusive within a certain period, the case was dismissed, any property at issue being divided between the two disputants. Beyond this, the issue might be taken to a leading elder of a powerful neighbouring village.

The elders entrusted with the settlement would have the power to exact a fine, of say a pig – which they, and not the 'winning' disputant, then ate. The purpose of this was no doubt to discourage unnecessary litigation and to encourage settling 'out of court'. Sometimes the fine was eaten in advance. It might be, for instance, that bamboos were regularly being stolen from a certain clump and the elders would announce that more thefts would entail a fine of a pig. If more bamboos disappeared, the elders would seize and eat a pig, and the whole of the village would mobilize to catch the thief, since if the thief were not caught the pig would have to be paid for by general subscription.[2]

Although fines were the most common penalty, in certain cases the elders could expel an individual from the khel or village, and for incest the offenders' houses and property would be destroyed. It is said that for murder within the village, the offender could be executed, but in all the Naga groups there was a strong revulsion against injuring physically a fellow-villager, and expulsion was

(top) Man holding a spear wearing a hat decorated with a hornbill beak and feathers, horns, and boar's tusks. Konyak, Namsang village. 1937. CFH.
(bottom) Man drumming. Konyak, Hungphoi village. 1937. CFH.

more likely. There is an interesting confirmation of this in the case of bamboo clubs found in some Konyak and Kalyo-Kengyu villages, specifically intended for use by villagers in fights: doing serious injury to a fellow-villager would be a serious crime, so these clubs were deliberately fashioned to be too light to cause serious injury to an opponent. [3]

This emphasis on talking and fining was in fact political rather than legal settlement, in the sense that the 'winner' was likely to be the one whose lineage members and clansmen rallied round him most vociferously; but nevertheless the issue turned on Naga law, and there was no recourse to force except in *extremis*.

Altogether different were disputes between villages, whether this was a private quarrel between individuals and their clans, or between whole villages united internally against each other. In these cases, fighting was likely, and (except in the case of the Lhota) fighting within the tribe was as likely as fighting between villages of neighbouring tribes. Even without the positive desire for fighting, there was little that could be done to stop it. Weaker villages might well opt for safety and voluntarily become 'sons' paying tribute, in return for protection, to powerful Konyak villages or Angami *khels*. The Konyak village of Chintang, for instance, had developed this strategy to the point of paying tribute to *morungs* of four neighbouring villages. [4]

Villages were nevertheless organised as political, autonomous fighting units, and there was no higher authority above the villages to regulate their relations peacefully. It is easy enough to see how the system perpetuated itself in these circumstances: in conditions of war, restraint was at best ill-advised and could be catastrophic. The best form of defence was, as an anonymous boxing coach once put it, to get your retaliation in first. And as we have seen, on top of this, violence was given a positive cultural validation – that is to say, warfare as a sport, game or way of life was a generally favoured, and exciting, activity (just as it has also been at times throughout European history). Therefore, to some extent the cause of an increase in raiding was simply a function of the demographic situation of a village. More young men eager, and competing, for heads, and more alert to any possible insult or slight from a neighbouring village, meant more head-taking. [5]

Before considering forms of fighting, however, it is as well to point out that two mechanisms did exist for attempting to mediate between groups. One mechanism was the oath (which was also used within the village). This removed the sanction to the supernatural level, and was taken very seriously. Oaths were ranked, but could be of the utmost gravity. In the Pitt Rivers Museum in Oxford, one Naga artefact is the tip of a Sema man's finger, cut off by an oath-taker to attest to the great seriousness of his oath in an adultery case in which his statement as a witness was questioned. [6]

Young man dressed for head-taking dance. Konyak, Tanhai village. 1936. CFH.

Man decorated for dancing with hornbill feather headdress, boar's tusk necklet, brass armlets, and painted white rings around the eyes. Konyak, Tamlu village. 1918-23. JHH.

Other oaths were less dramatic. In 1936, a dispute arose between Totok and Wanching villages, concerning an alleged trespass that signified hostile intentions. The two sides agreed to take an oath.

'From each side a man went with the dobashis to a tree trunk near the bungalow which had been struck by lightning, spoke the oath while his hand touched the tree, and then bit into the tree. The oath of the Wanching man said approximately, 'We went to Chi to see the dead man. Totok fired shots. Gha-wang you can see it all. May you strike me down if I tell a lie'. After this oath both parties were quite content.'[7]

It is admittedly the case that this form of dispute settlement was undertaken between two villages in the administered area which were obliged to settle the dispute peacefully, under the eye of the sub-divisional officer. In pre-colonial times it is possible that the same dispute might have led more rapidly to violence. Oaths were in fact a part of the feud process: they might delay aggression but could not in all probability replace it, and a disputed oath settlement might itself become ammunition in an ongoing political confrontation.

The second mechanism, at least in certain Naga communities, was the mediating figure of the *lambu*, often translated as 'herald'. In diverse situations an old man from a village might act as an intermediary between two parties. This might include acting as a middle man in an economic transaction,[8] but it could also include acting as a go-between in a dispute between two villages. The person of the *lambu* was held to be sacrosanct, and should not be attacked. His role, as far as can be seen, was strictly as a messenger, and he took no autonomous initiatives of his own towards negotiating a settlement. It appears, however, that in times of very serious violence, the sanctity of the *lambu* was not respected, and it was not a role that was eagerly sought.[9] His role was in other words not structural, in the sense of automatically being a part of the dispute process, but it was an option that might avert fighting.

These exceptions apart, relations between villages were – in pre-administration times, it must be stressed – always poised on the edge of violence. There were of course also peaceful relations between villages (political, trading, marriage). But – and this is the important point about Naga fighting – violence complemented and mirrored these peaceful relations. It is for these reasons that Naga warfare is categorised in what follows as essentially 'feuding' rather than 'warfare' *per se*.

The Nagas themselves distinguished different kinds of fighting, but largely on the grounds of tactics. The Semas, for instance, differentiated between the pitched battle, a raid on the enemy's fields, two kinds of ambush, a raid on the village, raids at midday,

Simulated attack with guns and *daos*. Konyak, Oting village. 1937. CFH.

(top) Village street. Angami, Cheswezumi village. 1936. CFH.
(bottom) Long bridge over the Dikhu river in a state of disrepair. Konyak. 1936. CFH.

dawn and night, killing a cow and the cow's owner who has set off in pursuit, and taking the head of a man met casually on the path. [10]

The first of these, the pitched battle, is of some significance given that since the earliest mid-19th century accounts, it is always the ambush or treacherous attack which has received most attention. The evidence is there, however, that pitched battles were not uncommon. One village challenged another, through an intermediary, to a battle at a set time and place, both sides turning up in full ceremonial dress. [11] Fatalities were low, in comparison with the typical stealthy raid, in which one party had the advantage of surprise. The women of the village (whose own heads, ironically enough, were the most highly-prized trophies, because they were held to be harder to obtain) might in this sort of battle bring up the rear, carrying and throwing stones.

Much more typical, however, were the various ambushes and attacks, which European writers found horribly fascinating because so many rules of European warfare were blatantly flouted. Women and children were prized targets of attack, there was glory in successful retreat (and none in falling in combat), and a treacherous attack on guests invited for a feast was legitimate.

How should this form of fighting be characterized? This form of institutionalised violence is best thought of as a kind of 'feud', though with some elements more like 'raiding' and 'warfare' proper.

'Feud', in the sense meant here, is an enduring social relationship between villages; containing mechanisms for achieving temporary cessations; conducted according to rules; with essentially political rather than economic motives. These definitional criteria can be taken in turn.

First, it might seem strange to think of head-taking as evidence of a 'social relationship'; yet the evidence is that violence mostly occurs between villages who know each other, are related, or have links of some sort. It is not random slaughter of unknown people (discounting here for the moment head-taking raids carried out against non-Naga Plains Indians and Europeans). W.G.Archer made in his field-notes of 1946 some significant observations on the feud between the Konyak villages of Longmein and Chonui: 'Began head-taking 9th March – before that on very friendly terms – intermarriage – war broke out – casualties: Chonui – 6 killed 4 wounded. Longmein – 2 killed 2 wounded and 1 likely to die. Longmein could only take away 1 head out of the 6 killed. Chonui took 2 heads from Longmein later in the day by surprising 2 of Longmein.' [12] The relationship between the two villages involved exchange, positively, of women, and negatively, of heads. Among the neighbouring Kachin in Burma, E.R. Leach found that 'to the Kachin way of thinking cooperation and hostility are not very different.' The Nagas too saw these as two sides of the same coin. [13]

Marriage relations between feuding villages in fact were of great importance for the second of the criteria given: continuing affinal ties provided an incentive, and a mechanism, for achieving a truce. [14] Clan ties did likewise. But, contrary to some authorities, it is in the general nature of the feud that the conflict is enduring, possibly unending: at best the settlement would be a palliative, not a definitive resolution, for the memory of a previous attack can be resuscitated, and time can amplify the grievance. It is also a logical consequence of a situation of general feuding that particular peace treaties or reconciliations do not produce a general decrease of violence, because peace between A and B might well lead to increased danger for C at the hands of both. [15]

It is significant that, generally speaking, the feuding unit was the *morung*, clan or (most usually) village. Individuals might take heads for individual reasons, but the perception from the victim's village's point of view was that the aggression came from the perpetrator's village. The relevant unit was emphasised in the head-receiving rituals: the captured head might be attached to the log-gong (symbol of the *morung*), to the head-tree (symbol of the village), to the *morung* itself, or was paraded around the perimeter of the village [16], even though later the individual might be permitted to hang the head in his own house.

An exception to this might appear to be the Angamis, where the feuding unit was the clan or *khel*, but this is because the village was a non-functional conglomeration of autonomous clans, each well defended and pursuing its own foreign policy. Thus in the Angami case, the clan was structurally analogous to the village among the other groups.

Equally, units larger than the village did not engage in a feud, because there were no units larger than the village for functional purposes, and because it would not be a 'feud' by definition. No 'tribe', it appears, ever united as a tribe against another 'tribe': no mechanism existed to bring this about. The Lhota observed a prohibition on taking other Lhotas' heads, but there could not be a situation in which, for instance, all Lhota villages were in conflict with all Aos. Even if this were possible, it would be war and not a feud, which is by definition a balanced, particular relationship between paired villages. Even when 6000 Angami warriors rose up to besiege the English at Kohima in 1879, [17] they did so as a confederacy of particular clans. Such alliances were found in a number of complicated feuds, in which two or more villages unite against a third; but this is a matter of political strategy and may not last long. What endures was the feuding arrangement of a pair of roughly equal villages.

This was recognised early on in European observation of the

Nagas. In 1873 H.H. Godwin-Austen commented that 'a sort of Debit and Credit account in lives goes on year after year.' [18] This observation is interesting, because (unlike the case of the Kachin) the idiom of 'debt' is not particularly noted in the Naga ethnography. And yet it can be argued that, just as with the Kachin, social relationships for the Nagas are precisely chains of debt. Without a debt, the social relationship cannot endure. Among the Kachin, the term *hka* covers this notion of debt. [19] It is not a purely financial kind of debt, and it cannot be repaid with mere currency units. It is rather a claim that one person (or rather a lineage) holds against another, until it is paid off, and it is paid with objects of ritual wealth. Giving feasts, giving brideprice, paying a fine, taking a head: these may all involve a kind of debt relationship, involving mutual claims between groups, who seek at least to meet the claim if not to outdo or reverse it.

The feud thus existed as reciprocal violence between villages. There were, however, rules – in the manner of fighting (children who have not cut their teeth are not killed), and in the goal of this activity. The main one was that a balance of heads gained and lost, should eventually be struck. The numbers were not in fact very great. The feuding villages were of roughly equal strength and were constantly on guard, and in any case it was understood that a balance was the goal. Mills provides one case from the early part of the century: 'Tamlu and Namsang, with only a valley between them, were at war for sixteen years. The casualties on both sides totalled four. He goes on to remark that in general, 'A village which lost on an average a head a year would consider itself subjected to a series of stunning blows.' [20]

The fourth criterion was that the aims of the feud were essentially political rather than economic. This is paradoxical in the sense that the immediate triggers might be material, such as an infringement of an exclusive trading route, or the deliberate cutting-down of a neighbouring village's fruit trees. [21] More often, however, the casus belli was symbolic: the failure of a 'formal friend' to honour his partner with a feast; a failure of the wife-receiving clan to honour brideprice obligations; an insult; or an intrusion during a village *genna*.

These actions in fact constituted 'the feud': the homicides which result were the culminations of the feud process. When a head was taken, and a formal reconciliation was established, other less dramatic feud actions might continue. There was a whole range of such actions. The Konyaks and Aos, for instance, would blow on an egg and wish ill-luck on an enemy village; they then would seek to place it in the enemy village. This was a form of aggressive magic, and fitted into a cycle of ritualised aggression that could culminate in overt violence. [22] Equally, the Aos and Konyaks made wooden models of enemies and decapitated them

(this in the past was also done with fellow-villagers in mind, but to seek a fellow-villager's death would indicate a very serious breakdown in normal social relations). [23] If a villager was suffering an illness, suspicion might well fall on a neighbouring hostile village for having practised magic of this sort. A similar ritual form of aggression was delivered to the District Officer in 1913, when he received from a Yachungr village a symbolic message, in the form of a small bundle wrapped in cloth. This conveyed a challenge to personal combat, sent by the chief of Saporr, consisting of a chilli transfixed by a splinter of wood (meaning, 'if you do not fight you are only fit to be impaled like a sacrificial dog or a chicken'). [24] Snubs and insults could also keep a feuding relationship going, short of homicidal violence. Some communities also had a tradition of competitive singing. When Ao villages meet, a champion singer from each village would sing songs of jovial mockery, each hinting at the superiority of his village or clan. Usually the insults are traditional and were accepted in good humour; but bad feeling could ensue if this was taken too far. [25]

The reconciliation itself might indeed provide further tinder to re-kindle the feud. In 1925 Yungya attempted to give Mongnyu a mithan in lieu of a slave, as compensation for Mongnyu's loss of a head to Yungya; Mongnyu was not happy about this, and chose to accept nothing at all; the unsatisfactory nature of the 'peace' that ensued was likely to rankle with Mongnyu for some time to come. [26]

The feud process was thus essentially political in nature. The aim was to prove superiority over a neighbour, but not essentially to do damage to his property or expropriate booty, which are technically the distinguishing characteristics of 'raiding'. Nor was it desired to decimate the population indiscriminately and finally as a matter of predatory greed, which are the features of 'warfare'. One authority on the general nature of feud notes that 'Apparently gratuitous violence, raiding or homicide for 'glory' and trophies of little material value, or to avenge insult and injury with no goals of an economic nature, are...akin to the sphere of 'policy'. [27] Once done, the victory is the important thing, not who exactly was killed: 'The reason for indulging in feuding relations is not so much the desire to inflict a loss on a given section, as to use this victory to enhance individual and group prestige within the home community and in the eyes of the world.' [28] This definition, written with reference to the circum-Mediterranean, works well enough in the Naga case too.

The parallel is also to be seen with regard to the question of victim equivalance. Just as in the circum-Mediterranean, the reciprocal death was defined as a category rather than as a person. That is to say, considerable care was taken to ensure that the

Spear throwing. Konyak, Punkhung village. 1937. CFH.

'balance' was not merely numerical but also qualitative: if the killer was man X of clan Y, then precisely this person, or at least a close male clansman, ought to die in turn. But the Nagas had little interest in fine calculation in this matter. To take the head of a woman or child, if of the right clan, *morung* or village was considered acceptable revenge for the loss of a renowned warrior. Nor was there any seeking-out of the killer's immediate family as the objects of revenge. This resulted in a phenomenon noted by various observers, that Naga feud killings were conspicuously impersonal, even without malice. [29] Rather, it is as if the emotion were channelled into celebrating the return of the head to the village, and hence the political status of the successful warriors.

In one aspect, however, Naga feuding did resemble 'warfare', although the unit involved (the village) remained the same. In most of the above cases, the tangible results of the feud were trophies. But when a Sema chief was seeking land for his sons to colonize, the purpose of fighting was material: economic control of a village and its land, and hence the deaths of large numbers of its population.

It must also be mentioned that in some cases warfare of this sort could lead to extremely high levels of casualties, far more serious than the one head a year loss referred to above. Between 1902 and 1905 an average of 90 heads a year were taken in a stretch of border country about 30 miles long. [30] On 9 June 1936, in the unadministered area, Ukha, Pangsha and Yangkao together took 96 heads from Agching; this horrifying tally was itself outdone in 1939 when one village, also in the unadministered area, was exterminated with the loss of 400 lives. [31] There is some evidence that after about 1900 villages in the unadministered area were indeed taking part in attacks (often into the administered area) resulting in very high loss of life. In 1948 another apparent upturn in violence was recorded by W.G. Archer, when the Konyak village of Choknyu was wiped out by other Konyak warriors from Chen, together with Naga from across the Burmese frontier, with the loss of 400 lives. [32] There are at least two possible ways of looking at this grim picture.

It may be that the picture of 'one head a year' was typical of the area nearer the plains (the area administered by the British), while high fatalities had always taken place in the more remote interior, near the border with Burma. In this case, the increase of fatalities noted in the period after 1900 was only the result of better reporting of the more remote areas, as the border of administration pushed eastwards and less-known groups were encountered.

But it is more likely that these levels of fatalities were the response to particular, identifiable, historical conditions. One changed circumstance, for instance, concerns guns. Despite attempts at licensing guns, it is clear that these examples of raids

Dancing in front of *morung* at the Spring Festival. Konyak, Wakching village. 1937. CFH.

'Great dance' at the Spring Festival. Konyak, Wakching village. 1937. CFH.

with high casualties were all raids which involved large numbers of guns; it is at least arguable that warfare with spears and *daos*, between roughly equal villages, could not result in such levels of death. By the turn of the century it was clear that attempts to control access to guns through licenses were failing. [33]

Beyond this, however, it is possible to argue that something structural had changed. To begin with, violence of this kind is not indefinitely sustainable; it is quite antithetical to the 'balanced' feud process outlined above, which there is no reason to suppose stopped on one side of a line that ran through Naga country. It is more symptomatic of a system which is in some sense breaking down, and there is a reasonable explanation for this: it was an unintended consequence of the British colonial policy towards the practice of head-taking.

British policy, from the Naga point of view, was fundamentally ambiguous. Head-taking within the administered area by unadministered villages, was deemed unacceptable and necessitated the gradual eastwards extension of administration. Since the mid-19th century, this had always been a reluctant, stop-start process, because it obviously did not end the problem, but rather simply shifted its location eastwards. Complete administrative control of the entire area, up to the Burma border, was the logical alternative, but was practically impossible. British officers on-the-spot were therefore charged with three tasks: ensuring that head-taking remained suppressed in the administered area; encouraging the people away from the practice in the intermediate 'control area'; and ignoring it altogether in the unadministered tribal area, unless it involved raids into the administered area.

These tasks were, in fact, performed with considerable imagination and success. Officers tried to help settle disputes, suggested appropriate compensation, witnessed peace treaties, and threatened fines or military reprisals should feuds break out. The results of this make paradoxical reading: 'I warned Totok that I could not have guns used in their raids on Shuwa and that if they raided Shuwa with guns I should stop their raiding there altogether, but that meanwhile I should not interfere with decent raids conducted on ancestral lines. Totok did not like this...' [34]

An interesting aspect of this was the attempt to find substitutes for heads, such as monkey skulls rather than human ones. But the objections to this substitution simply reveal the quandary of the policy:

'I found that the Wakching Konyaks are very sore that villages in the control area can go on taking heads while they themselves are deprived of them. Kongon, for example, spoke very bitterly of the results which attended the use of a monkey's head instead of a man's when they made their last log drum.

Head-taker's dance. Konyak, Wakching village. 1936. CFH.

(top) Girl wearing a grass skirt. Konyak, Hungphoi village. 1936. CFH.
(bottom) Spring Festival dance. Konyak, Wakching village. 1937. CFH.

(top) Steps and bridge leading over a stockade of thorns. Yimsungr, Yimpang village. 1936. CFH.
(middle) Thorn stockade with crowd outside. Chang, Chingmei village. 1936. CFH.
(bottom) Gate at Khonoma village. Angami. 1917-23. JHH.

"Ten men died and it was all due to that". Wangla will have to bring a new log drum next year when the Ang is married and they told me that they were determined to have a head on that occasion. There can be little doubt that continued head taking in the control area makes for general unrest in the administered tract, and it would make it much easier for the administered Konyaks to evolve suitable tribal substitutes for their head-taking rituals (as the Aos and Lhotas have done) if there was not this standing incitement from across the border.' [35]

Paradoxical this may have been, but alone it would not explain why there might have been a massive increase in deaths. The answer may lie partly in the effect of the dividing line separating (at any one time) the administered from the control area, on the 'rough balance' given above as a criterion of 'traditional' feuding. Weaker villages naturally looked to stronger villages for protection, in return for tribute and loyalty. The dividing line may well have cut off some villages from their protectors, leaving them vulnerable to powerful neighbours. This was, from early on, recognised by some officers as a consequence of the policy, as in this conclusion from 1905:

'These atrocities are perpetrated within sight of our subjects, in whom the only feeling they excite is one of envy. They are perpetrated almost before the eyes of the District Officers. Some of them are in a manner due to the extension of our boundary. Mangaki's village was raided mainly because we had annexed their former protectors. In common justice it must be remembered that a village which does not raid is sure to be marked as one from which heads can safely be taken, and to suffer accordingly so that undoubtedly self-defence is frequently one motive in what appears to us mere barbarity and lust of slaughter.' [36]

It must also be said that equally to blame was a simple failure of two cultures to communicate alien ideas to each other. In particular, it seems that whereas the British intended a permanent, general prohibition, in the nature of a moral imperative, the Nagas understood this to be a particular, possibly temporary, instruction that was an aspect of an ongoing political competition. The confusion over who exactly could, and who could not, take heads, and under which conditions, probably helped this difference of interpretation, which was further buttressed, oddly enough, by the policy of punitive expeditions. The Nagas could rationally argue that if one year they were punished with a punitive expedition, but not in the next two years, this was an admission by the British that they were deliberately turning a blind eye, or even that they were now in favour of head-taking for that particular village.

In 1936 a punitive Government expedition destroyed the village of Pangsha, as punishment for numerous head-taking and slave-raiding activities. Neighbouring villages appeared to interpret the British action as a particular contribution to an ongoing political competition, as manifested in feuding. On this expedition, British anthropologists contributed to the confusion out of their desire to see 'traditional' customs maintained against (as they saw it) the enervating tide of modernization and missionization. Heads were removed from hostile villages, and although intended for European museums some were divided up among various villages, setting off an explosion of rituals and dances for weeks afterwards. Mills and Fürer-Haimendorf debated with friendly Naga villages whether heads taken from the Pangsha skull tree could indeed be used in place of the skulls of the Pangsha men killed during the expedition. 'Mills strongly supported this view as he too wanted our coolies to be able to perform the head-hunters' *genna* and then wear the ornaments of the head-hunter.'[37] To say that the British condoning, if not actual encouragement, of these practices in the administered territory was contradictory, is to understate the case.

W.G. Archer noted in 1947 an upturn of violence, perhaps related to this issue, in the unadministered area:

'This recrudescence of war seems due to a number of factors. It is now four years since any villages were burnt and thus the restraining effects which former punitive expeditions may have had have long since worn off. The presence of military outposts in the area during the war made neutrality by Government advisable but this has in turn led the Konyaks to conclude that Government approve of head taking and even desire to maintain it. When Government had sufficient force in the area but did nothing for four years, they argue that head taking has Government support. Moreover, the fact that before the war various columns themselves took heads [that is, Nagas volunteering for Government service in the hope of surreptitiously gaining a head] has given further cover to the view that Government is not averse to head taking.'[38]

Archer considered this fighting to be a 'recrudescence', but left it unclear whether this meant a reversion/revival to an older pre-British system or rather whether the renewed fighting was evidence of a response to radically changed circumstances. The argument put forward in this account is that changing circumstances in the exterior world played a significant role in upturns in violence. The Nagas were responding to continuous changes in administrative boundaries, political control and punitive expeditions, and in addition found themselves close to the centre of a major theatre of war in 1945. The parallel that suggests itself is the case of the Ilongot, in the Philippines, whose own patterns of head-taking have been shown to be related to major changes in the external world happening around them.[39]

(top) Village granaries. Zemi, Laisong village. 1940. UGB.
(bottom) Granaries. Rengma, Tseminyu village. 1947. WGA.

This conclusion mirrors that of Blick in a recent study of 'genocidal' warfare in four tribal post-contact societies. [40] He finds that the pre-existence of a 'revenge complex' (i.e. feuding relationship), when faced with modern weaponry, could quite easily result in unbalanced, genocidal patterns of warfare. In the Naga case, this seems to be applicable, though in addition, also of importance was the change in administrative boundaries which left some villages without their traditional protectors and hence suddenly vulnerable to attack.

It should also be said, however, that over time, many Naga communities were, under British pressure, but also out of self-interest, willing and even eager to abandon head-taking, in return for a guarantee of peace and the possibility of material well-being. One case in point is the Sangtam Nagas, of whom W.G.Archer wrote the following in 1947:

'The outstanding example is the Sangtam villages just to the east of Mokokchung, which were first administered in about 1927. At that time they were so poor that they used to work for the Aos during the harvest and other busy seasons and in their external relations were dominated by the Changs, now Chare the largest Sangtam village is one of the chief sources of the supply of rice to Mokokchung Station. Instead of the male population spending half their time on sentry duty they can work in the fields and trade and work in the plains in the cold weather. The rest of the Sangtam tribe is continually clamouring for administration...' [41]

Finally, there are some anecdotal accounts, in their own words, of why individual Nagas agreed to give up head-taking. Chirongchu, a Sangtam Naga explained it thus in 1947:

My father took thirty heads. Then one day there was a fight and a Sangtam killed him. I myself took thirteen heads. One day Hutton Sahib called me. "You have taken enough" he said. "Why do you go on killing? You cannot eat them. Let them live". Since then I gave it up. Formerly it was the custom. Whoever took most heads was the greatest among us. So all of us went on taking heads. Now that it is stopped, we live in happiness and peace.' [42]

Men returning from a successful raid. Before entering their village they turn to face the enemy village, and leaning on their spears, chant "O Yemusale, Yemale". Sema, Baimho village. 1918-45. JPM SOAS.

Head-receiving ceremony at Oting. Konyak. 1937. CFH.

The carved house horns decorating the roof and the posts elaborately carved
with representations of human figures, heads, mithan horns, and female
breasts indicate that the house-owner has given many Feasts of Merit.
Tangkhul, Ukhrul village. J. Shakespear, SOAS.

Chapter 14

Naga Nationalism

India is a multi-racial, multi-lingual and multi-religious State with 25 million tribal people, and the Indian Constitution provides special safeguards for their protection and in their interests. The Naga problem is not an isolated one but one of many that faced India at independence. [1]

The Nagas will become a free nation. The Indian constitution cannot bind the Nagas. An appeal is made to India to declare to the world on Republic Day [26 January 1950] that the Nagas will be given the freedom of choice to become independent. [2]

The inauguration of Nagaland as the sixteenth state of the Indian Union ...brought the brave, proud and sturdy people of Nagaland irrevocably within the national mainstream and thus within the processes of nation-building, national integration, modernisation and political development. [3]

In these three quotations – the first from the Indian Government, the second from the separatist Naga National Council, and the third from the integrationist Naga leader Hokishe Sema – can be seen the three political positions which have set the Nagas and the Indian Government in confrontation more or less continuously since Independence in 1947, and which have kept the Nagas themselves divided as to their relationship with India.

The emergence of two kinds of Naga nationalism – labelled here separatist and integrationist – can be traced to a common origin. In what follows, the terms used are a kind of shorthand. In particular, the Naga resistance here termed 'separatist' would argue that they demand independence, not separation.

In 1919, a group of Nagas who had returned from military service in France, [4] met to form a Naga Club. The members of the Club were Christian-educated Government officials and a number of headmen from around the two principal villages concerned – Kohima and Mokokchung. The Club was informally supported by local British administrators. They ran a cooperative store, and held discussion meetings. When the Simon Commission came to Kohima in 1929, to seek opinions on the future of India, the Club submitted a memorandum, signed by 20 Nagas of different tribes: '...We pray that the British Government will continue to safeguard our rights against all encroachments from other people who are now more advanced than us by withdrawing our country from the reformed scheme and placing it directly under its own protection. If the British Government, however, want to throw us away, we pray that we should not be thrust to the mercy of the people [i.e. India] who could never have conquered us themselves, and to whom we are never subjected; but to leave us alone to determine

(top) Carving of a mithan head. Eastern Angami, Cheswezumi village. 1947. WGA.
(bottom) Carved house post. Yehimi village. Sema. 1947. WGA.

(top) Lady Reid, the wife of the Governor of Assam, with Mawang, the chief of Longkhai. Konyak. 1939. CP.
(bottom) Angami tribesmen in ceremonial dress meet the Governor of Assam, Sir Robert Reid in Shillong. 1937. CP.

for ourselves as in ancient times.' [5] The measures of partial self-rule for India which were effected in 1937 continued to treat the tribal areas separately, and the Naga territory was 'excluded' from Assam, remaining under direct colonial administration from Delhi, and Indian Plains people continued to be restricted in their rights to enter the Hills.

Separate tribal councils were subsequently formed, the first two being a Lhota council (1923) and an Ao council (1928), these councils being nurtured again by the British. Shortly after the war – in which many Nagas fought with bravery for the Allied cause – an overall tribal council was formed, the District Tribal Council. In 1946 this became the Naga National Council (NNC). Subsequently, Naga nationalists have either accepted the autonomy contained in the statehood granted to Nagaland in 1963, or have retained a fierce devotion to a totally independent state. The Naga Federal Government (NFG), that is, the Naga Government in exile proclaimed in 1956, continued to fight as an underground armed opposition movement. It is still fighting for the goal of independence, and hence finds itself in conflict – often a bloody conflict – with both the Indian Federal Government and the Nagaland State Government.

It has already been pointed out that the first stirrings of Naga nationalism were prompted or at least encouraged by certain British colonial officers, who felt that the distinctiveness of Naga culture would be at risk in a united India. It will be recalled that the crystallization of the 'tribes' was itself aided, if not created, by British administrators and anthropologists, and there was a certain logic in the subsequent development of a pan-Naga sense of solidarity and ultimately nationhood. From the start this was much more counterposed to India than to British colonialism (the target, of course, of 'mainstream' Indian nationalism at the same time).

The other factor in the development of Naga national consciousness (in both manifestations) was Christianity – specifically that of the Baptist Church.

The first US Baptist missionaries were invited into the Naga Hills by early British explorers such as Major Jenkins in the 1830s, but it was not until the 1870s that really significant missionary activity developed. The first settled mission was in the Ao country, at Deka Haimong (Molungyimchen), in 1876; but, as an early indication of a conflict that would last at least until Independence, the new religious practices divided the village, and the Revd. Clark and the converts left to found a new village, Molungyimsen, nearby.

The relationship between the British administrators and the American missionaries was not an easy one. In the first two decades of this century, Government officers continued to see conversion as an appropriate concern of the colonial enterprise. [6]

By the 1920s, however, although apparently unwilling or unable actually to expel the missionaries (who did after all supply the schools and teachers, the latter merely being paid by the Government, which also printed the textbooks), colonial administrators found themselves with a dramatically different perspective on the question of Naga development. This tended to be highlighted when, as district judges, they were asked to rule on disputes that had divided the Christians from the non-Christians in a particular village. The officers sought wherever possible to rule in favour of the traditionalists, giving rise to claims that the British punished people who converted. [7]

The British attitude was built on the premise that the social implications of Christianity (not necessarily its theology) were destroying Naga culture. The Baptists prohibited the drinking of rice beer, condemned sexual freedom and forbade young men to sleep in the morung. They destroyed house carvings, forbade songs and dances, expected converts to renounce and despise their 'heathen' neighbours, and banned Feasts of Merit (because of their apparently reckless celebration of conspicuous consumption). All of this implied not merely giving up 'customs' but also 'opting out' of the obligations normally attendant on every villager. Christians might refuse, for instance, to join in necessary communal agricultural tasks if they fell on the Sabbath, refuse to contribute rice for a festival in which they would not participate, or refuse to subscribe to village gifts for important visitors from neighbouring villages. [8] Christians were more likely to adopt Western dress and to lose interest in the ornaments which signified their position within traditional society. Catholic missionaries, arriving later, tended to take a more relaxed attitude to rice-beer and traditional songs.

The Nagas were therefore clearly caught between two alternative Western views of what they should become: a missionary attitude which banned everything traditional, but which offered education, 'modern' aspirations, and freedom from the burden of communal obligations; and an administrative perspective which banned head-taking but was passionately in favour of everything else traditional, and came close to advocating the isolation of Naga society in an unchanging primitive past. [9] Hindu Plains people were not allowed to travel or reside in the Hills without special permission. Protection from outside influence, rather than development *per se*, was the British goal. Recently, one Naga summed up this paradoxical paternalism thus: 'The British aim was not to educate the Nagas but to give them basic knowledge of reading and writing. They were not educated too much in case they began to think like the British.' [10]

The truly autonomous options for the Nagas in deciding their own future were therefore limited.

(top) Chapel with a picture of Jesus Christ on the cross-beam behind carved hornbills. Angami, Sangratsu village. 1986. SK.
(bottom) Chairman and staff of the tribal court. Lhota, Wokha village. 1948. CS.

Today at least 90 per cent of the Nagas are Christians. Some of the reasons for the spread of Christianity have been touched on: the possibility of escaping obligations and the lure of a clerical job for an educated Naga. Many Nagas also suggest that it was a rational theological preference – a move 'from uncertainty to certainty', a response to the promise of salvation and the fear of hell-fire [11], a choice to desert the propitiation of capricious spirits in favour of the security of Christ's benevolence. There is also a connection between openness to new religions and weakening of traditional village authority: the advent of the British meant that ultimately military power lay with British soldiers, not Naga warriors, and political-judicial power with colonial officers, not elders or chiefs. Traditional authority could be questioned, including traditional religious belief. [12] All of these explanations may be partly true. But of more significance is a conclusion that emerges from the sociology of conversion, during the period of conversion itself, before Christianity simply became the religion of the majority.

A puzzling feature of the years of conversion is the differential rate of conversion, apparently unrelated to the intensity of missionary activity. Conversion among the Aos was rapid, as might be expected given the 17 different missionaries working among them, 1876-1954. In the same period, the Angamis had seven missionaries, but only only one-fifth the number of conversions (despite the smaller size of the Angami population). Finally, the Semas had no missionaries at all until 1948 and yet in the period 1876-1948 converted at a rate very nearly equal to the Aos. [13]

The historian who has investigated these developments, concludes that the reason lies in the way in which traditional Naga beliefs related to traditional society, and how (consciously or not) missionary beliefs either fitted in harmoniously with these pre-existing systems, or else appeared to challenge them directly.

It will be recalled that Naga cosmological beliefs, across the different groups, tended to give different emphases to the High Gods, the sky spirits, and the earth spirits. Among the Ao, traditionally the Supreme God, Lungkijingba (Lungkizungba), was aloof and little involved in human affairs: far more important were the earth spirits, *tsungrem*. The first translators of the Bible into the Ao languages, opted to translate 'God' as *'tsungrem'* (rather than try and introduce the word 'God' or 'Jehovah'). This did not challenge Lungkijingba directly, and instead established the Christian God as partaking of 'spirit' in a familiar way, though possessing evidently rather greater powers than the average *tsungrem*. Subsequent events then served to reinforce the superiority of the new *tsungrem*. At the spiritual level, for instance, it turned out that no disaster befell when a particular *genna* was ignored; materially, the missionary tended to carry a hymn book in

(top) Grave stone decorated with mithan. Ao, Ungma village. 1946. CS.
(bottom left) Newly opened museum. Angami, Sangratsu village. 1986. SK.
(bottom right) A reconstructed *morung* with carved mithan and human heads and a model aeroplane hanging from the rafters. Chang, Tuensang village. 1986. SK.

one hand and painkillers in the other, [14] good health thus becoming associated with the new god, and less with the village shamans. But it was the initial shrewd translation which gave Chistianity its foothold.

There was a further useful coincidence between the traditional Ao belief in a Great Fire which will end the world, and the Biblical Day of Judgment: the missionaries used the Ao term, *molomi*, which proved effective. [15] In addition, the Ao appear to have had, perhaps to a greater degree than other communities, a belief that good and bad lives receive different rewards in the next life. [16] And of great importance, no doubt, was the fact that literacy (the word) and conversion (the Word) were presented as indissolubly linked. The truth of Christianity had an external authority beyond the custom of the ancestors.

The Sema and Angamis cases present interesting contrasts. Entirely without the aid of missionaries, by the 1920s many Sema villages had established Christian meeting places and held regular services. This was partly related to the problem Sema chiefs faced in trying to find new villages to conquer at a time when British administration had outlawed warfare: this failure inevitably meant a diminution in the authority of a chief, and Christian conversion perhaps was another way for weaker villages to signal their rejection of their dependant status. In turn, recognizing this logic and their own likely defeat, Sema chiefs in the 1930s started to invite in missionary teachers themselves, in an effort to preserve what they could of their authority.

At the cosmological level, the Sema High God, Alhou, was much more sharply defined than the Ao god Lunkijingba, and was acknowledged to possess qualities of omnipotence and omnipresence. It was a logical step to translate 'God' not as 'tsungrem' but as 'Alhou'. It would therefore be wrong to see this process only as the 'imposition' of an alien god; it was equally the adoption of a foreign god, autonomously, by the indigenous people, for their own purposes.

The case of the Angami is different again. In 1961, their percentage of Christian converts was half that of the Sema. [17] Two factors, according to Eaton, may explain this. The first is that as sedentarised farmers, their religious system was more stable and less flexible than that of the Ao and Sema, who were evidently able to adapt and adopt foreign concepts. There are certainly peculiarities of Angami religious beliefs, which were not part of a pool of shared Naga ideas, including the female High Goddess. But more important, perhaps, was again the question of translation. The first Angami translations (1890) attempted to introduce the name 'Ihova' into the Angami vocabulary, for both 'god' and 'God'. This did not work, as the experience of the Aos might have predicted. Later, 'God' was translated as 'Ukepenopfu' – the High

(top) Baptist chapel with corrugated iron roof. Ao, Akhoia village. 1936. CFH.
(bottom) Naga guerrillas of the anti-Government N.F.G. in 1961. Gavin Young. By permission 'The Observer'.

Deity. This might have seemed more promising, but it too failed, because of the contradiction between Ukepenopfu (female) and God the Father (male). 'Ihova', re-cast as 'Jehova', was once again employed.

The question of conversion is relevant to the question of Naga nationalism in two ways. The first is that the mechanics of missionary activity helped to crystallize a powerful pan-Naga sense of solidarity. In some sense this existed already: as has been pointed out, no group existed in isolation, and there had always been contact of different sorts between villages. But participation in the missionary network (especially the training of hundreds of Naga youth from different communities in the secondary and missionary training schools, and for the first time in a single common language, English) was a powerful force for promoting the overall sense of pan-Naga ethnicity. As non-Christian communities came into more contact with Christian, they may have compared their relative fortunes as this individual did in 1947: 'Everywhere it is the Christians who have flourished. The Aos became Christians and look at their school. The Semas became Christians and now they have 2 M.E. [Middle English] schools. What can the Sangtams do? They are lower than all of them.' [18]

The second is that the process of conversion is revealed in all three cases above to have been far from being merely an 'imposition' by a powerful culture on a weaker one. Rather, the Nagas, in a position of objective disadvantage with regard to the material and political aspects of a vastly larger world than had ever been imagined before, nevertheless sought to use what they could in the new religion, in both its explanatory and its instrumental features.

It would be unwise to assume that 'conversion' simply meant the wholesale adoption of one religion and the complete abandonment of the other. W.G. Archer noted in 1947 that, 'the Litami village is Sema and apart from six houses, it is now entirely Christian... I noticed on the house of Kolhoshe a formalised carving of a cross. This commemmorates three feasts which he has given and is obviously a Christian substitute for the carvings he would formerly have earned by Feasts of Merit.' [19] In the eyes of some it was more Naga than Baptist. For many, Christianity was thought of simply as an 'effective' way of getting material results. On the other hand, W.C. Smith, a sociologist and missionary, thought that the negative aspects of Christianity had become too dominant: 'There is grave danger that Christianity, as presented to these people, comes to be little more than the adoption of another set of taboos... Under the old system the Nagas had to refrain from working in the fields on certain days, lest their god Lizaba curse the village with an epidemic of blight the rice crop; now they must

(top) Men squatting in the long grass and objecting to the passage of a Government column. Unadministered area. Konyak, Yonghong village. 1918-45. JPM SOAS.
(bottom) Council meeting. Chang, Litim village. 1948. CS.

(top) Assembly at the closing of the V Force. Zemi, Laisong village. 1944. UGB.
(middle) Sub Divisional Officer giving an honorarium to Magulong village for their participation on VJ day. Zemi. 1946. UGB.
(bottom left) Presentation by the Viceroy to Angami men for their service during the war. Angami, Kohima village. 1945. Public Relations Directorate, CP.
(bottom right) Soldiers at the war memorial in Kohima. Angami. 1945. CP.

refrain from work on the Christian Sabbath, lest Jehovah, the God of Israel, smite them for their wickedness.' [20]

For both reasons, in the era of conversion there was evidently a good deal of prevaricating, and individuals might well convert and lapse a number of times, before taking Pascal's wager and converting once again on their death-bed. 'I used to be rich and I was told I should become richer still if I became a Christian. I became one. But instead of growing richer I grew poorer. So I have given it up and am getting on quite nicely now.' [21]

Today, however, Christianity is simply an accepted and vital part of Naga ethnicity. It clearly distinguishes them from the people from whom they most want to be distinguished – the Hindu or Moslem Indians. Arguably it has in recent years been the principal stimulus behind the renaissance of interest in Naga material culture. And it has a character which is *sui generis*:

'Europeans do not have the monopoly on Christianity...When Europeans became Christians they made it a European indigenous religion....Now I, like many Nagas, am a Christian, but I am not a European. I have a relationship with my God. Now my God can speak to me through my dreams, just as happened to my Angami ancestors. I don't have to be like the Anglicans or the Catholics and go through all those rituals. I don't need them. What I am talking about is Naga Christianity – an indigenous Naga Christianity.' [22]

To return to the larger issue of Naga nationalism, however, Christianity is common to both separatist and integrationist Naga nationalism, and an explanation for the diverging development of the two strains, requires further consideration.

After the foundation of the Naga Club, and its tentative moves towards a pan-Naga political sense of solidarity, the most significant event in the development of Naga nationalism was undoubtedly the Second World War. This had been foreshadowed to some extent in the First World War, in which many thousands of Nagas had volunteered for a Labour Corps, bringing men of different communities into contact with each other, and into contact with industrialized warfare in Flanders. The Second World War, on the other hand, brought the rest of the world to the Nagas: the Naga Hills was a crucial strategic focus of the war in the East, and it was here that, with the help of Naga irregular troops, the Japanese advance into India was repelled. [23] Improved communications, floods of material resources, and a large number of weapons, were all concomitants of the war.

Politically the most important development of the war years, was the emergence of a British Government plan for Naga independence. Britain had already offered India the prospect of Independence in return for loyalty during the war; also on the table was a plan for a Crown Colony for the Nagas and other hill peoples

(top) House horns indicating that the owner had given Feasts of Merit. Eastern Angami, Cheswezumi village. 1947. WGA.
(bottom) *Morung*. Rengma, Tesophenyu village. 1947. WGA.

in the India-Burma region. The Naga National Council (NNC) rejected this, and claimed the right to independence and not merely autonomy, insisting that anything less would leave them vulnerable to the assimilating tendency of the Indian nationalism of the Plains.

In 1947 a Naga delegation visited Delhi, in order to assert the Nagas' intention not to join the new Republic. Up to this point, both Gandhi and Nehru had said they were sympathetic to the Nagas, and would not support forced unions. The Nagas' own interpretation of their meeting with Gandhi in July was that this was still Congress policy. But in August, perhaps in response to fears of secession elsewhere in the new India (especially in the Princely States, as well as Pakistan), the Indian Government attitude hardened, and the Nagas were told that India would never allow independence. The Nagas' reacted by a Declaration of Independence, signed by nine members of the NNC on 14th August 1947.

In Nagaland itself, Independence Day was marked in a way quite different from that of the rest of India. Mildred Archer recorded the events in some detail.

'Yesterday evening, as we sat by the fire, Charles Pawsey, the Deputy Commissioner, told us about recent developments in Kohima..... Indian Independence Day, it seems, flopped badly. Pawsey had to hoist a flag on the office and take the salute. But apart from a few Assamese the great parade ground was deserted and not a single Naga was anywhere in sight. A little later the Civil Surgeon, a Bengali, hoisted his own flag, but it had only been up an hour when a crowd collected and some angry Nagas hauled it down. That was the only time the flag appeared. But if, in Kohima, Indian Independence Day was 'dry, chilly and lifeless' (as the Naga Nation described it) the move for Naga Independence also proved equally feeble and abject. On 14 August the Khonoma group had boldly drafted telegrams to the press declaring the independence of the Naga Hills. Twelve copies were made and addressed to the leading newspapers. But before they were despatched the postmaster referred them to Pawsey. He decided that they would only make trouble so he ordered them to be withheld. Nothing therefore reached the press, not a word appeared announcing their tremendous step. [24]

Although the Indian Government ignored the Naga Declaration (and because of the action of the Deputy Commissioner, there is some doubt as to whether anyone in the Government or press actually received the telegrams), the NNC entered into a dialogue with the Governor of Assam, Sir Akbar Hydari. In the agreement they reached with him in June 1947, the NNC appeared tacitly to recognise that they were, despite their

Declaration, citizens of India. In this 'Nine Point Agreement' a clause was included which appeared to give the NNC the right to reconsider their status within India, after ten years. The Nagas assumed that this included the right to opt out of the Union if they wanted. Its lack of clarity, however, contributed to the discord within the NNC itself, in particular between the generally more maximalist Angamis, and the more flexible Aos; [25] it was clear by this time that the smaller Naga communities had their own suspicions of the traditionally more powerful groups such as the Angamis.

The Indian Government in practice ignored this Agreement. This was to become the key betrayal in Naga eyes over the following years. The immediate posting of plains officers and policemen to the Hills, was also handled in a way that was from the Naga point of view, at best, insensitive. A plebiscite in the Naga Hills in 1950, which appeared to confirm the support of the majority for the NNC's position, was ignored by Delhi.

Z.A. Phizo, who had led the Naga delegation in 1947, met Nehru again in 1952, but stalemate ensued. Relations between the Nagas and Delhi grew increasingly bitter, Delhi accusing various foreign interests of stirring up Naga assertiveness. Adopting the Congress way, the Nagas launched a campaign of civil non-cooperation, including the non-payment of taxes and the resignation of Government-appointed headmen. NNC leaders were arrested, and in 1955 fighting began on a large scale. The Nagas declared a Federal Government of Nagaland in 1956. As in many cases of counter-insurgency, civilians were often the victims of torture and killings. The Government admitted 1400 Naga deaths, 1956-58, as opposed to 16 in the Indian Army. [26] Among the Nagas, too, political discord grew, as it became clear that many thought the NNC should adopt more 'gradualist' strategies for independence. For most of the NNC, however, this amounted to advocating collaboration.

The idea of statehood, within the Union, began to gain credibility by the end of the 50s, both among Indians (but not, initially, Nehru) and among Nagas (but not the NNC). The Naga People's Convention led the campaign for statehood as the best practical tactic in the short term, and in 1963 the new State of Nagaland was inaugurated. The NNC did not recognise statehood, and violent conflict continued with the Indian Army, which by now was a major presence in the area. In 1963 the Government admitted aerial bombing and strafing of suspected guerilla areas, and the Army developed a form of 'strategic hamlet' relocation. [27]

At about the same time, however, negotiations resumed between the 'Federals' (the 'underground' resistance) and the Indian Government, thanks largely to the mediating influence of the Reverend Michael Scott, who had helped Phizo settle in

(top) Men grouped in front of a house with horns. Angami, Kezoma village. 1946. CS.
(bottom) House horns. Angami, Ungoma village. 1936. CFH.

(top) Men of Laisong village. Zemi. 1946. CS.
(bottom) Man smoking pipe. Tangkhul, Ukhrul village. 1937. UGB.

London (where he remains in exile today) but who also had good relations with Nehru. Scott was one of a three-man Peace Commission (together with J.P. Narayan and the new Chief Minister of Assam B.P. Chaliha) which in 1964 secured an agreement for a cease-fire. From the Federals' point of view, by this agreement the Indian Government seemed to have acknowledged their existence as a significant actor; but little else could be explicitly agreed, given the incompatibility of the two rival claims to sovereignty. Although the political negotiation collapsed in 1966 (and Scott was deported), the cease-fire held a little longer; but this too was formally terminated by the Indian Government in 1972 and the NNC was banned. Since then the Indian Army presence has been at a high enough level to secure strategic Government control; the elusive Federals have slimmed down their fighting forces, and still evidently can command the support of the villagers (often the targets of Government actions).

The political organisation of the pro-statehood Nagas, the Naga Nationalist Organisation, found it difficult in the 1960s and 70s to assert itself as the legitimate representative of the majority of Nagas. Its sitting member in the Indian Parliament in Delhi, was not returned in 1971, and in 1975 Delhi suspended the Nagaland State Government, implementing President's Rule from Delhi instead. In 1977 the United Democratic Front defeated the NNO (now merged with Congress (I) in India) and called for renewed talks with the Federals. In the 1980s the Congress (I) candidates improved their position, perhaps indicating among Nagas a general weariness with continued conflict. To some extent the New Delhi combination of on the one hand military force, and on the other hand political concession and economic subsidy, seems to be working. But their civilian government is buttressed by a very heavy Army presence.

The 'separatist' Federals, based in the remoter areas of Nagaland and in Burma, continue to count on a certain level of support among villagers. They have not been removed even today from the picture, though their unity is tenuous. In particular, there is obvious disagreement arising from the emergence of new political ideologies, as in insurgent movements throughout S.E.Asia: in the late 1960s some Nagas began to receive military and political training in Yunnan, China. When an Underground armistice treaty with New Delhi, the Shillong Agreement of 1975, was signed by Federals living within Nagaland, it was condemned as treachery by the the National Socialist Council of Nagaland (NSCN) or 'Muiva group'. It is this group, based in the Burma border area and called after one of its leaders, which is largely carrying on the fighting at present, and is unwilling to entertain any thoughts of concessions. Its ideology is Maoist and class based, though, like the Naga National Council, Christian. Phizo, still in

London, remains the head of the NNC, which has distanced itself from the Shillong Accord. The NNC continues as a political and military force, advocating independence. [28]

The above account attempts to show that Naga nationalism partly arose out of the 'modernizing process'. The potentiality for nationalism inherent within the shared, unifying, generalized culture of the Naga communities, was catalyzed by British administration and American Christianity. Separatist and integrationist nationalisms both emerged as recognizably 'modernizing' movements, with national goals to be achieved through political organisation. But one parallel development in early Naga nationalism presents a radically different picture.

In the early 1930s a rebellion spread rapidly through the Kacha Zemi and Kabui communities – the southernmost of the Naga groups. The rebellion was led first by a seer called Jadonang, and then, after his execution by the British on murder charges, by a 17-year-old woman called Gaidiliu. The obvious features of the rebellion were its ritual means. The leaders of the rebellion announced that the day of the Nagas was at hand, and the Raj was soon to fall. A new set of religious practices was established, including the setting-up of temples containing purifying baths, shrines and clay statues of the gods of the new religion. Jadonang and Gaidiliu soon became the recipients of gifts of sacrificial cattle: such tribute, it was said, ensured prosperity and would help to usher in the new era of plenty. Jadonang and Gaidiliu were described as *maibas*, the traditional shamans of the Kacha-Kabui area, and indeed continued to foretell the future and cure the sick in the traditional way. [29]

But in addition there was a clear element of the conscious emphasis on, though not the introduction of, Hindu concepts from the neighbouring plains. Jadonang's god, Kangrellung, who would bring about the new era, appeared to him in dreams in the Naga manner, but was in fact the god of the Hindu temple in the nearby Bhuban Hills. He may indeed have been a form of the god Vishnu. The Naga god 'Buicheniu', who had long been a part of the Manipuri Nagas' pantheon, was said by villagers in the 1920s to live in the Bhuban Hills. [30]

The means included not only the gifts of mithan to Jadonang and Gaidiliu, but also the non-cultivation of plots. Gaidiliu claimed (or at least her followers claimed for her) special powers of appearing in two places at once. When Gaidiliu led Naga warriors against British troops near the village of Hangrum in March 1932, she assured them that despite the confrontation being in broad daylight with no cover whatever, they would be immune to the soldiers' bullets, which would turn to water.

In the Pitt Rivers Museum, Oxford, a set of notebooks belonging to Gaidiliu have been deposited. [31] The notebooks are

(top) Notebooks supposed to be writings of Gaidiliu. 1932. PR.
(bottom) Gaidiliu after her release. 1948. WGA.

Page 163.
(top) Notched ladder up to a platform at the back of the *Ang's* house. Konyak, Punkhung village. 1937. CFH.
(middle) Stone platform built over clan grave, *sikar tso*, in Tseminyu village street. Western Rengma. 1918-45. JPM SOAS.
(bottom) Fortified wall of the Thekronoma khel at Jotsoma village. Angami. 1913-1923. JHH.

(top) House set alight during punitive expedition into the unadministered territory. Kalyo-Kengyu, Pangsha village. 1936. CFH.
(bottom) A couple in the stocks. 1913-1923. JHH.

filled with regular and repetitive symbols, resembling writing but in no known language. It is said that Gaidiliu used these pages to enhance her power: they were sent as messages to her network of followers, though of course they also required a translation by the messenger. [32] This magical or pre-literate attitude to literacy is of significance. The more or less conscious adaptation of an outside symbol system in the context of an indigenous movement of resistance suggests that the Gaidiliu rebellion can be thought of as a crisis cult or millenarian movement.

In such a cult there is the desire to bring about a radically new state of affairs through new ritual means, in conditions of deprivation over which the participants feel they have little real control. It is certainly the case that of all the Naga communities, the Kacha-Kabui were perhaps considered by the British, by reason of their poverty and political weakness, the least likely to pose a threat to British administration. The Kacha-Kabui had long been dominated not only by Manipuri plainsmen but also by more powerful tribute-demanding Naga communities (especially the Angamis), and in the early 1930s were experiencing an obvious economic depression and loss of land to outsiders. [33] These are conditions in which a millenarian movement might well thrive, and as with other such movements, the rebellion did indeed succeed in crystallizing a latent unity, based on many shared cultural and social features, into a more united community with a conscious sense of its distinctiveness vis-a-vis outsiders. In this rebellion, long-held bitterness and frustration surfaced against their neighbours, the Angami Nagas, Manipuris, Kuki tribesmen and the British. The British response to the rebellion – punishment fines, forced labour and the burning of villages – fuelled distrust long after Gaidiliu was imprisoned in 1933.

Millenarian leaders are also often individuals who have had a brief but dramatic or catalyzing experience of the colonizers' world, producing a vision that seeks both to emulate and to destroy that world. Jadonang fits this role, if one can accept a tantalizing and unsubstantiated reference to the fact that Jadonang had been a soldier in the First World War, and that it was on his return that he began his prophecies of a Naga Raj and the advent of prosperity for 'all who ate from the wooden platter', that is, all Nagas. [34]

The means were thus strongly ritualistic, though with one exception. Jadonang and Gaidiliu promoted a house-tax boycott among the Kacha and Kabui Nagas, which was plainly secular and a direct (and effective) assault on the legitimacy of British rule. In this respect, it is worth making some reference to a contemporaneous rebellion, on a much larger scale, in Burma. In 1930-31, Saya San led a widespread rebellion by Burmese peasants, in which 9000 rebels were arrested or captured and 3000 wounded or killed. The conscious idiom of Saya San's leadership was millenarian: it drew on the folk Buddhism of the Burmese peasantry with its belief in an avenging Burmese king and a divinely sent creator of a Buddhist utopia. [35] The cause and target of the rebellion, however, was firmly located in the material world – the colonial state's taxes, and in particular the capitation tax (head tax).

There are plainly differences in the Kacha-Kabui rebellion, but the similarity is that a house-tax was the issue of contention. The deliberate non-payment of the tax was a strong statement against the economic and political power of the colonial state. In times of depression, the uniform imposition of the tax could mean the difference between the survival and non-survival of the subsistence household economy. Although a relatively small sum from the point of view of the state, its unvarying level could cause a considerable fluctuation in the fortunes of the villagers from year to year. [36] During the years of the Kacha-Kabui rebellion, the percentage of tax remitted by the state or withheld by the villagers increased enormously: the uncollected percentage of house tax rose from 0.3 per cent to a brief peak of 41 per cent before falling again. [37] Either way, this shows that the tax was unpopular and was recognised as an imposition that was beyond the means of many people.

Nevertheless, apart from the issue of the house-tax, the means employed in the Kacha-Kabui rebellion were essentially ritualistic. Their goal, however, was clearly parallel to 'mainstream' Naga nationalism developing at the same time as outlined above. The potentiality for unity between the Kacha and Kabui Nagas (that has today found fulfilment in the clear ethnic identity of the 'Zeliangrong' community) found an expression in this largely ritualistically-oriented rebellion, which drew equally on beliefs about a lost golden age and a promised future era of plenty.

Where the other Naga groups took advantage of British administration and Christianity to manifest and advance their desire for ethnic identity, the Kacha-Kabui looked to a different Great Tradition, Hinduism, and remained much less favourably disposed to the British. Armed irregulars associated with this movement long after Independence found themselves in violent clashes with the separatist Federal Nagas, whom they regarded as too Christian and too anti-India, and instead remained on reasonably good terms with the Indian Government: the Zeliangrong nationalist movements accept the legitimacy of the Indian constitution, though they argue for a united Zeliangrong homeland (at present they are distributed between the States of Manipur, Nagaland and Assam). This attitude towards India may have been a result of Nehru's perhaps naive advocacy, from his prison cell, of Gaidiliu as the Rani or Queen of the Nagas. [38]

Certainly it seems to be the case that in recent years the Zeliangrong have sought to identify Jadonang with the Gandhian civil disobedience campaign against British colonialism. [39] The Zeliangrong therefore stand in a somewhat different relation to the Indian state to both the integrationist and separatist Naga nationalists. Their history makes them both somewhat more anti-British than the integrationist Nagas, and less anti-Indian than the separatists.

(top left) Front of a *morung* with large stones on either side, a huge tassel hanging from the centre and bamboo poles projecting from the roof with tassels. Konyak, Wakching village. 1937. CFH.
(top right) *Morung* of Mongsen khel. Ao, Lungkam village. 1947. WGA.
(bottom left) Field rest house with mithan horn carvings. Eastern Angami, Thenizumi village. 1947. WGA.
(bottom right) Girls' dormitory in the house of an elderly couple. Rengma, Tseminyu village. 1947. WGA.

Morung carvings of an elephant's head with men on either side of tusks. The cross beam is decorated with men and hornbills. Konyak, Wakching village. 1937. CFH.

(top left) Man with fresh throat tattoo. Konyak, Chi village. 1923. JHH.
(top centre) Young girl carrying a puppy like a baby. Zemi, Hange village. 1941-42. UGB.
(top right) Rebuilding the *Ang's* house. Konyak, Chintang village. 1936. CFH.

(bottom left) Girls carrying large baskets of millet. Konyak, near Wakching village. 1936-36. CFH.
(bottom right) Young men and women dancing. Zemi, Laisong village. 1942-44. UGB.

Woman on sitting-out platform at the back of a house. Konyak, Punkhung village. 1937. CFH.

Page 168.
The *Ang* of Sheangha with huge rattan arm rings and a monkey-skull hat. Konyak. 1936. CFH.

Page 169.
Pangmi village headman of the Naga Hills of Burma. He became a Christian in 1982 but still wears brass heads round his neck (symbolising the seven skulls he took in his youth). HNL, 1985.

Angamis wearing traditional festival dress for a gate-pulling ceremony.
Kohima. 1976. JA.

Chapter 15

Nagaland Today*

The outline of Naga society given in the previous chapters is a historical portrait. Naga society is described as it was in the long period of the colonial encounter between the Nagas and the British, up to the time of Indian Independence in 1947. It is not the intention of this chapter to bring the story fully up-to-date. Such a task would require a separate work altogether. Nevertheless, some of the areas of continuity and change between the past and present can be briefly described here.

In terms of social organisation, it remains the case nowadays that every Naga is born a member of a clan. This is an important part of an individual's self-identity, and finds concrete expression in the mutual obligation clan members owe to each other. Clan members come together at funerals and marriages, and help each other with farming and other economic tasks. In addition, lineages and clans continue to own land and will appeal to the village court should a clan-member attempt to sell farm or forest land to which other clan members, possibly quite distant, might claim a right. The clan system is in this sense held together by a denial of the rights of women to own land outright or dispose of it to outsiders. The ban on marriage within the clan is still, at least theoretically, firmly upheld. [1]

Nagaland remains predominantly an agricultural economy. Seventy per cent or more of the population works in agriculture. Most Nagas therefore continue to live in villages, which today may well contain both traditional houses and stone sitting circles, and modern shops and amenities. Most agriculture remains slash-and-burn farming, with households making their own canework baskets for carrying and storing rice, as in previous generations. But there has also been investment in irrigation, machinery and reclamation with a view to expanding the proportion of permanent terraced agriculture. Commercial growing of fruit, coffee and tea has developed, as have new industries such as fish-farming. Timber exploitation for export has resulted in a near-crisis of deforestation. Where once the household was a self-sufficient unit of production, today agricultural labour is increasingly done on a wage basis by Nepali, Bangladeshi and Assamese labourers.

Nagaland is evidently pursuing a policy of economic and social 'modernization'. This is evident in, for instance, the widespread

* My thanks are due to Vibha Joshi for research which has been of great help in writing this chapter, and to Mrs. Lily Das for her insights into Nagaland today. The views expressed remain those of the author.

(top) Angamis pulling a gate. Kohima. 1976. JA.
(bottom) Don Bosco school in Kohima. Children arriving the the school bus. c.1980 Milada Ganguli.

provision of piped water, electricity and a network of roads of at least jeepable quality. A sizeable proportion of the population now largely derives its income from non-agricultural jobs, in the public and commercial sectors. In 1984 five major state industries employed 1426 people, and seven private sector companies employed 740. As a symptom of the increased use of the market and declining importance of the domestic unit in production, the production of traditional artefacts so much admired in the West (cloths, ornaments and carvings) is increasingly in the hands of a handicrafts industry. Much of the distinctiveness of pattern and colour, which once identified groups and individuals with great precision, has subsequently been lost.

Education and health services have expanded considerably. There is at least one primary school for each of Nagaland's 1,112 villages, and there are a number of higher educational and training institutions. Naga students attend university in Delhi and elsewhere, and their contact with India is a factor behind the growing electoral preference for the all-India Congress (I) party. The literacy rate in 1981 was 41.99 per cent. Since 1963 the number of hospitals has more than doubled and the number of dispensaries has increased fourfold. There has been a huge expansion in the state bureaucracy. Population growth has been rapid, though it includes large numbers of non-Naga immigrants: in 1971 the population stood at 516,449, increasing to 774,930 by 1981. Urban growth has been particularly rapid, bringing with it familiar problems of 'development', including unemployment and drug addiction. Per capita income in Nagaland, partly thanks to very high levels of Indian Government investment and subsidy, is notably higher than the average for India. [2] Despite these high levels of investment, Nagaland's economic base remains weak and development projects fail to materialise.

The number of Naga communities or tribes remains to some extent a subjective matter. Government sources tend to cite fourteen major tribes in Nagaland itself. [3] Administratively Nagaland has been divided since 1973 into seven districts. [4] The State constitution recognises the right of village and tribal councils to exercise customary Naga law, though there is also appeal to the higher national court system. The village council, often called the *panchayat*, as in the rest of India, exercises particular responsibility in matters such as land ownership. The secular power of chieftainship has declined, but chiefs still command respect and are often found to be the Chairmen of village councils. The elected town council exercises a parallel authority to the village council at a local level.

Nagaland has a State Assembly and sends elected members to both houses of the Union Parliament in Delhi. In the 1987 State elections the Congress (I) obtained an overall majority, reversing

(top) Outdoor school, Konyak. 1970. CFH.
(bottom) College in Mon, Konyak. 1970. CFH.

the trend in the 1970s of majority support in Nagaland (as elsewhere in N.E. India) for regional over all-India parties. The result suggests decreased support for the views of the opposition Naga National Democratic Party (formerly the United Democratic Front) and the Nagaland People's Council, which have in the past favoured more conciliatory policies towards the Naga insurgents. The latter remain a force, albeit a diminished one. They uphold an alternative sovereignty in Nagaland, and call their capital, which is moved between different free zone areas, Oking. Their continued presence within Nagaland is the ostensible reason for the very heavy Indian troop concentrations in the State.

The army presence is perhaps the other side of the coin of investment by the Indian Government in economic and social development. Many villages have grave stones saluting those who died fighting the Indian army. Reliable accounts exist of harassment, burning of villages and killings of civilians by the Indian army in the 1950s and 1960s. Some reports describe army abuses continuing into the 1980s, on a lesser scale. At all events, the Indian army presence, together with factors such as the increasing economic and cultural influence of non-Nagas in Nagaland, leads some Nagas to consider that a form of Indian colonialism has replaced and modified that of the British. [5]

These conditions reveal Nagaland to have undergone a process of material change from the days in the 1930s when the entire area of the Naga Hills was governed by one deputy commissioner stationed at Kohima, one sub-divisional officer at Mokokchung, and a small number of clerks and Assam Rifles. To what extent, however, has the 'traditional' Naga world of that era – the world of *gennas* and sacrifice, of *morungs* and Feasts of Merit – also changed ?

This is of course in many ways a false question, since it appears to counterpose the old and the new as if the former were itself somehow outside history and unchanging. Nevertheless, it is inevitably a question that springs to mind, and some tentative answers can be given.

The most obvious point to be made is that the 'modern' and the 'traditional' correlate strongly with the division of town and country. This is so in the outward signs such as dress and tattooing, but also at the level of belief and social organisation. It appears to be the case that much of 'traditional' Naga society has indeed changed dramatically throughout Nagaland, and more so in the towns and their immediate hinterlands. Village gates are not always tended and *morungs* have fallen into disuse. Feasts of Merit, in which material wealth was redistributed in return for status, are still occasionally given by rich men[6] but in general they have given way to the accumulation of capital, and the acquisition of status through consumption in the market economy. The Feasts

(top) Kabui Nagas in traditional dress. 1980. D.H. Zemi.
(bottom) Zemi girls. 1970. CFH.

173

Nagas on the Burmese side retain a way of life that is comparable with that of India half a century ago. HNL, 1985.

given by richer people today are more likely to be parties at Christmas or on other occasions in the Christian year. Marriage is more commonly found within the theoretically exogamous groups (clans or lineages) than in previous generations, and takes place before the church pastor rather than before the elders and village priest. *Gennas* are decreasingly observed. Individualism has resulted in fewer communal activities and rituals in which the whole of a village or *khel* might join. Most obviously it is the wholesale rejection of traditional cosmology and 'animist' beliefs that seems to distinguish the old from the new. Ninety per cent of Nagas today are Christians (mostly Baptist), though some villages retain pockets of determinedly animist believers. Funerary practices are a case in point. Christian coffin burial is now the norm; but in the more remote Konyak villages the skull of an *Ang* is still removed, before the body is interred, and placed in a stone pot.[7]

At first sight it seems clear that Christianity is connected with the decline of 'traditional' features of Naga society. As has already been mentioned, it was a deliberate intention of the evangelical Baptist churches to attack central Naga institutions and beliefs which were deemed incompatible with their view of Christianity. One recent study of the Angami village of Jotsoma concluded that, 'All the traditional rituals and festivals have given way to the Christian celebrations. Rituals concerning sowing, transplanting and harvesting of the rice crop have lost their importance.'[8]

Jotsoma indeed presents some interesting aspects of the relationship of traditional and modern, for here this contrast appears to be directly correlated with the difference between Christians and 'animists', or *nanyu* to use the Angami term. *Nanyu* are a minority in Jotsoma as a whole, but are the majority group in one particular *khel*. The *nanyu* observe traditional *gennas*, keep their *morung* in good repair, and respect traditional beliefs about spirits. They continue to drink *zu* beer, in clear contrast to the Christian majority of the other *khels*, for whom beer drinking is grounds for expulsion from their church. In the matter of illness, *nanyu* are likely to make a sacrifice and to consult the shaman (*themumia*), who uses his supernatural contact with malevolent spirits (*terhoma*) to alleviate suffering, which is still seen essentially as a matter of 'soul loss' or the presence of a foreign body.

Nevertheless, the dichotomy of 'traditional' and 'modern' obscures the reality of synthesis. There are a number of significant points of contact between *nanyu* and Christians. First, although Christians are more likely in the case of illness to consult the dispensary and to adhere to the germ theory of illness, Christians tend nevertheless also to believe in non-medical causes of disease. Where the *nanyu* ascribe illness to spirits, Christians see illness as the manifestation of 'sin'. Second, individuals see no contradiction in straddling, on occasion, both world-views. One herbal specialist in Jotsoma practices an ancient pre-Christian art learned from village elders, but works as a laboratory assistant in the Kohima Science College. Christians and *nanyu* equally consult other pre-Christian specialists such as the fish-bone specialist, who uses a mixture of massage and mystically-acquired force to remove fish-bones caught in the throat. Christians and *nanyu* join together in the gate-pulling ceremonies, which is one of the few activities which continue to bring together all *khel* and village members. It may even be the case that the healing powers ascribed to charismatic church pastors today are a continuation of those powers traditionally held by the pre-Christian *zhevo* or priest. The most important of the Angami *gennas*, the Seikranyi *genna*, is respected by both Christians and *nanyu*, though the two groups interpret it differently. This *genna* ensures the health of the community and as such is compatible with both belief systems. Joshi notes, however, that in both gate-pulling and the Seikranyi *genna*, 'the social aspects have a primacy over the religious ones.'[9]

This general conclusion is therefore one way of looking at Naga belief and customs today. It seems also to be true of agricultural-cycle festivals, which continue to be celebrated throughout Nagaland. This represents something of a revival after the extreme puritanism of the early missionary years. Today most Nagas, Christians or not, participate in festivals as communal occasions, even if the pre-Christian cosmology and ritual is ostensibly jettisoned. At an Angami Christian wedding, the gifts may include the freshly cut head of a bull, strings of dried meat, shawls and utensils.

But another way of looking at this process reveals not so much a dichotomy between Christian and non-Christian, but rather a blurred area of adaptation. Christian Naga theology should not be reduced to a simple matter of a wholesale 'aceptance' of a Western model of Christianity. As with many interactions between an indigenous belief system and that of a colonizing power, the result may be a new, syncretic and distinctive belief system. For example, Christian Nagas may well observe the *genna* prohibitions on working in the fields on a sacred or festival day. It would be wrong to assume that this is done solely as a matter of social custom rather than belief.

The trend towards 'modernization' seems set to continue, partly, but not wholly under the influence of Christianity. The market economy, urban life, education and modern communications have together exerted an influence on Naga society. In looking at the decline of say, Feasts of Merit or beliefs in traditional spirits, it is as likely to be due to the proximity of a nearby town or College, as to the presence of a Church *per se*.

Konyak women from the Burmese side of the Naga Hills. HNL, 1985.

Man proudly displaying a Western style jacket in front of Y poles (which also have ritual significance for Burmese Nagas). HNL, 1985.

Moreover, in the process of modernization, traditional functions have often been transformed, rather than lost. Although the *morung* as an institution appears to be declining, it is possible to see the multiplicity of civic associations (Youth Association, Women's Association and so on) as performing a similar function. Elsewhere, traditional structures may if anything have been strengthened by the process of modernization. 'Tribal' allegiance, which in the past was often inchoate and intangible, may have been reinforced, even at the same time as pan-Naga national identity has also grown. [10] An example of this is the way in which the democratic process has had the effect of reinforcing tribal identity. It is noticeable that support for the main political parties correlates strongly with tribal identification. The Ao and Sema Nagas on the whole are associated with Congress (I), and the Angamis with the opposition parties. These three tribes (or, as some term them, nations) appear to have acquired considerable weight and authority. All Chief Ministers of Nagaland have been Ao, Sema or Angami Nagas.

In conclusion, it would be altogether wrong to see the Nagas as passive victims of a process of deculturation. There never was a pristine or unchanging Naga society. Rather, we may discern the ways in which Naga ethnicity is being actively and consciously remoulded in the present era. What emerges is a vigorous sense of history and identity at the level of individual, tribe and nation.

Heavily tatooed Konyak man from the Burmese side of the Naga Hills smoking a water-pipe. HNL, 1985.

Large wood carving inside the *morung* of Kesan Chanlam village on the Burmese side of the border. Until 1983, human skulls were kept in the *morung*; during that year, Indian Nagas from the rebel National Socialist Council of Nagaland (NSCN) converted the villagers to Christianity (at least nominally) and destroyed the human skulls, but allowed the villagers to keep buffalo and mithan skulls. HNL, 1985.

The Indian Naga rebels (the NSCN) has its own gospel group who entertain the villagers on the Burmese side of the frontier. Christianity was introduced in the remotest parts of the Naga Hills of Burma by Indian Naga rebels, who established a base inside Burma for cross-border raids into India, from about the mid-1970s. HNL, 1985.

Colour Plates

Kacha Nagas. c.1873-1875. RGW. PR.

(left) Wife of the *Ang* of Chopnu village.
(right) Naga *Ang* or chief of Chopnu Village. Sketch. 1873-1876. RGW. PR.

Coloured drawing of Captain Butler surrounded by British officers and
assembled Nagas. 1973-75. RGW. PR.

Collection of head-taking trophies used as symbols of martial prowess and as a means of acquiring fertility for the taker and the entire village. PR.

(top left) Carved wooden head used as a chest ornament by head-takers or attached to head-takers' baskets. Glass inlaid eyes. MOM.
(top right) Monkey skull decorated with tufts of dyed goats' hair. Eye sockets filled with pith. Originally worn as a chest ornament by warriors. Mounted in collector's glass case. CUMAA.

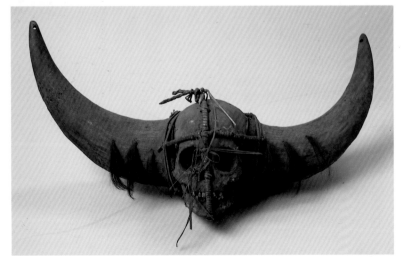

(bottom left) Trophy skull decorated with mithan horns and with goat's hair tassels. CUMAA.

(bottom right) Left: German helmet brought back from France after the First World War by a Chang member of the Naga Labour Corps and made into a dance hat with the addition of mithan horns and hair. Centre and right: two trophy skulls decorated with horns. PR.

Decorated human and monkey skulls, one placed in a phallic stone cist. Probably all Konyak. PR.

Collection of head-taking baskets decorated with carved wooden heads,
monkey skulls, goats' hair and fibrous tassels. Pitt Rivers Museum display.

Head-taker's baskets with woven baldrics. Monkey skulls, carved wooden heads, and boars' tusks were often used as a tally of the number of heads taken. Probably all Konyak. PC.

(top left) Head-taker's basket with monkey and rodent skulls and boars tusks. Konyak, Wakching village. CUMAA.

(top centre) Head-taker's basket, *dangsa*, with monkey skull and six cane balls representing additional heads taken. Chang, Tuensang village. CUMAA.

(top right) Carrying basket used by chief's children of a style similar to head-taking baskets. Konyak, Shiong village. CUMAA.

(bottom left) Head-taker's basket with monkey skulls and horns. MOM.

(bottom right) Left: Carrying basket decorated with 'Job's tears', seeds and goat's hair fringe. Konyak. C19th. Right: Carrying basket with attached carved wooden hand. MOM.

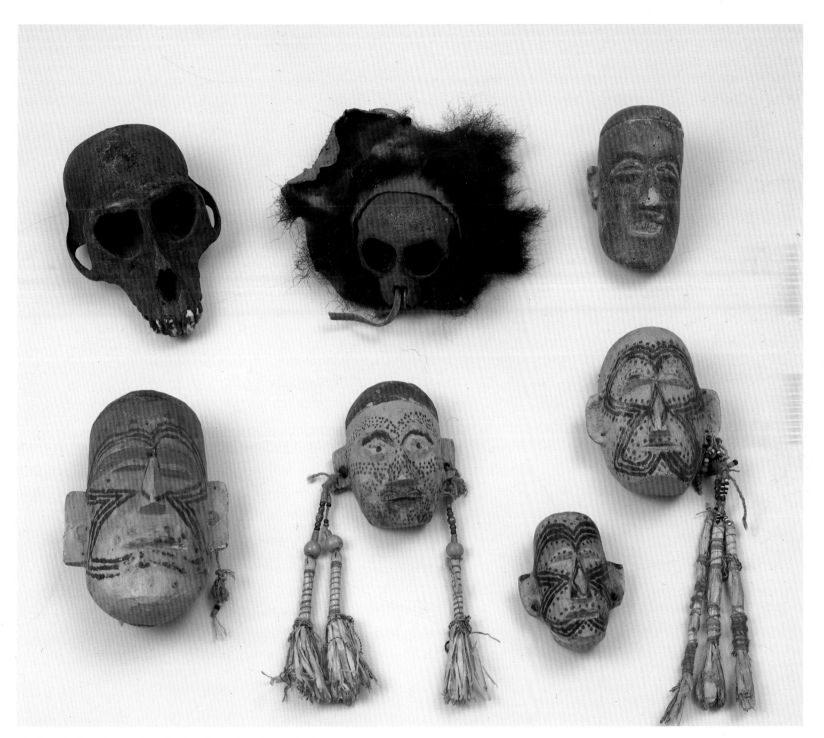

Monkey skulls and carved wooden heads used as chest or basket ornaments
to indicate head-taker's status. PR.

Various carved wooden heads and skull used as warrior's chest ornaments or attached to head-taker's baskets. Konyak. PC.

Carved wooden heads, some showing tattoo facial markings used to indicate head-taking status among the Thendu Konyak. Top left: Wooden torque with five head-shaped protrusions of a style more commonly executed in brass (see colour plate page 259). Probably all Konyak. PC.

Carved wooden heads used as chest ornaments by warriors. Konyak. PR.

Hairpin and chest ornaments used to indicate head-taking status. Konyak.
CUMAA.

Head-takers' chest ornaments. PR.

Chest ornaments used to indicate head-taking status, some showing tattoo facial markings typical of Thendu Konyak warriors. Also hip ornament and carving of a man with face tattoos. MOM.

Head-takers' chest ornaments. The head on the top left is suspended in a newly-built *morung* until a real head is procured. Ao. PR.

Carved wooden figures. Some are models of larger *morung* carvings. Konyak.
PR.

Three carved wooden models.

Left: Model of a bride wearing skirt with bead girdle, bead necklace and cowrie shell ear ornaments. She is carrying a basket containing carded wood and a spindle whorl, and a food dish. Sema.

Centre: Seated male figure wearing imitation hornbill feather headdress, hairpin, ear ornaments and bead necklaces. Konyak, Longkhai village.

Three figures with heart-shaped faces typical of Angami carvings.

Right: Male figure in ceremonial dress. The style of facial carving, ear ornaments, and 'kilt' with imitation lines of cowrie shells are typically Angami. Model of life-size grave carving. PR.

Left: Wooden female head with woollen ear ornaments and necklet. Carried on ceremonial occasions by a man who has killed a woman from a hostile village. Eastern Angami.
Right: stone models of a man and woman. Eastern Angami, Chizami village. PR.

The figures bear a handwritten label:

Figures in unbaked clay of warriors in full ceremonial dress.

EASTERN ANGAMI, KHIZABAMI, NAGA HILLS, ASSAM.

Pres. by J.H. Hutton, C.I.E, 1927.

Clay figures. Eastern Angami. PR.

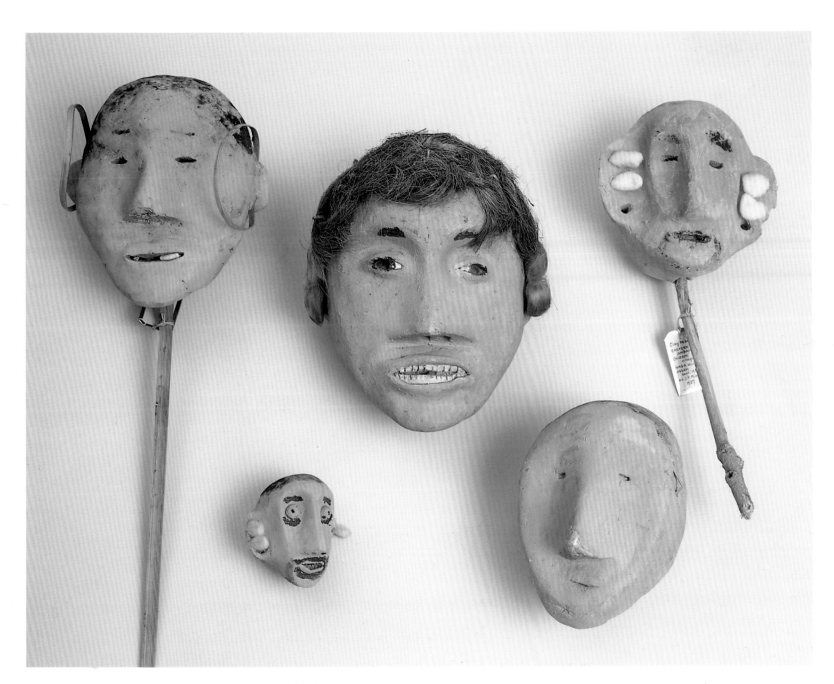

Clay heads used as house ornaments. Eastern Angami. PR.

Carved wooden models.
Left: Model of a Chang woman by Kaolom of Hukpong village; the model has human hair. PR.
Right: Representation of a warrior in full ceremonial dress. Sema. PR.

Left: Warrior figure in ceremonial dress carrying a trophy head. Made by Kaolom of Hukpong village and said to represent Yankai of Niengching village, a noted warrior whose head he had taken. Chang. PR.
Right: Pair of wooden figures. Woman's legs show tattoo markings received at puberty. She carries a baby on her back. Konyak, Punkhung village. CUMAA.

Carved wooden figures of a man and wife.
The man is Litamluem, a village elder from
Mongsemdi village. They were made by the men
in the neighbouring village of Susu who had a
long-standing quarrel with the former.
They were kept in the *morung* with other figures
with the intent of decapitating them on a particular feast day in order to cause the illness or
death of the person represented. Ao. PR.
(See photograph by J.H. Hutton, page 47).

Three memorial figures created in the memory
of a person whose skull was placed between the
'horns' on the head. The male figure in the
centre carries a model basket with a head.
Konyak, Angfang village. PR.

Carving made for Christoph von Fürer-Haimendorf depicting the figures found on the inner central post of the Ang *morung*. Konyak, Longkhai village. CUMAA. (See photograph by Christoph von Fürer-Haimendorf page 118).

(top left) Naga copies of *morung* carvings with human figures, hornbills, a tiger, mithan horns and an elephant. PR and MOM. (bottom left) Model of a chief's stool with stylised hornbills heads on the sides.
(top right) The model of a *morung* carving features an elephant. All PR.

Carved wooden tobacco container with human figures and tigers in deep
relief. The heads are removed when the lid is taken off. Konyak. PR.

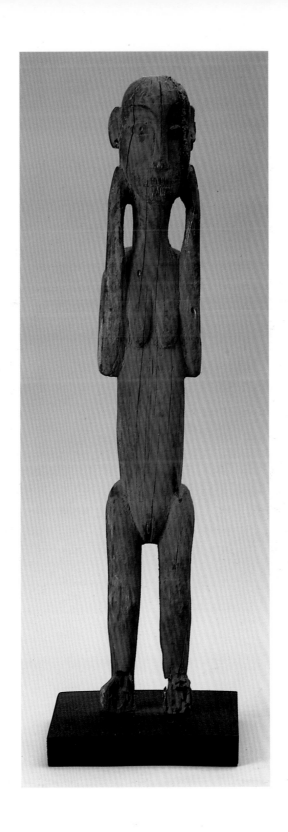

Carved female figure. Probably Konyak. PC.

(top) Two hairpins worn by warriors in a hairknot at the back of the head.
(bottom) Carved wooden figure with inlaid bone eyes. Both probably Konyak.
PC.

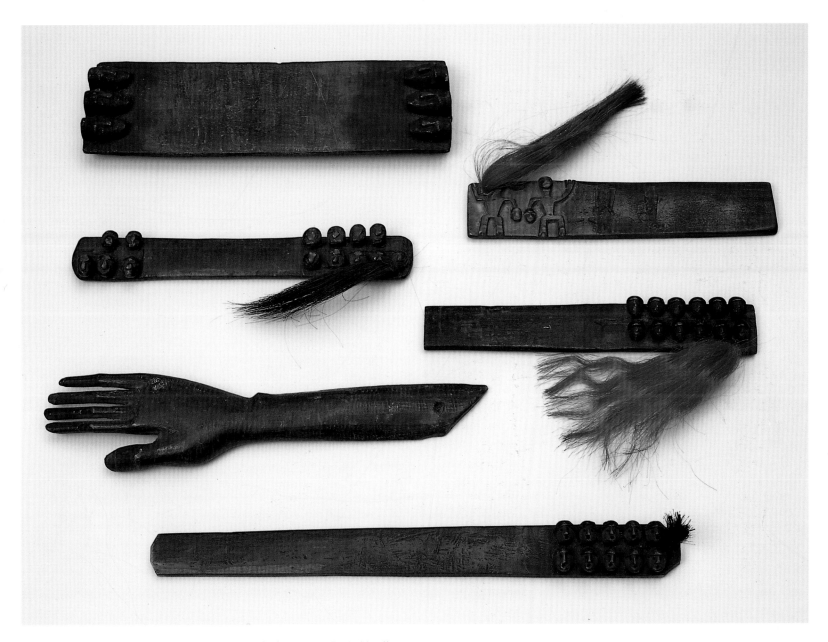

Carved wooden hairpins indicating the number of heads taken. Probably all
Konyak. PC.

Incised and carved wooden hairpins worn by men. The carved heads were
used as a tally of the number of heads taken. PR.

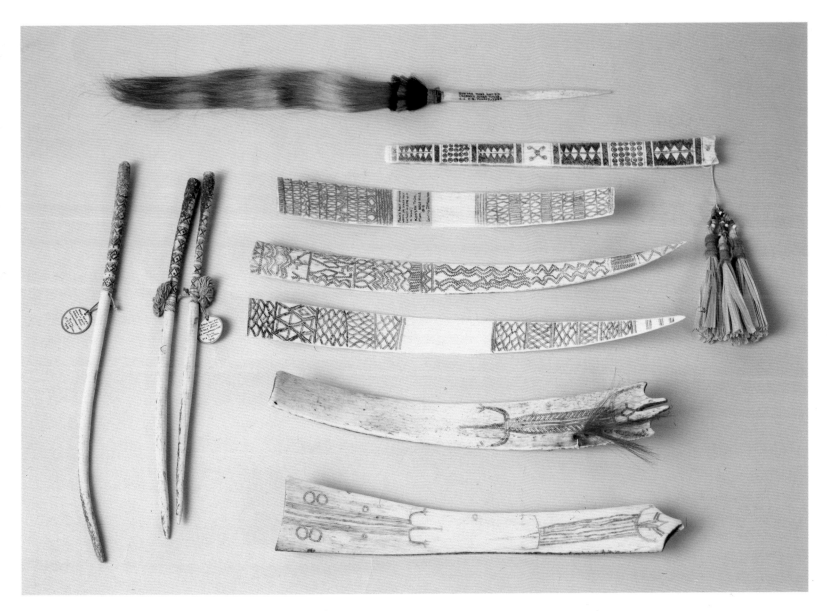

Incised bone hairpins worn by men in a hairknot at the back of the head. The
animal figured on the bottom two is probably a tiger. PR.

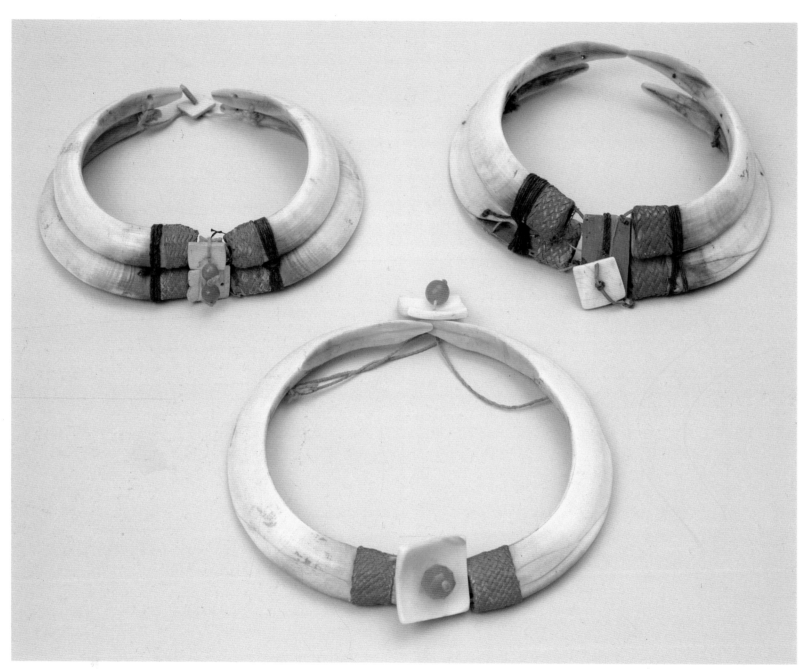

Men's boar's tusk necklets with central pieces of cut shell with cornelian beads. They denote status gained through feasting and warfare. Worn by diverse tribes. PC.

Chief's cane helmet with a plume of red dyed goat's hair and sections of boar, tiger, and leopard jaws. The atypical basketry straps suggest it may be Burmese Naga. CUMAA.

Left & Right: Hemispherical caps with black goats' hair, one on a basketry
base and the other on a perforated leather base. Sema.
Centre: Bear fur circlet or 'sweat-wig' with three hornbill feathers. Sema.
CUMAA.

Left: Cane hat with boar's tusks and a circlet of pig's bristles. Konyak.
Centre: Cane hat decorated with hornbill feathers, slices of mithan horn, and
a goat's hair plume. Konyak.
Right: Child's cane hat with yellow orchid straw and goat's hair. Kalyo-
Kengyu. 19th C. CUMAA.

Hats. Three are decorated with pangolin scales. Top left to right: Yimsungr, Chang and Konyak. Bottom left to right: Konyak, Chang and Lhota. PR.

Left: Thick cane hat decorated with a hornbill beak, two thin slices of mithan
horn, and a circlet of pig's bristles. Yimsungr, Kyntsukilong village.
Right: Cane hat decorated with the forelegs of a monitor lizard, two thin
slices of mithan horn from which hang long fringes of human hair, two
carved wooden heads, and crescent-shaped pieces of brass. Konyak, Longkhai
village. PR.

Cane hats decorated with yellow orchid stem, hornbill feathers, horns, bear's
fur, boar's tusks, and red dyed goat's hair. The basic conical design is Kalyo-
Kengyu, but the variations were worn by diverse groups. PC.

Hats decorated with hair, feathers and bristles.
Top left to right: Kalyo-Kengyu, Phom and Chang or Phom.
Bottom left to right: Konyak and Phom. PR.

Hats decorated with wood, beetle wings and brass discs. Top left to right:
Tangkhul and Yimchungr. Bottom left to right: Rengma, Ao and Rengma. PR.

Head ornaments. Top left to right: Konyak, Konyak and Zemi. Bottom left to right: Konyak, Konyak and Sema. PR.

Left: Tangkhul women's bridal headdress.
Right: Male headdress of hornbill feathers, and jaw piece decorated with red seeds and hair fringes. Feather box in front. Tangkhul. PC.

(top left) Wristlets of dyed goat's hair. MOM.
(top right) Hairpins. Right: ear ornament, decorated with dyed goat's hair. MOM.
(bottom left) Wristlets decorated with goat's hair and cowrie shells. PR.
(bottom right) Ear ornaments decorated with dyed goat's hair. MOM.

230

Various ear ornaments. PR.

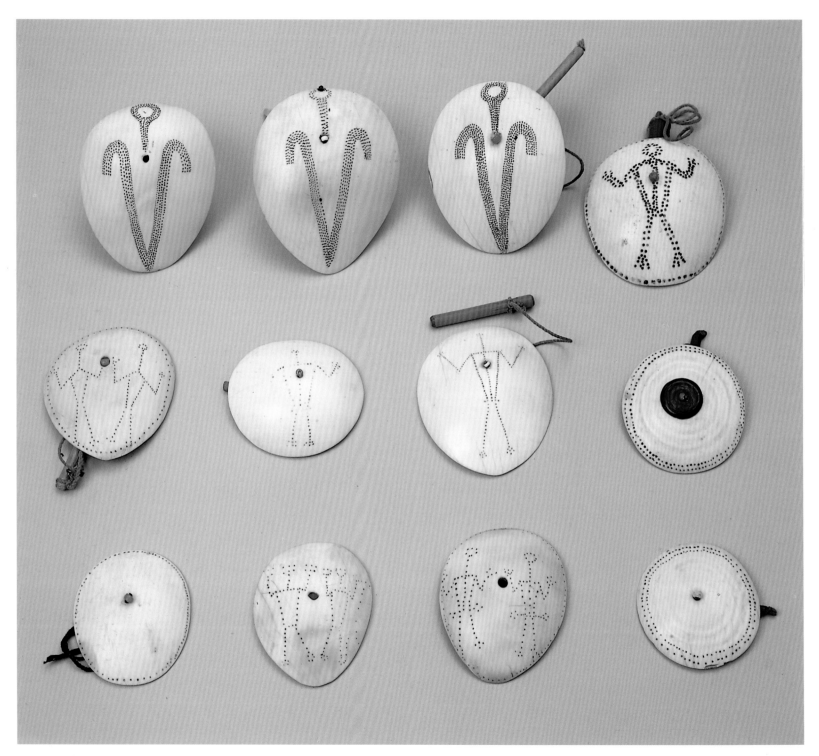

Conch shell ear ornaments with poker-work decoration.

Top left: the stylised design is similar to the tattoo markings found on the chest of Konyak head-takers. PC.

Left: conch shell and bead head ornaments.
Right: brass and bead ear ornaments. Konyak. PC.

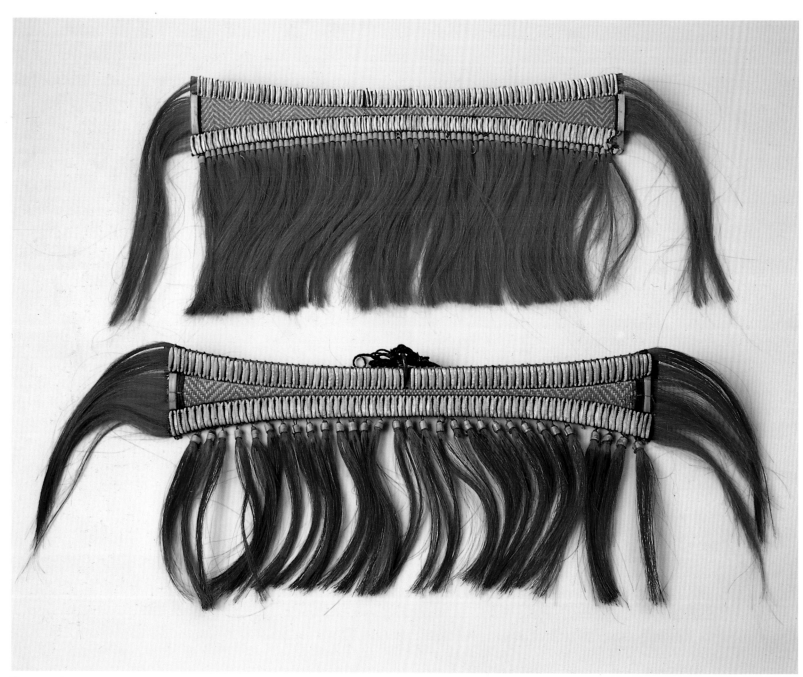

Head-takers' shoulder ornaments, enemy's teeth or *aghuhu*. The plaited
cane and orchid straw represent the mouth, the cowrie shells the teeth, and
the red goat's hair fringe the blood flowing from the victim's mouth.
Top: Sema. Bottom: Ao. 19th century. CUMAA.

Men's baldrics or sashes of woven cotton and dyed hair. PC.

Man's ceremonial dress. Angami. PC.

Different forms of men's shoulder ornaments, *aghuhu*, or breast ornaments, *thatsu*. Angami. PR.

Ceremonial tails and hip baskets used for carrying *panjis*, sharpened bamboo spikes stuck in the ground to impede the progress of one's enemies. PC.

Ceremonial tails and hip baskets decorated with human and goat's hair. Bottom right: Head of a hornbill worn as a shoulder ornament by warriors. PR.

Various hip ornaments worn by men on ceremonial occasions. Probably all Konyak. PR.

Various hip ornaments with human hair tassels, serow horns or wooden representations. Probably all Konyak. PC.

(top left) Breast ornaments. Angami. PR.
(top right) Hip ornaments. Konyak. MOM.
(bottom right) Hip ornaments. Konyak. That on the right, 19th century.
CUMAA.

242

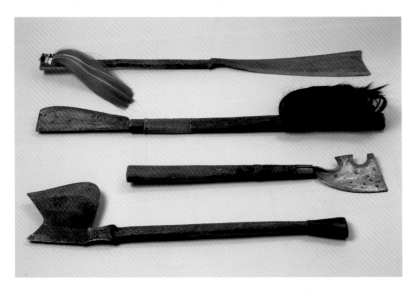

Daos. These all-purpose choppers were used for agriculture, house building, wood carving and warfare. The Kalyo-Kengyu were noted for the production of *dao* blades which were traded to other groups. (top left) PR.
(bottom left) Top: Kalyo-Kengyu *dao* with a decorative detachable end-piece which was made by the Sema. CUMAA.
(right) *Dao* decorated with dyed goat's hair. Konyak. Incised wooden *dao* holder, worn in the small of the back, and woven belt decorated with goat's hair fringes. Sema. CUMAA.

Various styles of *dao* holder and belt. Left: MOM. Right. PC.

Daos decorated with cane and dyed goat's hair. PC.

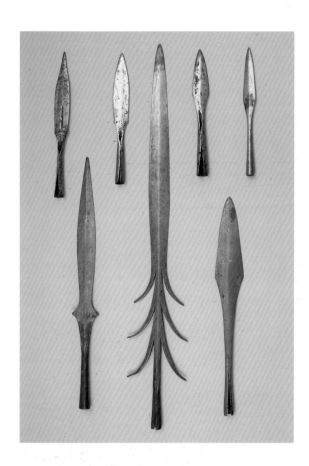

(top left) Detail of spear blade. PC.
Spears decorated with tufts of goat's hair. PC and PR.

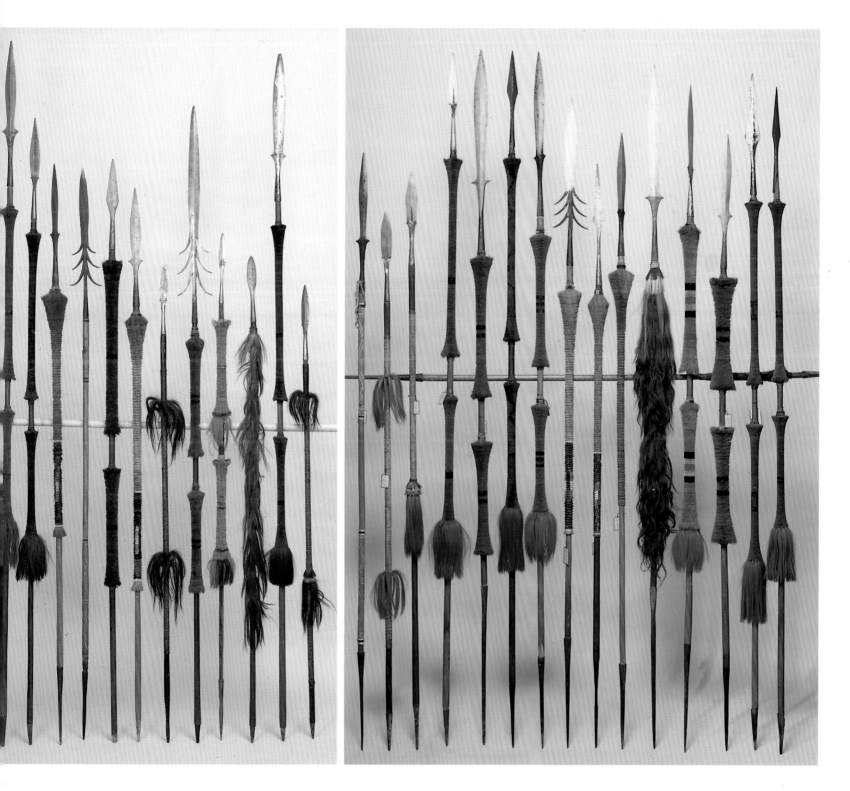

(left) Painted hide shields with goat's hair 'horns' of a type made by the Konyak, Ao and Phom. PR.

(right) Right & Left: Large ceremonial shields decorated with feathers goat's hair 'horns' and vertical line of heads made of bearskin, some with coix seed mouths and beetle's wing eyes. Centre: cane shield with painted designs and wooden and goat's hair 'horns'. All Angami. PR.

250

(left) Large ceremonial cane shields covered with leopard, bear, and tiger skin. Probably all Angami. PR.
(right) Hide shields some with painted designs decorated with goat's hair tassels and fibrous tassels. Konyak, Ao or Phom. PR.

Wooden and metal heads traditionally worn as chest ornaments to indicate head-taking status. Bottom left: Made from an Indian box lid imported from Manipur. PR.

Brass heads worn as chest ornaments to indicate head-taking status. Indigenous manufacture but style probably copied from Indian box lids imported from the plains. PC.

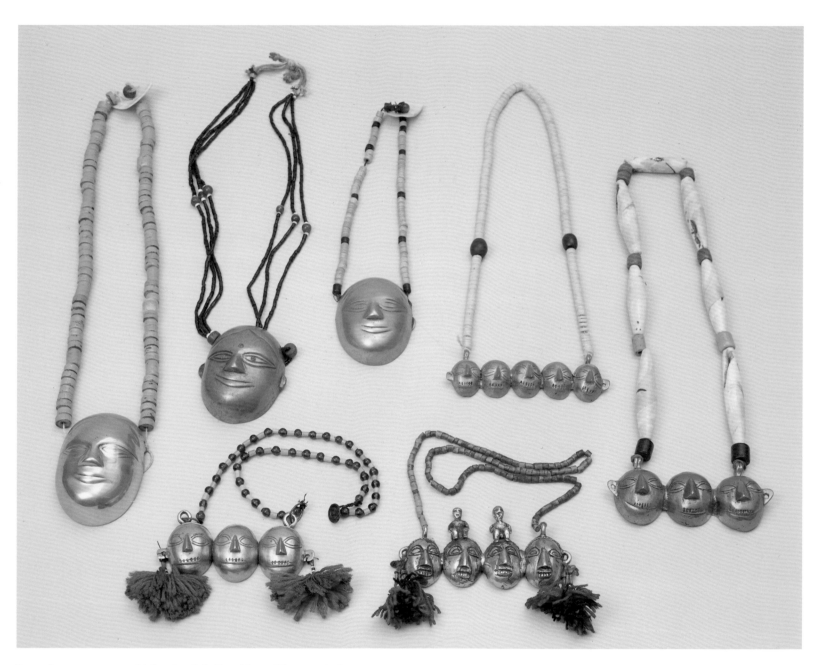

Brass chest ornaments with bead and shell necklaces. Three made from
Indian box lids imported from Manipur; the rest are of indigenous
manufacture. PC.

Brass 'fish tail' chest ornament. The shape imitates cut conch shell. May have been used as a substitute for brass heads to indicate head-taking status. PR.

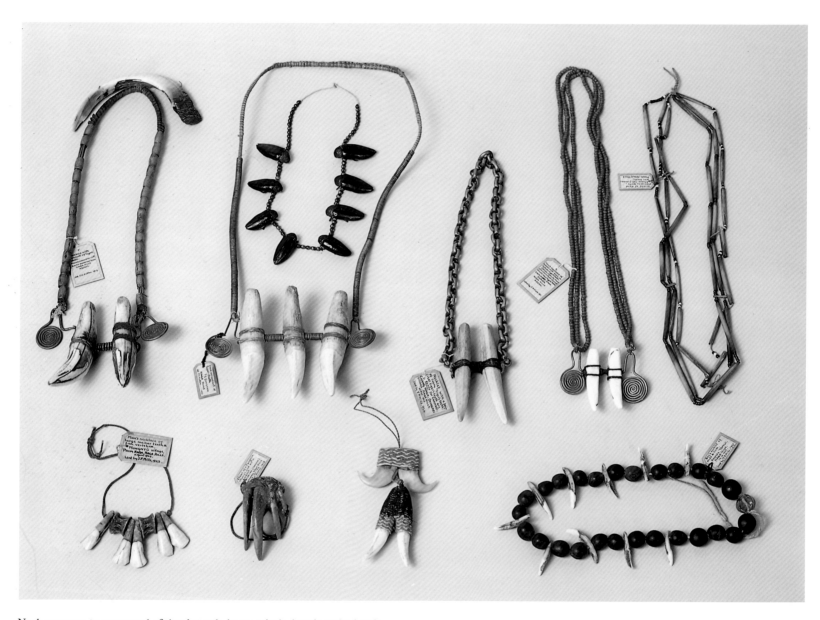

Neck ornaments composed of tiger's teeth, brass spirals, boar's tusks, beads, beetle wings, quills, cane-work, and pangolin claws. PR.

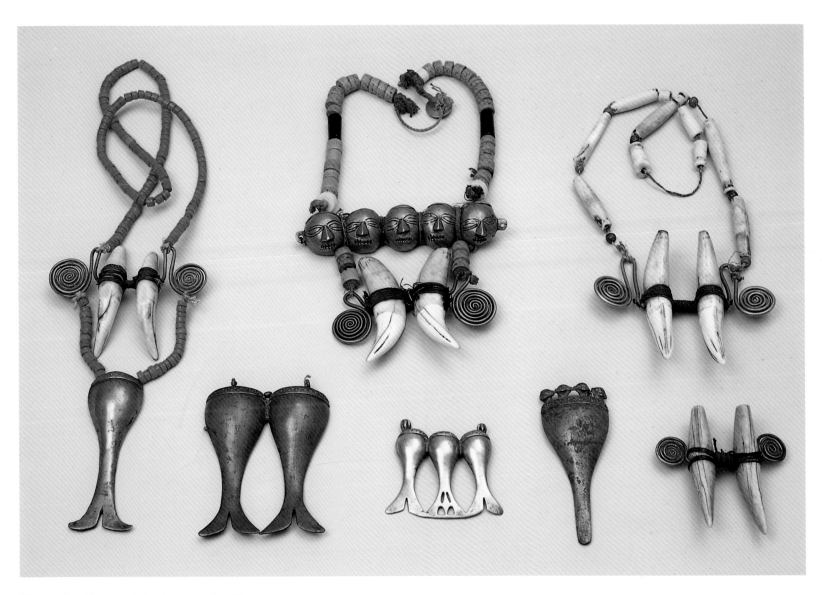

Warriors' necklaces and chest ornaments. PC.

Warriors' necklaces and chest ornaments. Probably all Burmese Naga. PC.

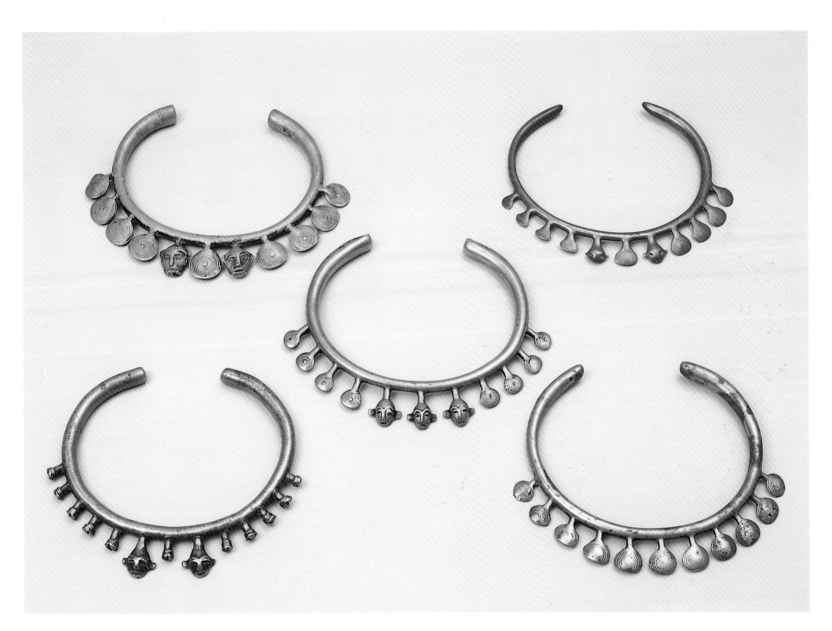

Brass torques with head-shaped protrusions, worn by warriors. PC.

(top left) Brass belts worn by men. Konyak. MOM.
(top right) Left: brass belt. Right: brass bridal headdress decorated with strands of cowrie shells and beetle wings. Possibly one of the Manipur Naga tribes. PC.

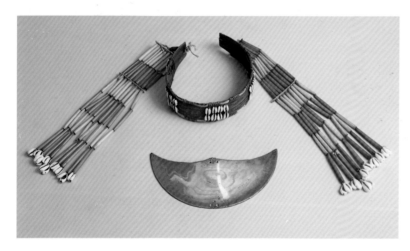

(bottom left) Top: head fillet. Konyak. Bottom: Brass crescent attached to the front of a man's helmet. PR.
(bottom right) Women's ear ornaments. Left: Ao. Right: Angami. PC.

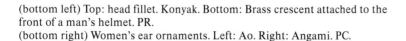

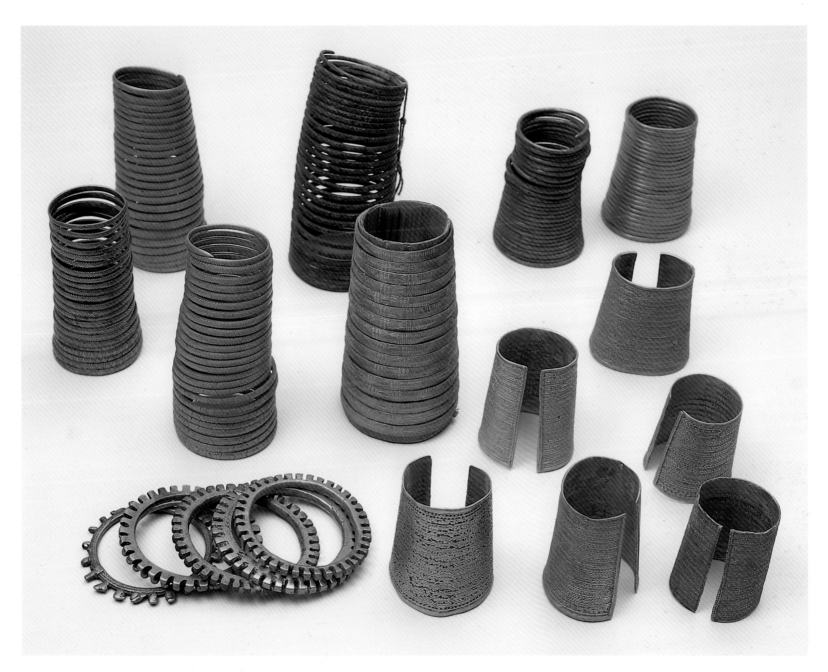

Spiral brass gauntlets made of brass wire which has been shaped around a wooden frame and then incised with geometric designs. Wristlets made by lost wax casting. Probably all Konyak. PC.

Brass and aluminium arm ornaments. Those with fluted ends were made in
Manipur. PC.

Solid brass ornaments of a style commonly made by the Tangkhul.
The heavier ones often have pitch inside to facilitate wearing. PC.

Heirloom arm ornaments highly valued by the Nagas. Many have been repaired countless times. Their origin is uncertain although some are said to have originated from Maibong, the 16th century Kachari capital in the North Cachar Hills. Others are made of an alloy resembling Tibetan bell metal. CUMAA.

Heirloom arm ornaments. PC.

Ancient heirloom arm ornament. PR.

Ancient heirloom ornaments. PC.

Thick ivory armlets worn above the elbow were highly desired ornaments for men. They indicated high status usually obtained through head-taking or feasting, but their specific meaning varied from group to group. Originally the ivory came from locally killed elephants and was rare although by the twentieth century Angami traders were buying ivory in Benares and Calcutta, some of which originated from Africa. PC.

Cane armlets and head fillets decorated with yellow orchid straw and cowrie shells. All Konyak except top left pair which was obtained from the Chang but made by the Kalyo-Kengyu. 19th century. CUMAA.

Various wristlets made of cane decorated with cowrie shells, yellow orchid straw and dyed goats' hair. Top centre: worn by the Kalyo-Kengyu as a protection against *dao* blows. CUMAA.

Leggings made of finely plaited cane with yellow orchid stem and bear's fur. Wristlets decorated with 'Job's tears' seeds. PR.

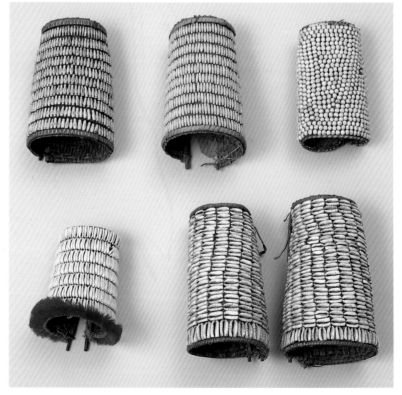

Various wristlets decorated with cowrie shells and 'Job's tears' seeds. MOM.

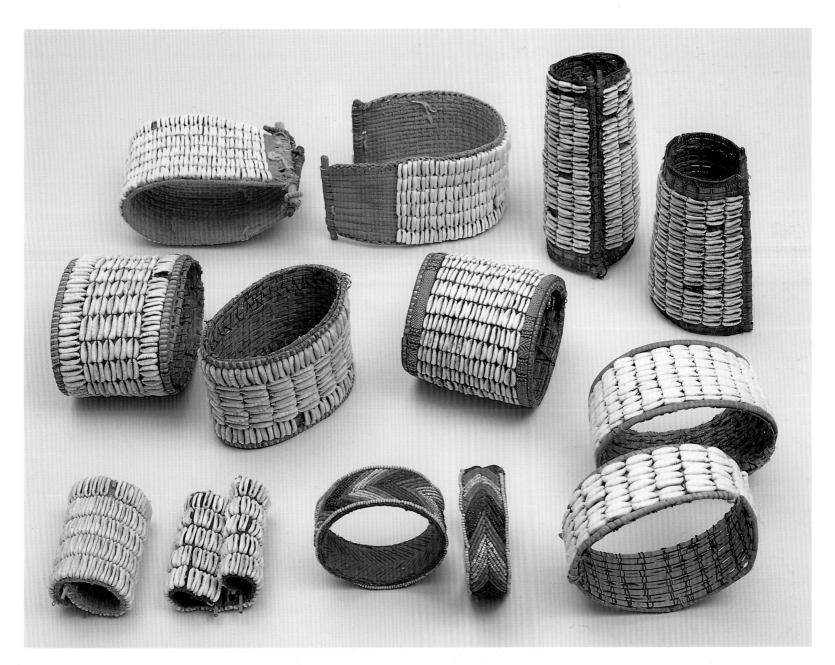

Various armlets made of cane decorated with cowrie shells and beads. PC.

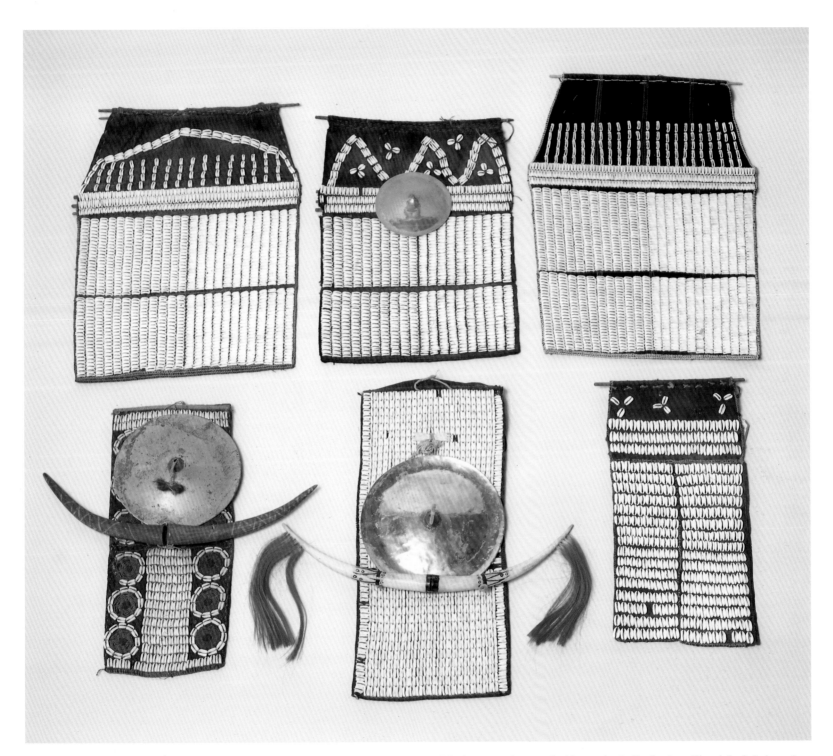

Men's loin cloths decorated with cowrie shells and brass discs.
Top left to right: Chang, Sema and Sema. Bottom left to right: Rengma,
Chang and Sema. PR.

Men's aprons decorated with cowrie shells, dyed goat's and dog's hair, and
horns.   Top left to right: Lhota or Sema. Bottom left to right: Chang, Konyak
and Sema. PR.

273

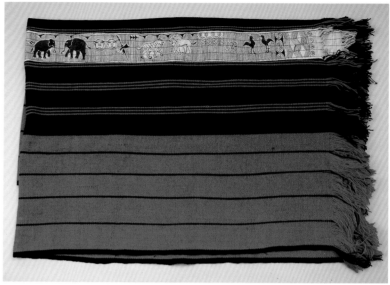

(top left) Youth's painted bark belt with human and animal figures. The tassels are worn at the back. Konyak. CUMAA.

(bottom left) Two pieces of palm spathe with sketches of men and animals. Used as a house decoration. Angami. PR.

(top right) Body cloth with painted band with elephants, tigers, and heads. Ao. PC.

274

Painted loin-cloths. Ao. PR.

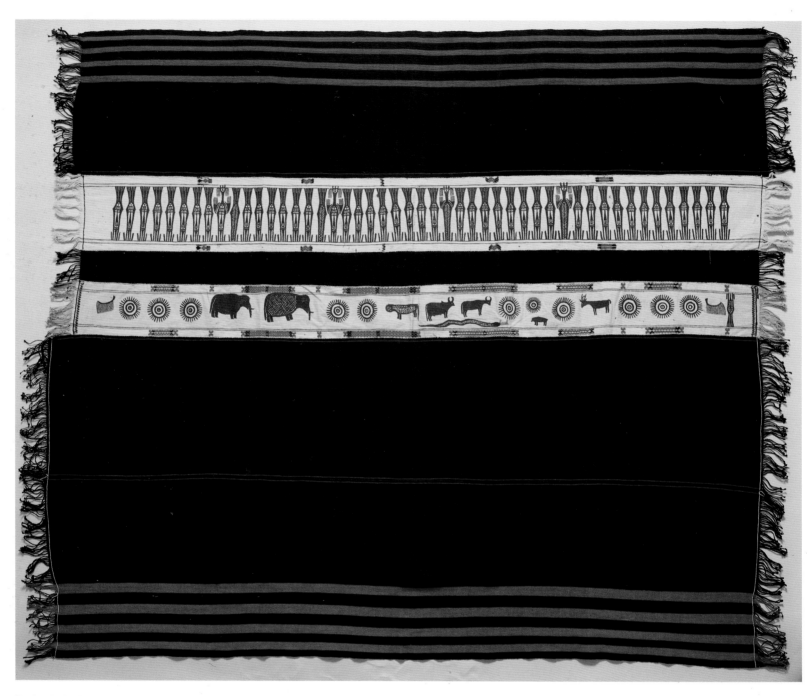

Body cloth with two painted bands. Western Rengma. PR.

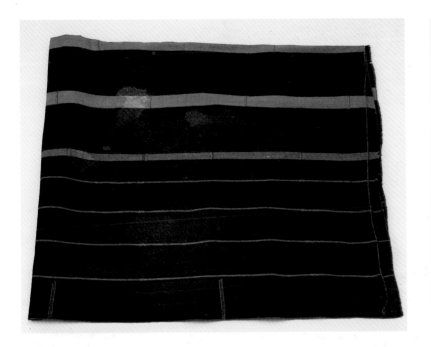

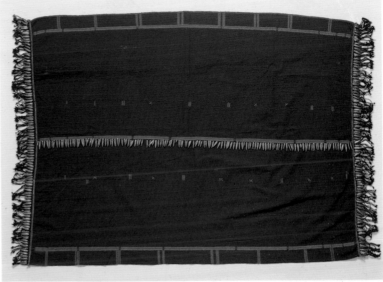

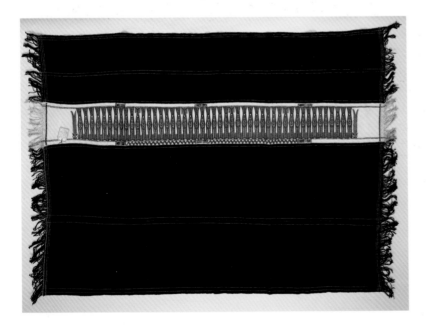

(top left) Body cloth. Lhota. PC.
(top right) Unmarried girl's cloth. Sema. PR.
(bottom left) Body cloth. Western Rengma. PR.
(bottom right) Body cloth. Angami. PR.

Body cloth, *rongsusu*, with thick bunches of dog's hair, and edged with tassels of red and black goat's hair ornamented with cowries. This cloth can only be worn by a man who has done the full series of Feasts of Merit and whose father and grandfather have done likewise. Ao. PC.

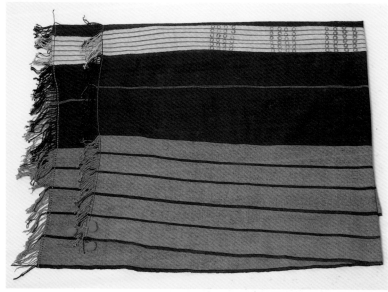

(top left) Body cloth. Ao. PC.
(top right) Body cloth. Chingmei village, Chang. PC.
(bottom left) Body cloth. Lhota. PC.
(bottom right) Body cloth. Rengma. PR.

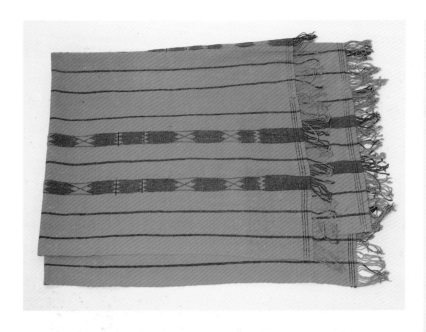

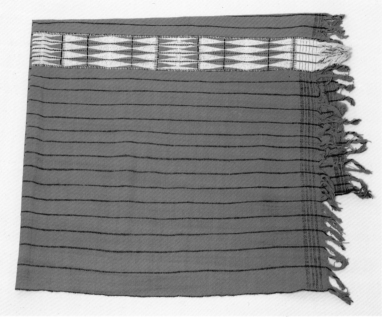

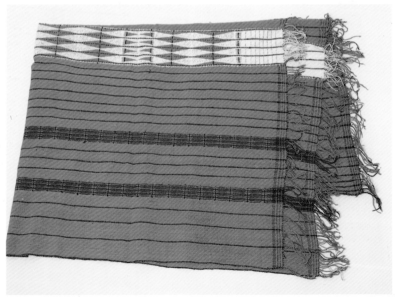

(bottom left) Body cloth. Ao. PR.
(bottom right) Body cloth. The additional two blue bands suggest that the wearer had sacrificed a mithan as well as taking heads. Chang. PR.

(top left) Body cloth. Ao. PR.
(top right) Body cloth. Very similar to Ao *suvangsu*, or head-taker's cloth. Chang. PR.

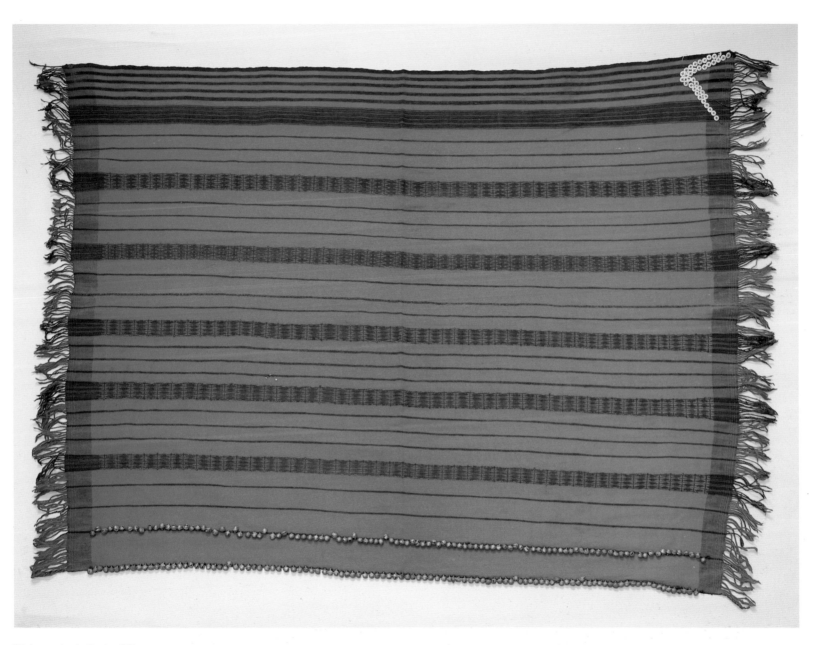

Rich man's cloth. Ao. PR.

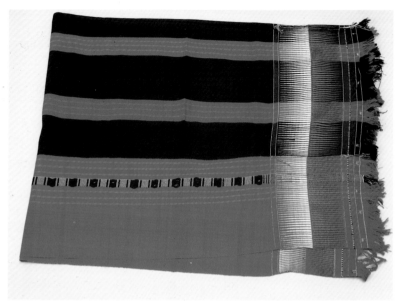

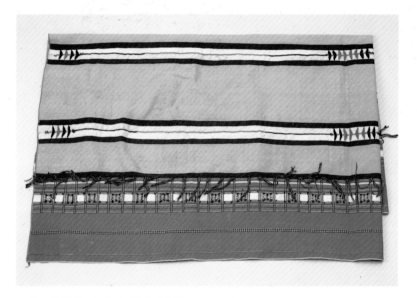

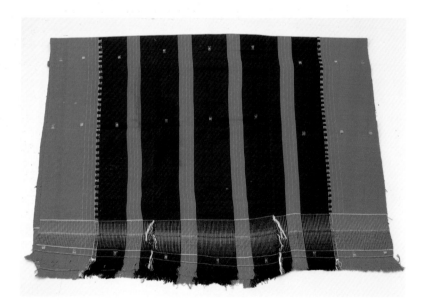

(top left) Body cloth. Kabui. PC.
(top right) Body cloth. Tangkhul. PC.
(bottom left) Body cloth. Zemi. PC.
(bottom right) Body cloth. Tangkhul. PC.

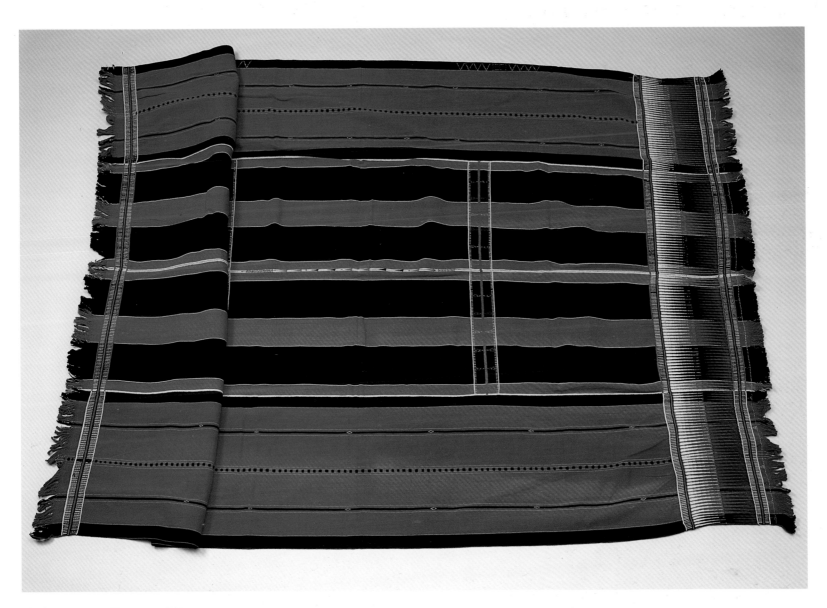

Man's body cloth. Tangkhul. CUMAA.

Body Cloth. Tangkhul. PC.

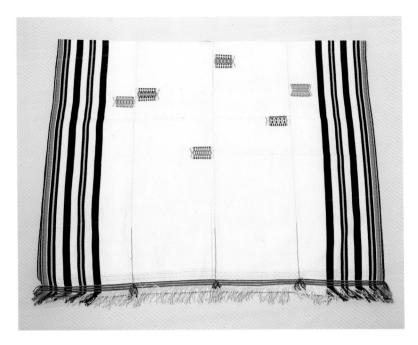

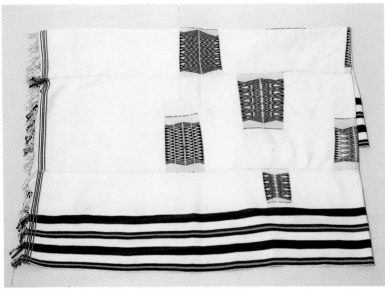

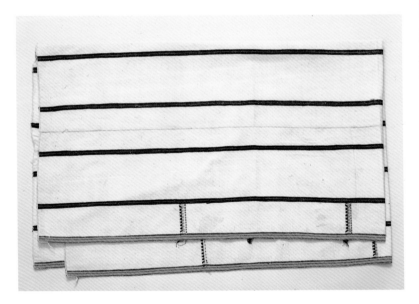

(top left) Body cloth. Angami. PR.
(top right) Body cloth. Angami. PR.
(bottom left) Body cloth. Western Rengma. PR.
(bottom right) Body cloth. Zemi. PR.

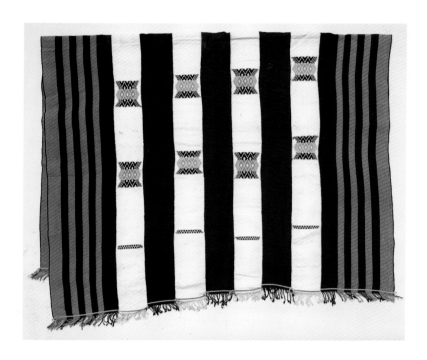

(top left) Body cloth. Doyang Valley, Sema. PC.
(top right) Body cloth. Western Rengma. PC.
(bottom left) Body cloth. Sema. PC.
(bottom right) Body cloth. Western Rengma. PC.

(top left) Body cloth. Sema. PR.
(top right) Body cloth. The bad dyeing of Longmisa village was much admired. Ao. PR.
(bottom left) Taboo cloth *chinipi*. Sema. PR.   (right) Body cloth. Ao. PC.

287

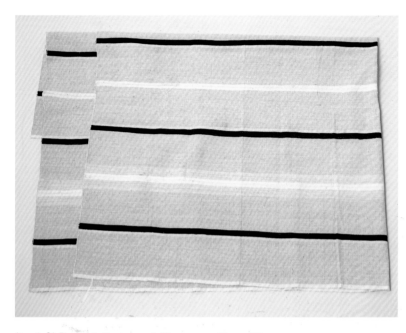

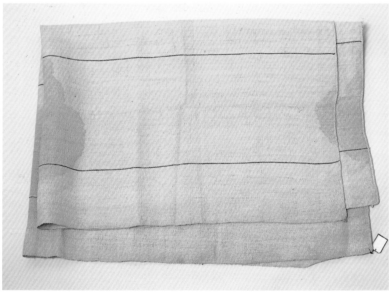

(top left) Body cloth. Angami, Khonoma village. PR.
(top right) Body cloth. Chang. PR.

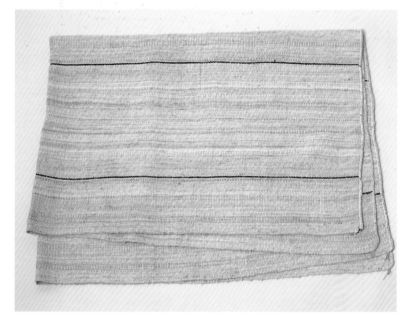

(bottom left) Body cloth. Angami. PR.
(bottom right) Body cloth. Angami. PR.

Body cloth. Wui village, Kalyo-Kengyu. PR.

Body cloth. Sakhalu, Sema. PR.

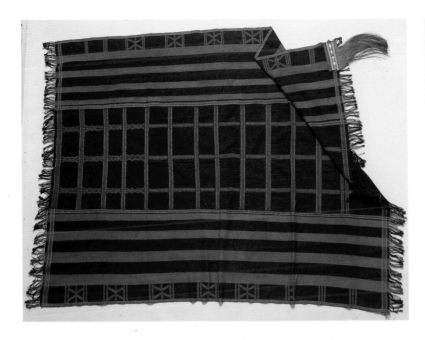

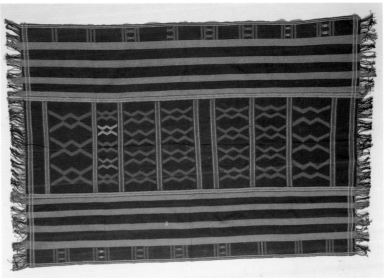

(top left) Body cloth. Sema. PR.
(top right) Body cloth. Sema. PR.
(bottom left) Blanket made of wool. An unusual design. Ao. PR.
(bottom right) Woman's skirt. Angami. PC.

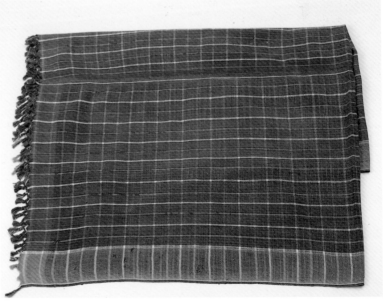

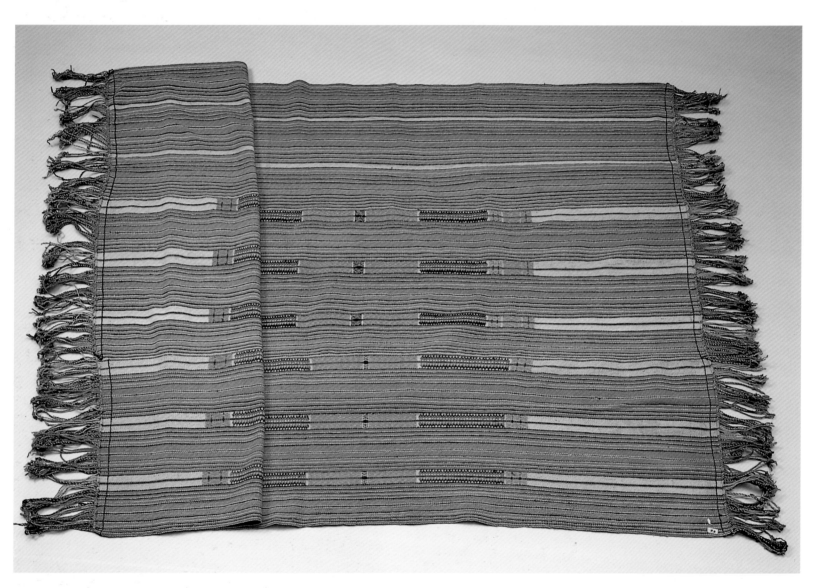

Body cloth of a man who has given the full series of Feasts of Merit. Konyak,
Tamlu village. CUMAA.

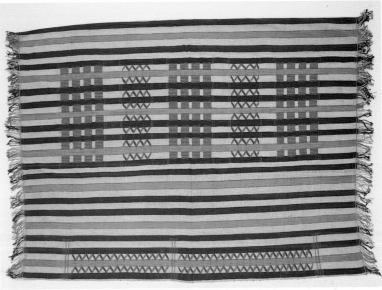

(top left) Body cloth of a man who have given the full series of Feasts of Merit. Konyak. PR.
(top right) Body cloth of a man who has taken heads. Yimsungr. PR.
(bottom left) Body cloth. Eastern Rengma, Meluri village. PR.
(bottom right) Body cloth of a man who has taken heads. Yimsungr. CUMAA.

(top left) Body cloth. Chang, Tuensang village. PR.
(top right) Body cloth. Chang, Tuensang village. PR.

(bottom left) Body cloth. Chang, Tuensang village. PR.
(bottom right) Body cloth. Southern Sangtam. PR.

Body cloth. Sema, Satoi village. PR.

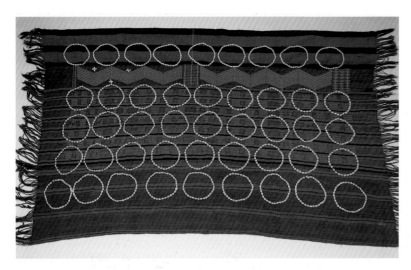

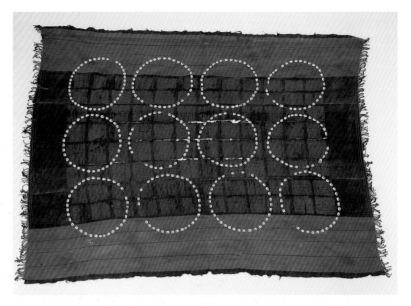

(top left) Body cloth of a man who had given full series of Feasts of Merit and taken heads. Chang. CUMAA.
(top right) Body cloth. PC.

(bottom left) Body cloth, *asukeda-pi*, with squares of red dyed dog's hair and circles of cowrie shells. The large tassel worn over the shoulder is decorated with cowrie shells, plaited yellow orchid straw, glass beads, and

beetle wings. Indicates the owner had taken heads and given Feasts. Sema, Hetoi village. CUMAA.
(bottom right) Body cloth. Another version of the *asukuda-pi*. Sema. PR.

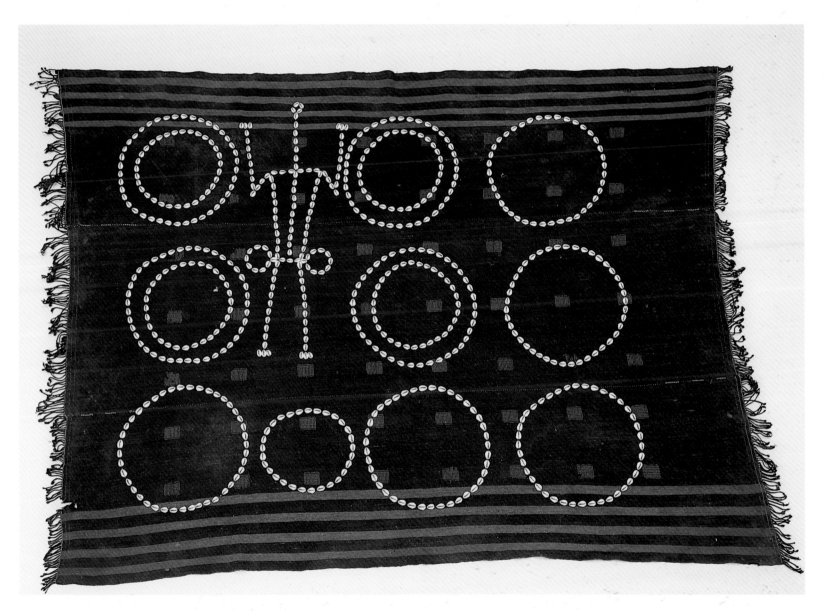

Body cloth with cowrie circles and anthropomorphic design over squares of red dog's hair. This style is common to the Sema, Chang, Kalyo-Kengyu and Sangtam. PC.

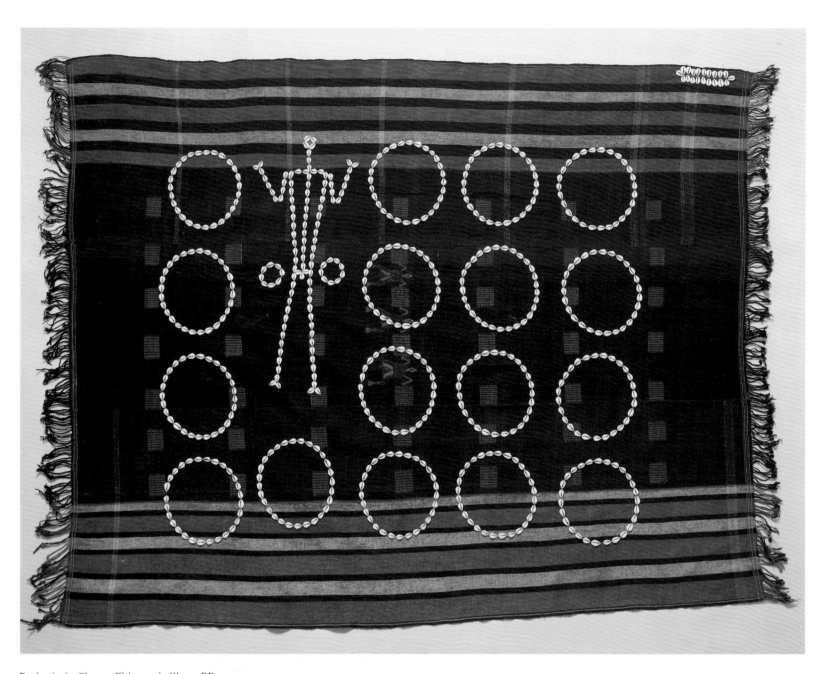

Body cloth. Chang, Chingmei village. PR.

(top left) Women's breast cloths. Zemi. PR.
(top right) Embroidered sashes. Kabui. PC.
(bottom left) Man's loin cloth. Chang. PR.
(bottom right) Shoulder bags. Kerami Nagas (Burma). PC.

299

(top left) Women's skirts. Probably Ao. PR.
(top right) Woman's skirt. Northern Sangtam. PR.
(bottom left) Woman's skirt. Chang. CUMAA
(bottom right) Woman's skirt. Zemi. CUMAA

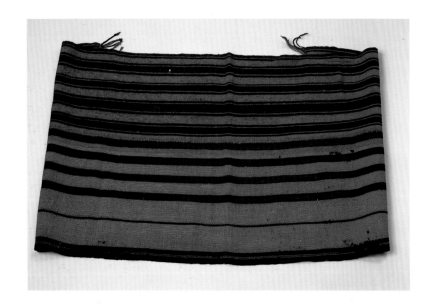

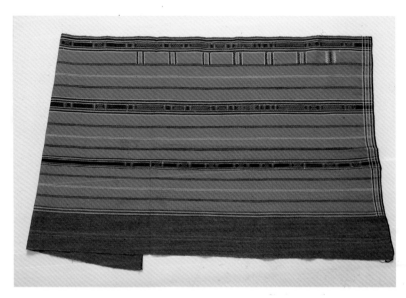

(top left) Woman's skirt. Sangtam. PR.
(top right) Woman's skirt. Sema. PR.
(bottom left) Woman's skirt. Sema. PR.
(bottom right) Woman's skirt. Yimsungr. PR.

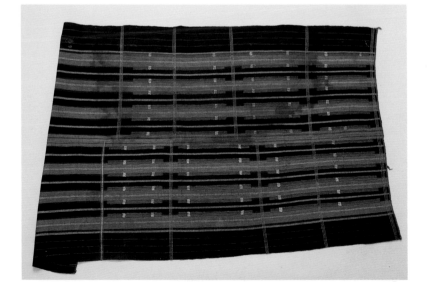

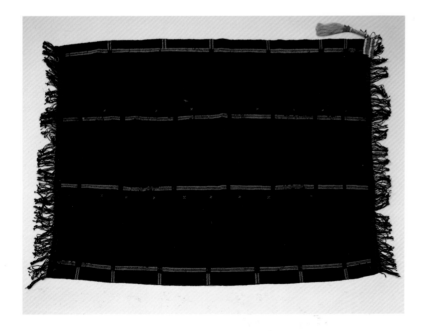

(top left) Woman's skirt with tassels of yellow orchid stalk. Lhota. CUMAA
(top right) Woman's skirt, *subeti*. Ao. CUMAA.
(bottom left) Bridal cloth with goat's hair tassel ornamented with yellow orchid stalk. Sema. CUMAA
(bottom right) Woman's skirt embroidered with dyed dog's hair. Sangtam. PR.

(top left) Woman's skirt. Sema. PR.
(top right) Body cloth. Sema. PR.
(bottom left) Woman's skirt. Angami. CUMAA 37.1019
(bottom right) Woman's skirt, worn by the Sangtam but bought from the Kalyo-Kengyu. PR.

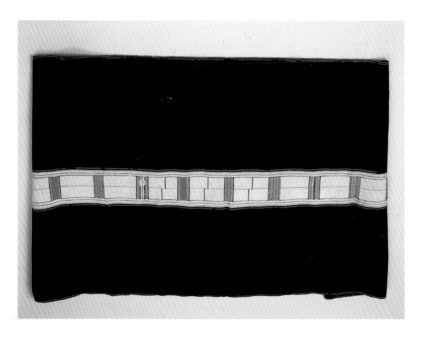

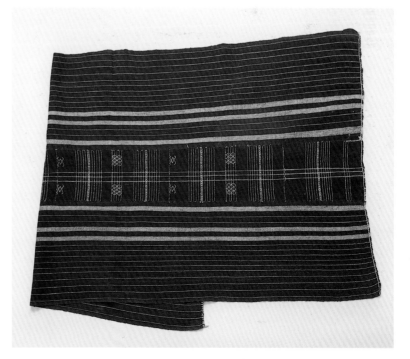

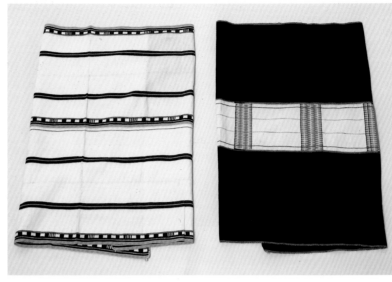

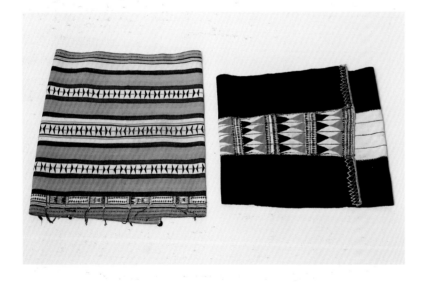

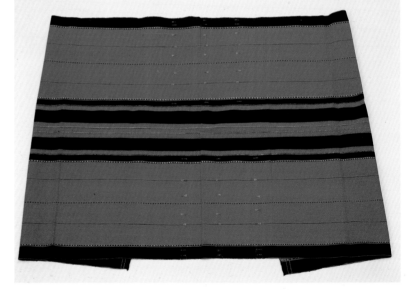

(top left) Women's skirts. Probably Tangkhul. PC.
(top right) Women's skirts. Angami. PR.
(bottom left) Women's skirts. Zemi. PR.
(bottom right) Woman's skirt. Probably Tangkhul. PC.

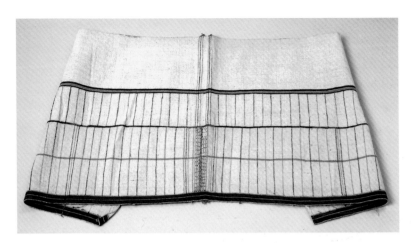

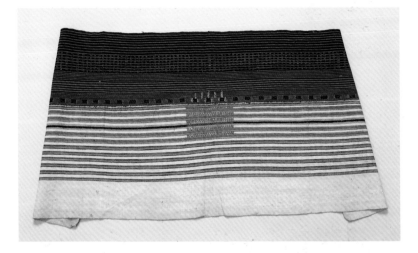

(top left) Women's skirts. Left: Sema. Right: Lhota. PC.
(top right) Woman's skirt. Either Eastern Rengma or Southern Sangtam. CUMAA
(centre right) Woman's skirts. Eastern Rengma. PR.

(bottom left) Women's skirts. Left: Ao. Right: Eastern Rengma. PC.

(bottom right) Woman's skirt. Eastern Rengma. CUMAA.

305

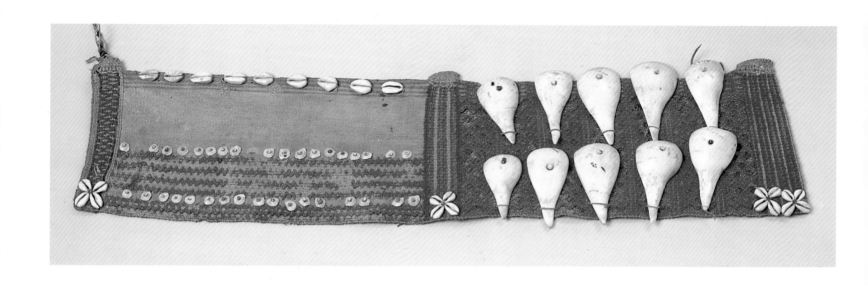

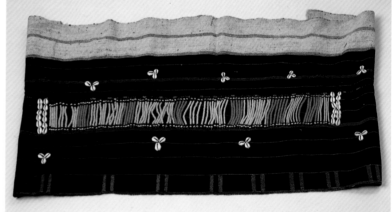

(top) Skirt or belt with cut conch shells and cowries. Chang. 19th century.
CUMAA.
(bottom left) Left: narrow skirt covered with beadwork and shell discs.
Konyak. Right: Beaded over-skirt. Probably Sema. PC.
(bottom right) Bridal skirt for chief's daughter decorated with a band of
beadwork and cowrie fleurets. Sema. CUMAA.

Necklaces of beads, dyed hair, and conch shell. Konyak. PC.
(bottom right) Bead and goat's hair hip ornaments. Konyak. PC.

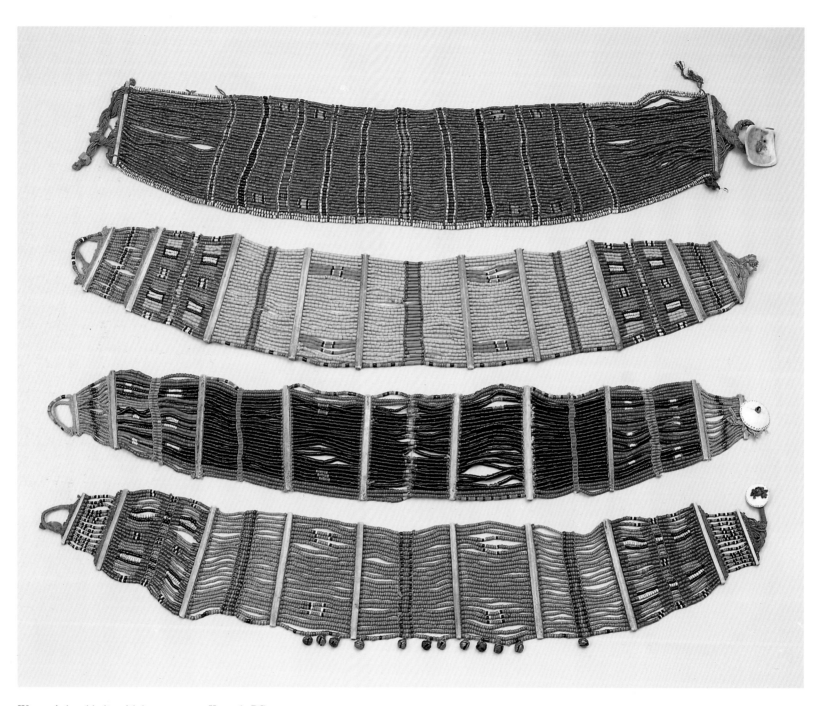

Women's bead belts with bone spacers. Konyak. PC.

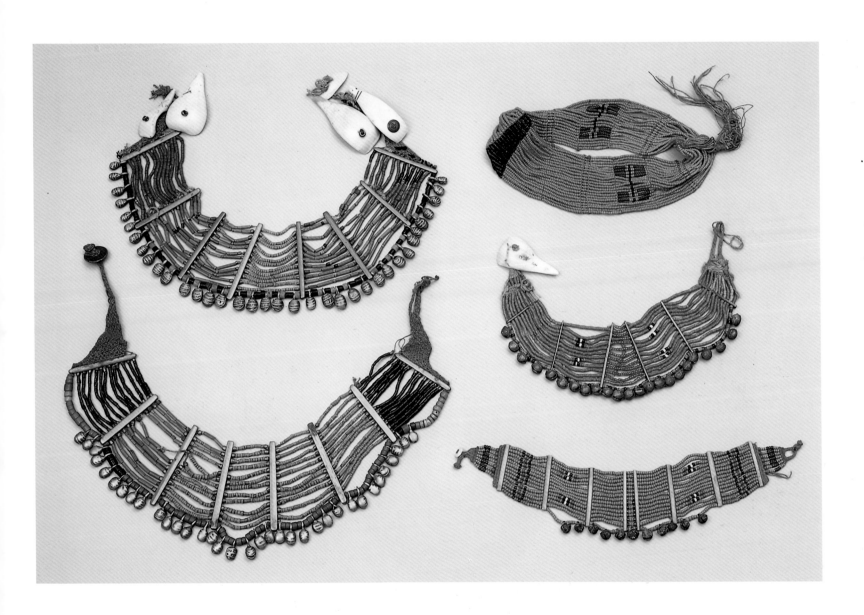

Left: two bead necklaces with bone spacers.
Top right: beaded head ornament.
Centre right. child's bead necklace.
Bottom right: child's belt. All Konyak. PC.

309

Bead necklaces. Probably all Konyak. PC.

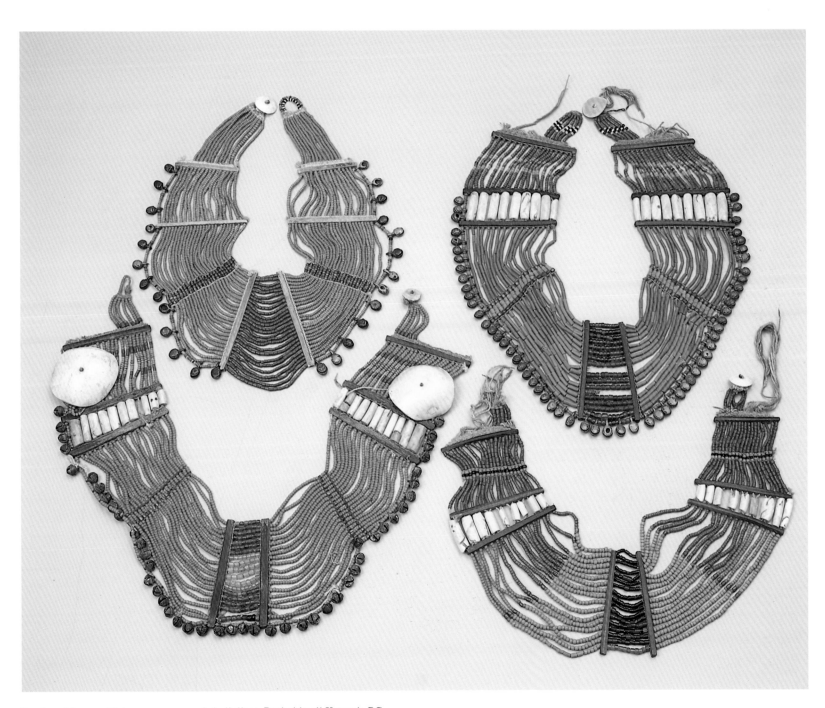

Bead necklaces with bone spacers and shell discs. Probably all Konyak. PC.

Bead necklaces. PC.

Bead necklaces. PC.

Bead necklaces. PC.

Bead necklaces. PC.

Bead necklaces with bone spacers, brass bells and cut shell. Probably all
Konyak. PC.

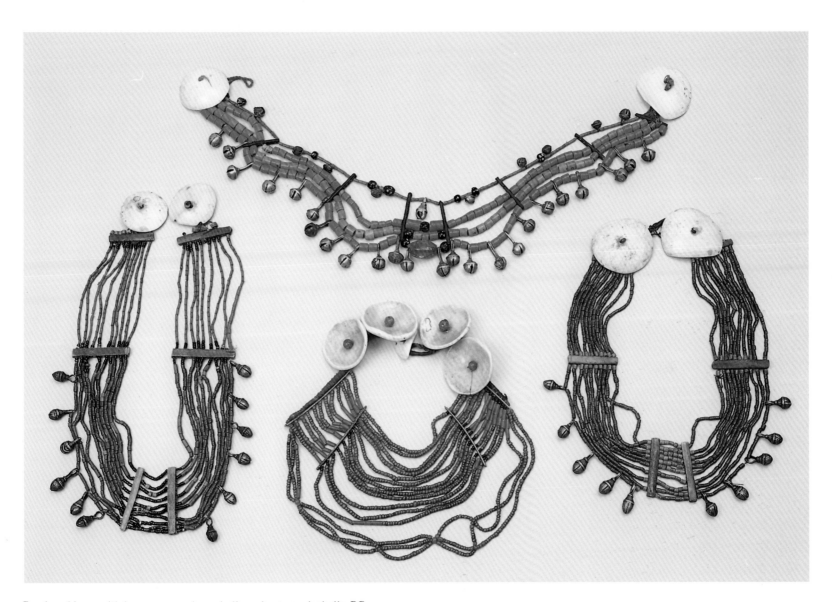

Bead necklaces with bone spacers, brass bells and cut conch shells. PC.

Necklaces with crystal beads and two pairs of crystal earrings characteristic of the Ao. PC.

Left: bead necklaces. Ao. Right: three necklaces each with a large piece of cut conch shell, of a style worn by the Sangtam. PC.

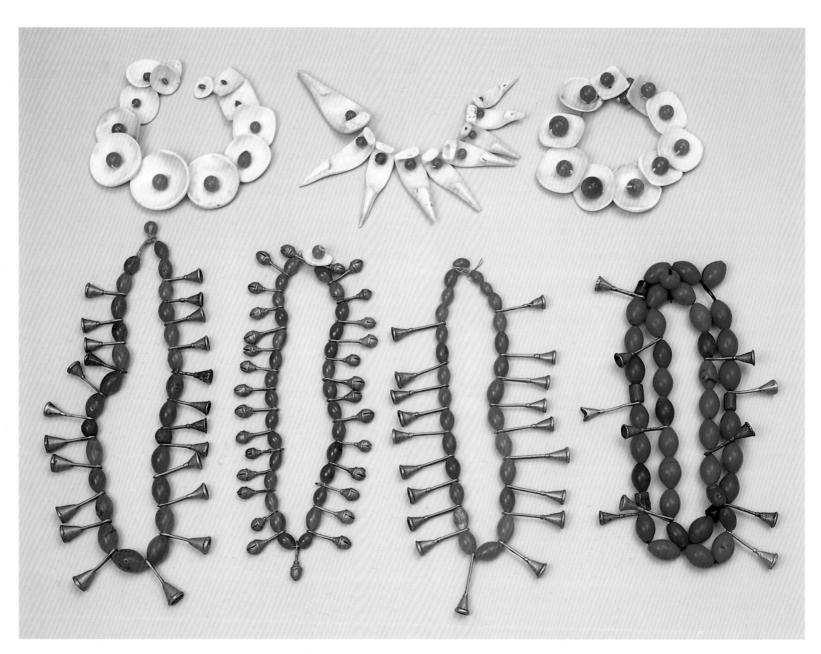

Above: cut shell necklaces with cornelian beads. Below: Necklace with cornelian, blue glass, and fluted brass beads. Ao. PC.

Large necklace with cornelian, blue glass, and fluted brass beads with bone spacers and a row of cut conch shell along the back. Ao. PC.

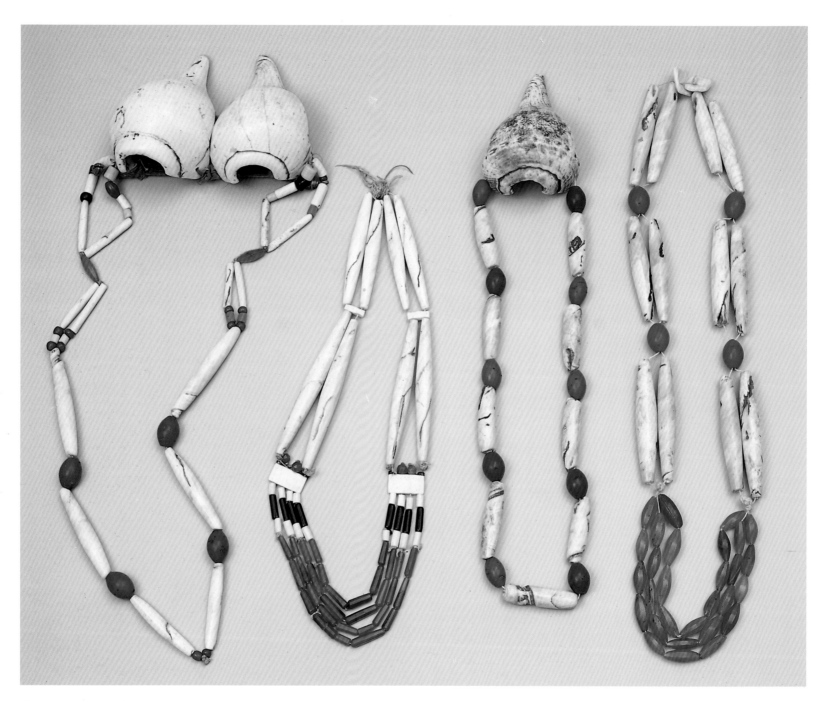

Cornelian and shell necklaces. The large conch shell were usually worn at the
back of the neck. PC.

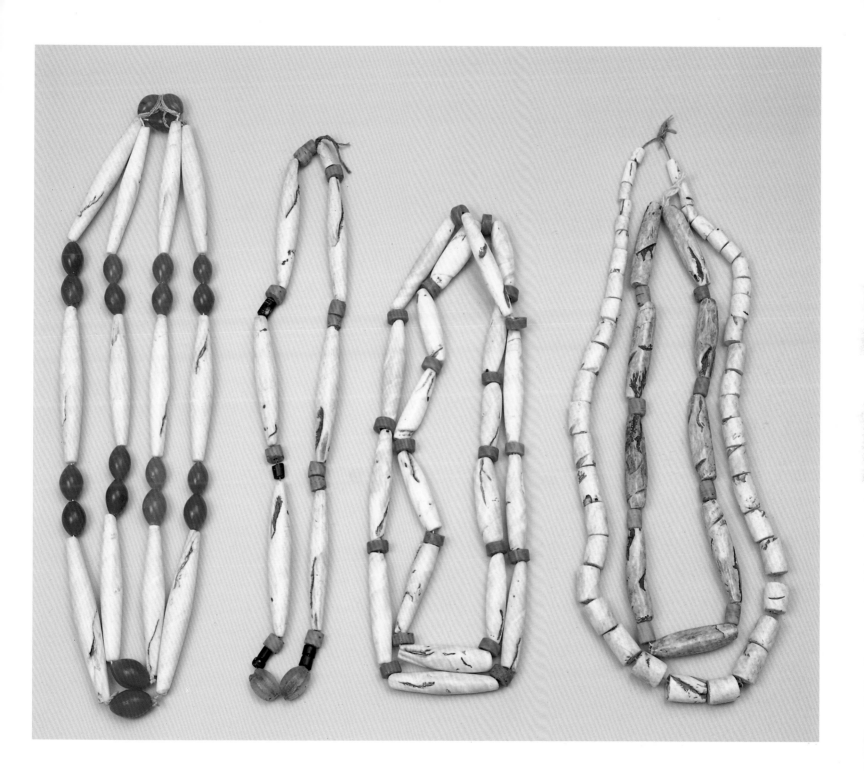

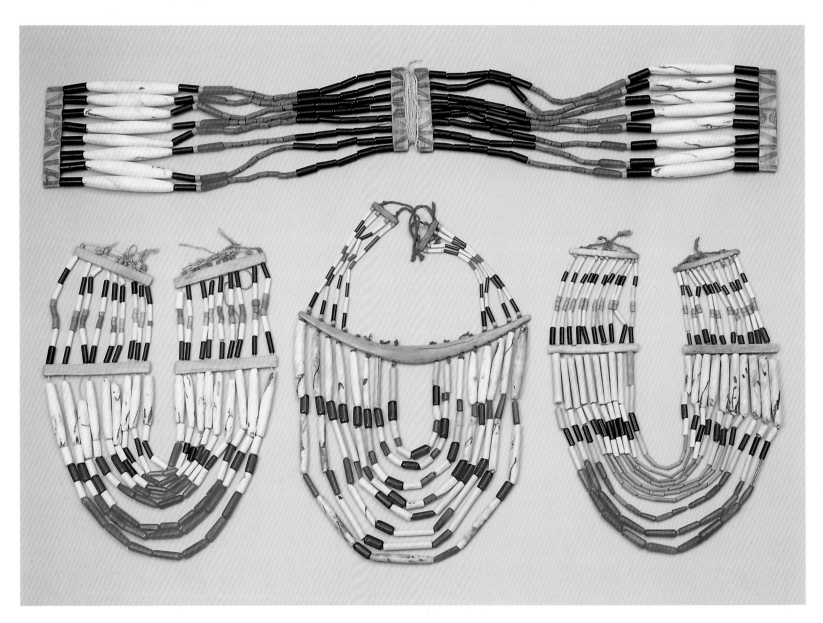

Necklaces with shell, cornelian, and glass beads with bone spacers. Angami.
PC.

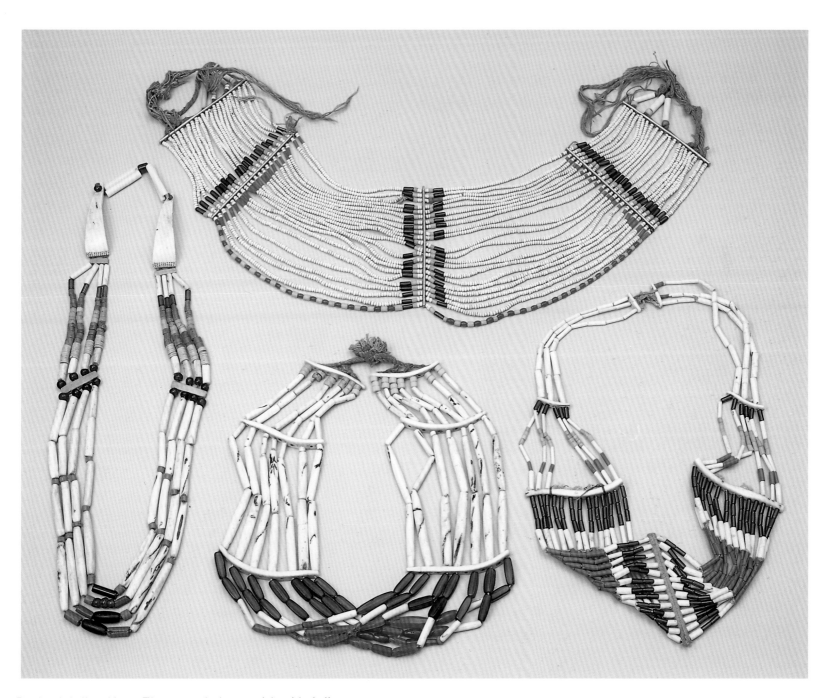

Bead and shell necklaces. The two on the bottom right with shell spacers are probably Tangkhul. PC.

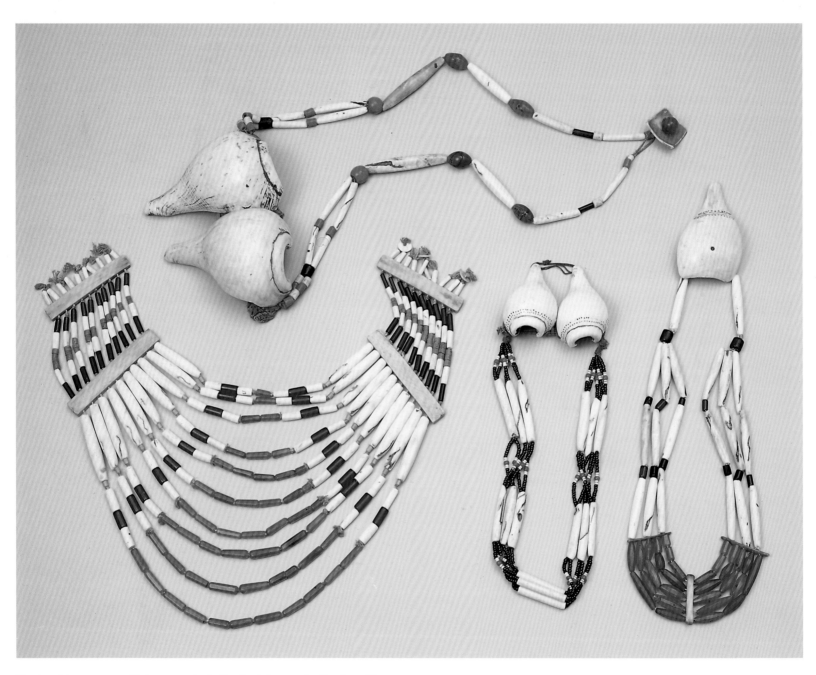

Bead necklaces some with large conch shells of a style worn by the Angami.
PC.

Bead and shell necklaces. PC.

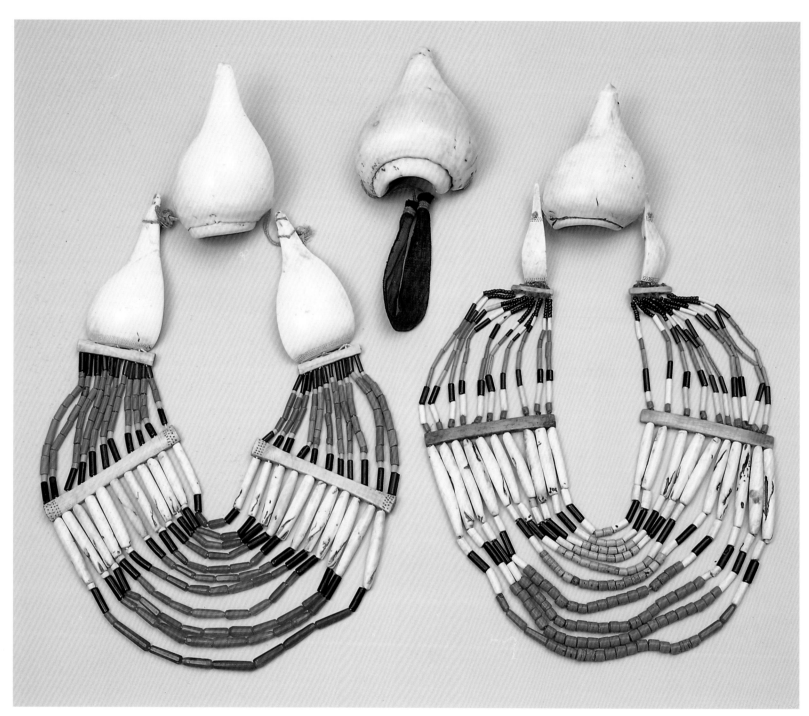

Bead and shell necklaces with bone spacers and conch shell neck ornament.
Angami. PC.

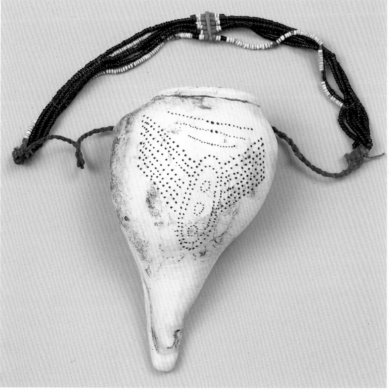

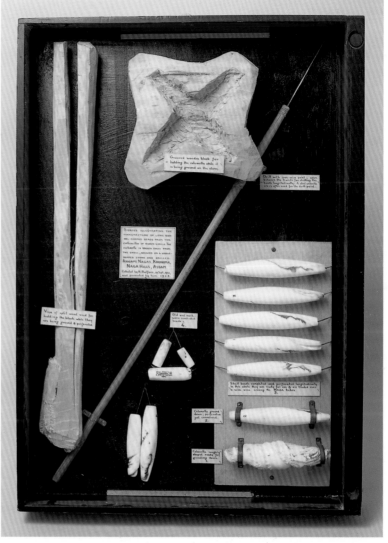

(top left) Two shell necklaces and a whole conch shell worn as a wrist ornament. PC.

(bottom left) Conch shell necklet with poker-work design. PC.

(right) Display demonstrating the manufacture of shell beads by Angami Nagas. PR.

333

Various pipes made of wood, bamboo and brass some with stems decorated with plaited cane and yellow orchid stem. The pipes with carved bowls in the shape of a head are probably Konyak or Phom, those of bamboo with black designs, Chang. PR.

Various pipes. PC.

Various bamboo vessels, *chungas*, used for drinking liquids. Left front: bark water container. Right front: the design is identical to the tattoo marking found on the chest of some Konyak warriors. Mainly Chang and Phom. PR.

Bamboo drinking vessels, *chungas*, with relief carving indicating head-taking status and sexual fertility. Left front: water pipe.
Right: Bamboo containers with poker-work designs. Chang. PR.

Horns used as drinking vessels. PR.

Household and agricultural containers and utensils. PC.

(top left) Models of storage and carrying baskets and gourds. PC.

(top right) Left: bamboo container decorated with incised lines, use for the stimulants 'pan' leaves and the bark used in betel-chewing. Konyak. Centre: shallow dish used to contain appetisers (chillis etc.) to eat with rice beer. Angami. Right: basket-work dish. Angami. CUMAA.

(bottom left) Left: Bamboo salt container (salt was an important trade item largely controlled by the Konyaks whose territory was rich in salt wells). Centre: earthenware pot with cane handle and frame. Right: large wooden rice dish. All Konyak, probably Wakching village. CUMAA.

(bottom right) Cane carrying basket with strap which was placed across the forehead. PC.

340

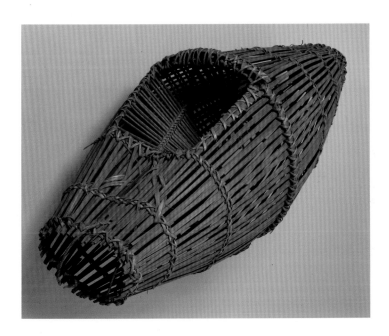

(top left) Bamboo fish trap, *shim*. Konyak, Longkhai village. CUMAA.
(top right) Two stone hammers with cane handles. Used by blacksmiths in the production of spear and *dao* blades. CUMAA.

(bottom left) Top: belt made of woven cane and yellow orchid stem with border of 'Job's tears' seeds. Konyak. 19th century. Bottom: finely plaited canework belt. Konyak. CUMAA.
(bottom right) Brush and comb. Konyak. CUMAA.

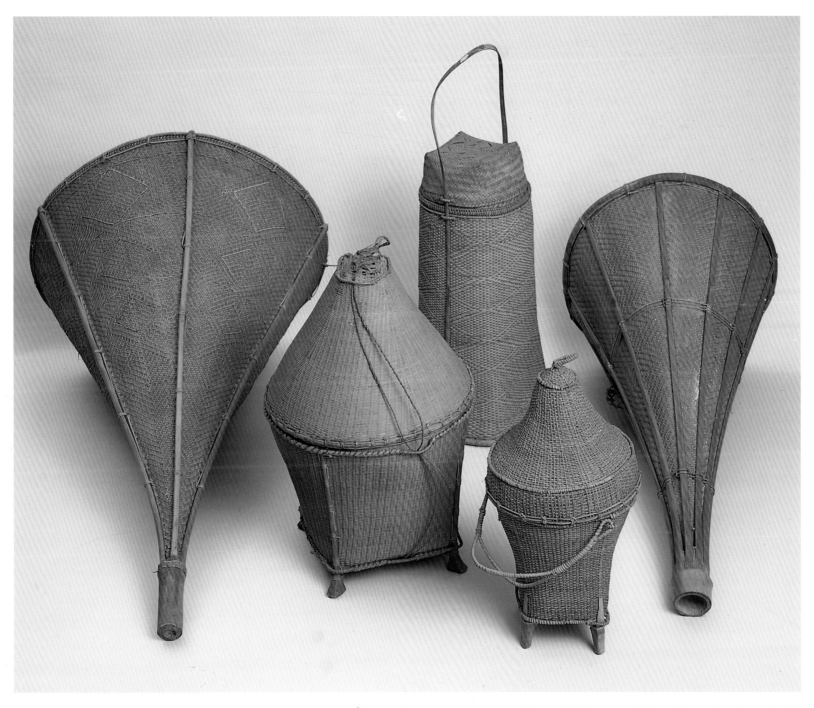

Canework baskets used for carrying and storing grain. PR.

(top) Carved wooden food dishes. PR.
(bottom) Wooden dishes and cups. Angami and Zemi Naga. PR.

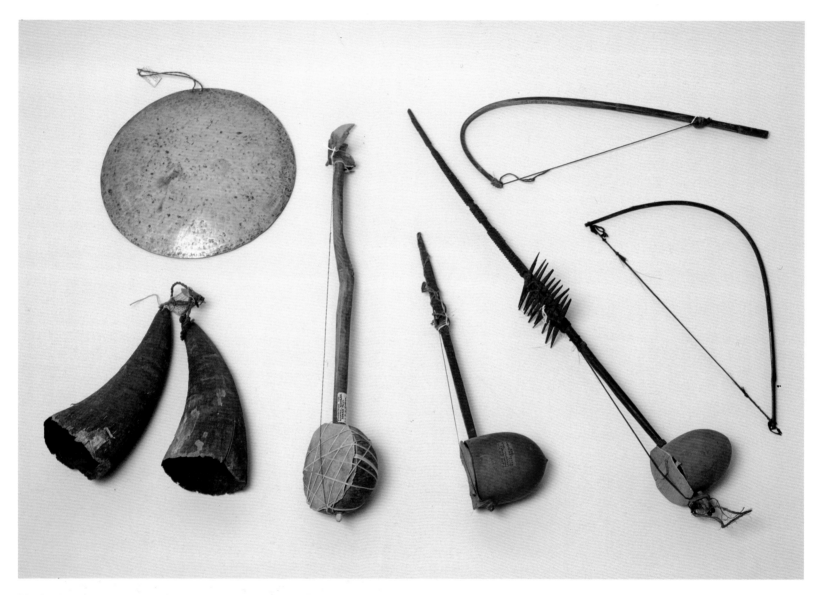

Musical instruments including chordophones with bamboo sounding box
and bow. PR

(top) Horn, bamboo jew's harps, and flutes. PR.
(bottom) Bull roarers which make a humming noise when twirled around the
head on a string. PR.

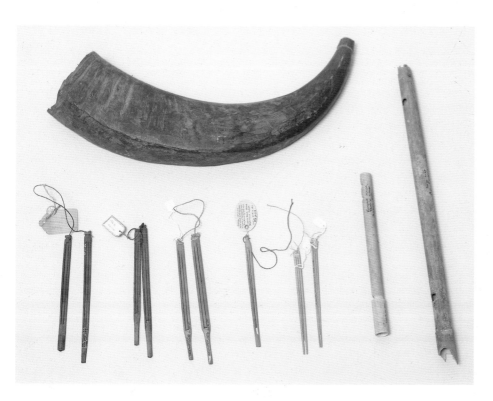

Left: pottery making tools. Right: pottery and wooden containers. PR.

Painted clay figure of a mithan. A household ornament. Angami. PR.

For over a decade fakes of Naga°objects, particularly wood carvings of varying
sophistication, have been circulating in the international art market and have
found their way into prestigious collections and have been displayed in public
exhibitions.

Footnotes

Chapter 1 Introduction

[1] Bower, *Papers*, box II, file 2, 'The Birth of the Spirits'.

[2] An extensive compilation of historical records relating to the Nagas of Burma is currently being compiled by Mr J.D. Saul of 27 Zandra Avenue, Florida Glen 1710, Roodepoort, S. Africa.

[3] Fürer-Haimendorf' *Diary*, 25.9.36; Fürer-Haimendorf, *Notes*, 25.9.36.

[4] Cf. Horam, *Social*, 24

[5] Barnes, 'Iconography', 17-18.

[6] This body of research has been the basis of the Cambridge Experimental Videodisc Project on the Nagas, based in the Department of Social Anthropology, University of Cambridge, which has brought together in a single medium photographs, films, books, recordings and unpublished manuscripts.

[7] For contrasting interpretations, cf. Sema, *Emergence* and IWGIA, *Naga Nation*.

[8] This brief treatment of an exceedingly complex subject has been considerably influenced by, in addition to those works cited in footnotes, Bellwood, *Conquest*, 83-92; and Sollheim, 'Reworking'.

[9] The classic treatment is that of Robert Heine-Geldern. Cf. 'Ancient Homeland' and 'Prehistoric Research'.

[10] Dani, *Prehistory*.

[11] Fürer-Haimendorf, *Problem*, p74.

[12] Not to mention, in addition, Ecuador (at least, in the view of J.H. Hutton). Mills, *Ao*, 52, fn3.

[13] Hutton, 'Mixed Culture', 19.

[14] Hutton, *Sema*, 378-9.

[15] Hutton, *Sema*, 219; Hutton, 'Fijian Game'.

[16] The two aspects of Naga origin stories are seen in the following account noted by Fürer-Haimendorf in the Konyak village of Wakching in 1937: 'There are two versions about the origin of mankind not only of the Konyak. According to one, all people and animals emerged from the great pumpkin 'Maikokwemniu'. Then Ghawang [the high god] divided the earth among them by saying, 'You have this piece of land, you that', etc. According to the other version, all beings emerged from the mythical bird 'Yangwemniu'. Then before he died he gave the gift of language to all humans and animals. Only the 'ou-shim' dove was not present at his death and therefore did not receive any power of speech. Up to the prsent day it only goes 'um, um.'.....No-one can say where the people emerged from the pumpkin or bird but the region called Yengyudang is considered to be the earliest home, a mountain which is identical with the Piankong of the Aos. At first they supposedly lived in the land of the Ao and some of the gaonburas went so far as to say that they had come from the direction of Mokokchung, in particular even from Wokha, but I do not think that the latter is an old tradition. All agree that from Yengyudng they migrated via various places to Chinglong. The villages on the way where had settled are Mohung, Hanching, Choha and Ngaching. From Chinglong they founded the village Wakniudzing, between Wanching and Wakching. Only there the people of Wanching and Wakching divided and founded their own villages. Against this traditon, however, stands the opinion that they had come from the Assam plains up the Dikhu River and then to Wakching....The people themselves solved this problem by saying that they came to the plains from the land of the Ao and from there then went into these hills....To the question of how this however coincides with the migration via Hanching, Choha etc., they have no other reply than that the people of Wakching came together from different sides.' Fürer-Haimendorf, *Diary*, 4.4.37.

[17] Cf. Hutton, 'Carved Monoliths'; Hutton, 'Fijian Game'; Mills, Ao, xiii, 8, 98, 278-9; Hutton, 'Mixed Culture', 22; Bellwood, *Conquest*, 86.

[18] Leach, *Political Systems*, 230.

Chapter 2   The Observers and the Observed

[1] There is a growing literature on the representation of the Other and the confluence of power and knowledge. For a particularly challenging interpretation of the role of photography in this regard, cf. Green, 'Classified Subjects.'

[2] Balfour, 'Welfare', 27.

[3] Butler, 'Rough Notes', 309-10.

[4] Pitt Rivers Museum , B. 19/II/1; B. 19.2.1–2. Published as frontispiece to Woodthorpe, *Survey*. rchieve see plate 000

[5] Fürer-Haimendorf, *Tribal Populations*, 80; Horam, *Social*, 74-5.

[6] Cf. Sahlins, 'Segmentary Lineage', 97-106.

[7] Hutton, 'Two Tours', 55; Hodson, *Naga Tribes*, 32-3.

[8] Godden, 'Naga', 165-167; Hutton, *Angami*, Appendix III; Elwin, *Nagaland*, 405; Horam, *Naga Polity*, 27; Yonuo, *Rising Nagas*, 7.

[9] Butler, *Sketch*, 152.

[10] Vetch, 'Visit', 255-75

[11] Brodie, 'Reports', 286-7

[12] Butler, *Travels*, 44-5

[13] The British perception of the process of expansion was summed up in the following way: 'The whole history of our tenure of the Naga Hills has been a gradual but reluctant extension of our borders.' W.J.Reid, District Commissioner, Naga Hills, 1905, in Archer *Notes*, 13:1. An early account of Naga resistance notes, 'The party was opposed in its progress from Yang to Papoolongmaie by the Angami Nagas, and having no idea of the effect of fire-arms, their opposition was most determined. They rolled down stones from the summit of the hills, threw spears and did their utmost by yelling and intimidation to obstruct the advance of the force, but all in vain.' Moffatt Mills, *Report*, 240.

[14] *Assam Administration Report*, 1887-8, 10.

[15] Butler, *Tour Diary*, 7 February 1870.

[16] *Census 1931*, vol.III, part 1, Appendix A.

[17] According to a Sangtam villager, 'When we were administered we had to sell our buffaloes to pay the tax.' Archer, *Notes*, 5:14.

[18] See chapter 8.

[19] Archer' *Notes*, 13:8.

[20] cf. Kirsch, 'Feasting', 32

[21] Woodthorpe, 'Notes', 55.

[22] Owen, 'Notes', 33.

[23] For an enlightening comparison with similar relationships elsewhere in the colonial world, cf. Thomas, 'Material Culture'.

Chapter 3 The *Morung*

[1] Fürer-Haimendorf, *Diary*, 15.7.36.

[2] Fürer-Haimendorf, *Diary*, 23.10.36.

Chapter 4 Environment and Economy

[1] Peal, 'Nagas', 103.

[2] Mills, *Ao*, 108.

[3] Brown, 'Narrative Report', 588-589.

[4] Cf. *Waromung*, 55.

[5] Bower, 'Cycle-Migration'.

[6] Mills, *Lhota*, 48, 151; Fürer-Haimendorf, 'Sacred Founder's Kin', 932-3.

[7] Cf. McCulloch, 'Account', 71.

[8] Archer, *Notes*, 16:25.

[9] Cf. videodisc frame 692.

[10] *Assam Adminstration Report'* 1886-87, 5; Mills, 'Effect'.

[11] Fürer-Haimendorf, *Diary*, 10.12.36.

[12] Hutton, *Angami*, 71.

[13] *Assam Administration Report*, 1883, 92.

[14] Fürer-Haimendorf, *Notes*, diary 1, 31.8.36.

[15] Fürer-Haimendorf, *Notes*, diary 2, 30.10.36.

[16] Fürer-Haimendorf, *Diary*, 28.10.36.

[18] Fürer-Haimendorf, *Diary*, 4.8.36; Hutton, *Tour Diary*, 18.6.25.

Chapter 5 Technology

[1] Mills, *Ao*, 100-101; cf. also the similar story of the Wancho, close neighbours of the Konyak Nagas, in Elwin (ed.), Myths, p.258.

[2] Archer, *Notes*, 12:41 (23.2.47); see below, ch. 9.

[3] Mills, *Rengma*, 68.

[4] Archer, *Notes*, 2:16; Mills, *Rengma*, 69.

Chapter 6 Social Organisation

[1] Fürer-Haimendorf, *Konyak* Nagas, 48.

[2] Mills, *Ao*, 268; Bower, *Papers*, Box II, ring binder 1, 'Birth', 'Personal Names'; Mills, *Tour Diary* (a), 7.9.28.

[3] Bower, *Papers*, Box II, ring binder 1, Birth.

[4] Archer, *Notes*, 4:12.

[5] Hutton, 'Mixed Culture', 21.

[6] Hutton, *Sema*, 134-5.

[7] Hutton, *Angami*, 219.

[8] Videodisc frame 962.

[9] Fürer-Haimendorf, *Diary*, 10.3.37.

[10] Fürer-Haimendorf, 'Morung System', 363.

[11] See Note to Chapter 7.

[12] Mills, *Rengma*, 266.

[13] Mills, *Lhota*, 155.

[14] Archer, *Notes*, 16:25.

[15] Fürer-Haimendorf, *Diary*, 11.12.36.

[16] Fürer-Haimendorf, *Diary*, 26.7.36.

[17] Fürer-Haimendorf, *Diary*, 24.4.37.

[18] The influence of Andrew Gray's radical re-analysis of Naga society is particularly evident in what follows. Cf. Gray, 'Structural Transformations'.

[19] Cf. Hutton, *Sema*, 151-2.

[20] West, 'Costume', 61.

[21] Hutton, *Angami*, 113.

[22] The Eastern Angami *Tevo* or *Thevo* is the equivlent of the Western Angami *Kemovo*. Fürer-Haimendorf, 'Sacred Founder's Kin' 923; Butler, Travels, 146; Hutton, Angami, 142.

[23] Bower, 'Village Organisation', 35.

[24] Mills, *Lhota, xxx*, 87.

Chapter 7 Chiefs and Democrats

[1] Fürer-Haimendorf, *Konyak Nagas*, 41.

[2] Archer, *Notes*, 4:14; Fürer-Haimendorf, *Diary*, 4.10.36.

[3] Fürer-Haimendorf, *Diary*, 24.8.36.

[4] Fürer-Haimendorf, *Notes* 10.12.36.

[5] Fürer-Haimendorf, *Konyak Nagas*, 55, 40.

[6] The evidence for these possible changes is of course, shaky, since military explorers would not have been best placed to assess these sociological distinctions. Vetch, 'Visit', 256-8.

[7] Fürer-Haimendorf, *Notes*, reporter's notebook No.3: 33,48; Fürer-Haimendorf, *Diary*, 20.7.36.

[8] Fürer-Haimendorf, *Notes*, notebook no.7, 23-24.9.36.

[9] Hutton, *Tour Diary*, 13.9.34.

[10] Butler, *Travels*, 145-6.

[11] Hutton, *Sema*, 11.

[12] Leach, *Political Systems*, 292; the Chin, to the south of the Nagas, also have autocratic and democratic communities. Cf. Stevenson, *Economics*, 14.

[13] The Nagas did keep slaves, and although their treatment varied considerably, it would be hard to identify them in either case as a class. On the one hand it would seem that it was possible for slaves within a generation to be adopted into the clan of their owners. Cf. Mills, *Lhota*, 111; Mills, *Ao*, 211. On the other hand, a considerable trade in slaves in the unadministered area bordering Burma continued up to Independence, largely as an aspect of escalating warfare and for ritual ends. Cf. Archer, *Notes*, 13:9 *passim*, and this diary entry by Fürer-Haimendorf: 'As we went on, Chinyang told me that in his youth they still were buying slaves occasionally. Once people of Chongwe offered Wakching a slave from Phom. 'Do you want to take him or not?' they asked. 'Here's he from?' 'He is a Phom.' 'Well, if he is a Phom we will take him.' Between the two villages the Wakching people received him and immediately cut off his head. It was a captured boy whose parents had been killed during a raid. The Oukheang *morung* people took the head and paid twenty layas, a pig and a lump of salt.' Fürer-Haimendorf, Diary, 10.4.37.

[14] Leach, *Political Systems*, 203.

[15] Fürer-Haimendorf, *Return*, 94.

[16] Nianu is in fact a Wanchu Naga village now in the state of Arunachal Pradesh, but the Wanchu are described as being very similar to the Konyak. Fürer-Haimendorf, *Return*, 214.

[17] Fürer-Haimendorf, *Konyak Nagas*, 58-61.

[18] Fürer-Haimendorf, *Diary*, 4.5.37; Fürer-Haimendorf, *Notes*, notebook 5, 4.5.37.

[19] Cf. Gray, 'Structural Transformations', 67f; and Friedman, *Tribes.*

[20] Cf. Kirsch, *Feasting.*

[21] Janowski, 'Chiefskip' 5. Stevenson, *Economics,* 18.

[22] Fürer-Haimendorf, *Diary*, 9.12.36.

[23] Fürer-Haimendorf, *Diary*, 13.2.37.

Chapter 8   Feasts of Merit

[1] Godwin-Austen, *Journal*, 14.1.1873.

[2] Mills, *Rengma*, 190.

[3] Mills, *Lhota*, 138 f.

[4] Archer, *Tour Diary*, 29.1.47.

[5] Cf. Kirsch, *Feasting.*

[6] Archer, *Notes*, 15:10.

Chapter 9   The Ritual World

[1] Archer, *Notes*, 5:19.

[2] Archer, *Notes*, 5:37.

[3] Fürer-Haimendorf, *Diary*, 18.7.36.

[4] Mills, *Lhota*, 114.

[5] Bower, 'Village Organisation', 24.

σ Higgins, 'Kabui', 3,7,60,80,83.

[7] Fürer-Haimendorf, *Konyak Nagas*, 93.

[8] Archer, *Notes*, 16:28; Fürer-Haimendorf, *Diary* 21.4.37.

[9] 'At the beginning of time day and night were the same, and the dead lived in the same world as the living and worked at the same time. But since the dead and the living were in different villages, their 'gennas' when they abstained from work in the fields, fell on different days. Often when the living were observing a 'genna' day, the dead used to go to their deserted fields and pick things, and so break the 'genna', and the living did the same thing to the dead. This led to so many quarrels that God divided time into day and night, and gave the day to the living in which to work, and the night to the dead. And He moved the dead to another world, too, for when the dead and the living lived in the same world they were so numerous that there was danger of there not being enough land to jhum'. Mills, *Rengma*, 271.

[10] Fürer-Haimendorf, *Diary*, 26.7.36; Archer, *Notes*, 16:19,22.

[11] For the Zemi Nagas, for instance, to dream of eating meat or sugar betokens illness and to dream of losing a tooth means death or illness for a near relative. Bower, *Notes*, 'Dreams'.

[12] Hutton, *Angami*, 261; Hutton, *Sema*, 128.

[13] Fürer-Haimendorf, *Diary*, 17.3.37.

[14] Archer, *Notes*, 5:50.

[15] Fürer-Haimendorf, *Diary*, 17.3.37.

[16] Mills, *Ao*, 224.

[17] Fürer-Haimendorf, *Return*, 200.

[18] Fürer-Haimendorf, *Diary*, 24.2.37.

[19] Fürer-Haimendorf, *Diary*, 19.9.36. The Zemi version is somewhat different. 'Earthquakes are caused by a *herapeo* [spirit] trying to turn the earth over with a crowbar. The scavenger beetle goes and tells him there are no men left, so he starts to turn the earth over, the top down and the underside up; so everyone shouts out: 'There are people here There are people here' so that he will stop. An earthquake is followed by a day's abstention from fieldwork.' Bower, *Notes*, 'Earthquakes'.

[20] Similar beliefs are common over a wide area of South East Asia. Hutton, 'Two Tours', 32.

[21] Füler-Haimendorf, *Notes*, notebook 4, p.100, 12.9.36.

[22] Fürer-Haimendorf, *Notes*, notebook 12, p.128, 21.4.37.

[23] Fürer-Haimendorf, *Notes*, notebook 4, p.97, 12.9.36.

[24] Fürer-Haimendorf, *Diary*, 8.2.37.

[25] Fürer-Haimendorf, 'Sacred Founder's Kin', 923.

[26] Archer, *Notes*, 5:14. A villager of Sangsoma described the origin of the drum thus: 'In early days villages were small and very far apart. All around was the great forest. If a man was far out in the forest, no one could make him hear. One day they found a hollow tree. A man struck it and it gave out a great sound. Men who were far away heard it. Then they felled the tree and struck it once again. Again it gave out a great sound. Then they considered how to take it to the village. They cut off the branches and made it into a long log. They pulled it to the village. There they beat it and far off in the forest its sound was heard. Then they offered it a pig and cock. That year the crops were very good. They said it is the doing of the drum. Since then they have kept a drum and worshipped it.' Archer, *Notes*, 5:10.

[27] Mills, *Lhota*, 28, 166.

[28] Archer, *Tour Diary*, 7.2.47.

[29] Bower, 'Village Organisation', 24.

[30] Archer, *Notes*, 12:33.

[31] Arhcher, *Notes*, 12:31.

[32] Archer, *Notes*, 12:41 (23.2.47). Cf. Marwah and Srivastava, 'Khel Gate'.

Chapter 10   Ornaments and Status Symbolism

[1] Mills, *Ao*, 58.

[2] J.P. Mills to Henry Balfour, 23.2.34, in Mills, *Papers*.

[3] Cf. J.P. Mills to Henry Balfour, 3.10.19, in Mills, *Papers*.

[4] Mills, *Lhota*, 44; Hutton, *Sema*, 11; Hutton, *Angami*, 203.

[5] Fürer-Haimendorf, *Diary*, 10.7.36.

[6] One reason why the 1920s ethnographers were able to record these seemingly random variations so well, is that as district officers, it fell to them to adjudicate on exactly these kinds of disputed rights. Mills, *Ao*, 50.

[7] Fürer-Haimendorf, *Return*, 159.

[8] Fürer-Haimendorf, *Diary*, 24.2.37.

[9] Mills, *Lhota*, 109.

[10] Fürer-Haimendorf, *Diary*, 29.4.37.

[11] Formerly rare objects such as elephant tusks were increasingly imported from the Plains. J.P. Mills noted in 1931 that 'More Naga ornaments are worn now than in the days before the hills were taken over". Mills, 'Effect'.

[12] Fürer-Haimendorf, *Konyak Nagas*, 9.

[13] Hutton, *Angami*, 371.

[14] Mills, *Ao*, 31.

[15] Videodisc frame 50230.

[16] Balfour to J.H. Hutton, 30.5.23, in Hutton, *Papers*, Box Ms. Box 3, 69-70; Mills to Balfour, 26.4.23, in Mills, *Papers*; Archer, *Notes*, 5:5, 6:2.

Chapter 11   Fertility

[1] Hutton, 'Significance', 399.

[2] Hutton, 'Meaning', 243.

[3] *Videodisc frame 48046.*

[4] Cf. Hutton, 'Meaning'.

[5] Fürer-Haimendorf, *Notes*, reporter's notebook 1, 7.7.36.

[6] Mills, *Ao*, 6.

[7] Hutton, 'Carved Monoliths', 58.

[8] Fürer-Haimendorf, *Return*, 20.

[9] Bower, 'Village Organisation', 59; videodisc frames 422, 651.

[10] Mills, *Rengma*, 22.

[11] Fürer-Haimendorf, *Diary*, 28.8.36.

[12] Cf. Hutton, *Angami*, 159.

[13] Cf. Fürer-Haimendorf, 'Morality', 155.

[14] Hutton, *Sema*, 174-6.

[15] Bower, *Notes*, 'Head-taking'.

[16] Archer, *Notes*, 5:14.

[17] Hutton, 'Two Tours', 51.

[18] Archer, *Notes*, 13:13.

[19] Archer, *Notes*, 13:27.

[20] Needham, 'Skulls'.

[21] Mills, 'Aspects', 34.

[22] Archer, *Notes*, 9:15.

[23] Archer, *Tour Diary*, 19.1.47.

[24] Archer, *Notes*, 5:41.

[26] Fürer-Haimendorf, *Diary*, 28.10.36.

[26] Mills, *Ao*, 100-1.

[27] Archer, *Notes*, 4:18.

[28] Mills, *Rengma*, 28.

[29] Archer, *Notes*, 13:27.

[30] Hutton, 'Significance', 401-2.

[31] Hutton, 'Mixed', 31.

[32] Cf. Hutton, 'Mixed', 25,28.

[33] Videodisc frames 47325, 47330.

[34] Archer, *Notes*, 9:33.

[35] Archer, *Tour Diary*, 24.1.47.

[36] Videodisc frame 48709; Archer, *Notes*, 9:4.

[37] Archer, *Notes*, 9:6.

[38] Archer, *Notes*, 9:5, 9:7.

[39] Hutton, *Angami*, 227.

[40] Hutton, 'Two Tours', 28.

[41] Archer, *Notes*, 9:21.

[42] Archer, *Notes*, 9:17.

[43] Videodisc frame 48521.

[44] Videodisc frame 47534.

[45] Videodisc frames 1301, 1305, 978.

[46] Hutton, 'Disposal', 63.

[47] Archer, *Notes*, 2:16.

[48] Fürer-Haimendorf, *Diary*, 18.11.36.

[49] Mills, *Ao*, 283-6; cf. Fürer-Haimendorf, *Diary*, 10.7.36.

Chapter 12   The Relations of Male and Female as seen in Ritual

[1] An exception appears to be the female elder of the Ao village of Khabza. Hutton, *Sema*, 96 n.2.

[2] Mills, *Rengma*, 159.

[3] Hutton, *Angami*, 239.

[4] Stonor, 'Feasts', 4.

[5] Stonor, 'Feasts', 3.

[6] Mills, *Lhota*, 3, 193; Mills, *Rengma*, 165-6.

[7] Mills, *Ao*, 117.

Chapter 13   War and Feud

[1] Mills, *Ao*, 192.

[2] Mills, *Ao*, 195.

[3] Fürer-Haimendorf, *Diary*, 4.12.36.

[4] Fürer-Haimendorf, *Diary*, 28.10.36.

[5] Hutton, *Angami*, 156.

[6] Videodisc frame 612.

[7] Fürer-Haimendorf, *Diary*, 1.8.36.

[8] Mills, *Ao*, 105.

[9] Mills, *Tour Diary (b)*, 22.11.36.

[10] Hutton, *Sema*, 170.

[11] Hutton, *Angami*, 33; Archer, *Notes*, 5:9.

[12] Archer, *Notes*, 13:23.

[13] Leach, *Political Systems*, 153; cf. Fürer-Haimendorf, *Diary*, 10.8.36.

[14] Bower, 'Village Organisation', 36.

[15] Cf. Rosaldo, *Ilongot*, 273.

[16] Hutton, *Sema*, 175.

[17] Maitland, *Report*, 25 f.

[18] Godwin-Austen, *Journal*, 22.1.1873.

[19] Leach, *Political Systems*, 144.

[20] Mills, *Ao*, 209.

[21] Fürer-Haimendorf, *Diary*, 11.7.36.

[22] Mills, *Ao*, 242.

[23] Videodisc frame 979; Mills, *Ao*, 241; Fürer-Haimendorf, *Notes*, notebook 6, 13.9.36.

[24] Videodisc frame 904.

[25] Mills, *Ao*, 330.

[26] Hutton, *Tour Diary*, 16.6.25.

[27] Black-Michaud, *Cohesive Force*, 6-7.

[28] Black-Michaud, *Cohesive Force*, 26.

[29] Cf. Fürer-Haimendorf, 'Morality', 179; this impersonality is also of course true of warfare in the high-technology nuclear age.

[30] Archer, *Notes*, 13:1.

[31] Archer, *Notes* 13:2 (25.4.47); Archer, *Notes*, 13:1 (24.3.45).

[32] Archer, *Notes*, 13:21 (29.1.48).

[33] Cf. *Assam Administration Report*, 1886-7, Section 2, para 41.

[34] Hutton, *Tour Diary*, 13.9.34. British use of force amounted to collective punishment or deterrence, through the destruction of property and wells. Such acts were frequently omitted from the published versions of Tour Diaries.

[35] Archer, *Notes*, 13:8.

[36] Archer, *Notes*, 13:1.

[37] Fürer-Haimendorf, *Diary*, 12.12.36.

[38] Archer, *Notes*, letter to Deputy Commissioner, 13:8 (III).

[39] Cf. Rosaldo, Ilongot , ch. 8.

[40] Blick, 'Genocidal Warfare'.

[41] Archer, *Notes*, 13:3. Cf. also, 'It is good that head taking has been stopped. Formerly no woman could go alone to the forest. We had to have sentries everywhere. Even then we were killed. Only a few could work in the fields. Nowadays the women can go freely to the forest and all the men can work in the fields. Formerly we could not get enough to eat. Nowadays we grow more and eat more'. Chuba of Chongtore village. Archer, *Notes*, 5:46.

[42] Archer, *Notes*, 15.1.47.

Chapter 14   Naga Nationalism

[1] Indian Government official in 1961, quoted in MRG, *India*, 9.

[2] Naga National Council declaration, 26 January 1950, quoted in MRG, *India*, 5.

[3] Sema, *Emergence*, 163.

[4] 2000 Nagas made up a volunteer labour corps in 1914. A dramatic object, resonant of the strangeness of this particular colonial conjuncture, is a spiked Germany Imperial army helmet decorated, as a traditional Naga skull trophy would have been, with large mithan horns. An example of this sort of dance hat is to be found in the Pitt Rivers Museum, Oxford: 1928.69.200. Videodisc frames 914-5.

[5] Alemchiba, *Brief Account*, 164.

[6] Eaton, 'Conversion', 21.

[7] IWGIA, *Naga Nation*, 105.

[8] Mills, *Ao*, 420.

[9] Fürer-Haimendorf, *Diary*, 14.7.36.

[10] IWGIA, *Naga Nation*, 105.

[11] Sema, *Emergence*, 53-55.

[12] Cf. Eaton, 'Conversion', 28.

[13] Eaton, 'Conversion', 25.

[14] Eaton, 'Conversion', 40.

[15] Eaton, 'Conversion', 34-6. A number of other points of convergence between Naga and Christian beliefs no doubt aided the process of convergence. The Konyak Nagas amongst others, for instance held a belief in an original great flood great. Fürer-Haimendorf, *Diary*, 20.3.37.

[16] Fürer-Haimendorf, *Diary*, 19.7.36.

[17] Eaton, 'Conversion', 44.

[18] Archer, *Notes*, 5:22.

[19] Archer, *Tour Diary*, 31.1.47.

[20] Mills, *Ao*, 418.

[21] Mills, *Ao*, 412.

[22] IWGIA, *Naga Nation*, 107.

[23] The setting up of the Naga 'V' Force is described in Ursula Graham Bower's Naga Path. The bravery of the Naga troops was acknowledged at the highest level. Not all Nagas, however, identified their interests with the Allied cause. Some villages advocated neutrality (cf. Bower, *Naga Path*, 187) and it appears that nationalist sentiment may have led some Nagas to seek tactical alliances with the Japanese. Rustomji, *Frontiers*, 25.

[24] Archer, *Journey*, 23.8.47.

[25] Archer, *Journey*, 23,24.7.47.

[26] MRG, *India*, 6.

[27] IWGIA, *Naga Nation*, 29.

[28] MRG, *India*, 10-11. A recent account suggests that the NSCN has 500 men under arms, and the NNC 160. Lintner, 'War', 49.

[29] Higgins, 'Kabui', March [1934]. 6th, 15th, 18th, 23rd; Hutton, *Tour Diary*, 21.5.34

[30] Higgins 'Kabui', pp. 60, 80, 83

[31] Mills I.116; Videodisc 867

[32] This was not the only case of the ritual use of writing. In around 1922, a girl of the Memi Naga tribe (a group living in Manipur, closely r of the Nzemi Nagas to the Angami Nagas), was reported to be writing in a magical manner. The Deputy Commissioner noted that she 'produces sheets of scribblings representing the names of natural objects at the dictation of ten familiar spirits, six male and four female. There is no doubt but that this child, aged about seven, is very much in earnest. She got her mother to obtain writing materials from Kohima at the dictation of the spirits that reside in her and when they arrived fasted seven days of her own accord as a preliminary genna before beginning to write.' It is an intriguing coincidence that Gaidiliu was the same age as this girl. Hutton, *Tour Diary* 15.5.22.

[33] One of Gaidilu's acts was to destroy the megaliths which symbolized the subjection of the Nzemi Nagas to the Angami village of Khonoma. Comment by Ursula Graham Bower, Mills, *Tour Diary* (c), 5.3.27.

[34] Yonuo, *Rising Nagas*, 126.

[35] Scott, *Moral Economy*, 149.

[36] Cf. Scott, *Moral Economy*, 156.

[37] Figures compiled from Assam *Administration Reports*, 1927-34.

[38] Nehru, *Unity*, 187-8.

[39] Mukherjee et al, 'Zeliangrong Movement', 72 f.

Chapter 15 Nagaland Today

[1] Das, 'Aspects', 71, 164-5.

[2] Sema, *Emergence*, 176; *Census* 1981, 255; Ganguli, *Pilgrimage*, 270-1; *Nagaland '86*, Directorate of Information and Public Relations, Kohima, pp. 12, 52. The literacy figure of 49 per cent represents a level of literacy in English, which is the official language of Nagaland. As a lingua franca, the pidgin language 'Nagamese', a mixture of Naga, Assamese, Hindi and English, also continues to be used. In theory Non-Nagas cannot buy agricultural land, but can buy town land; this is evidently flouted in practice.

[3] Angami, Ao, Chakhesang, Chang, Khiemungan, Konyak, Lhota, Phom, Rengma, Sangtam, Sema, Yimchunger, Zeliang and Kuki. The inclusion of the Kuki, not recognised as a Naga group in the colonial era, is a concrete example of the flexible and subjective manipulation of the tribal categories. In the neighbouring State of Manipur the principal Naga tribes are Mao, Memi, Maram, Kabui and Tangkhul. Chakhesang is a term uniting the Chakru, Khezha and Sangtam groups. The Khiemungan were formally known as the Kalyo-Kengyu. The Zeliang are a combination of the Zemi and Liyengmai; together with the Rongmai (formerly known as Kabui) they constitute the Zeliangrong group.

[4] The seven districts are Kohima, Phek, Wokha, Zunheboto, Mokokchung, Tuensang and Mon. Kohima is the most populous (250,105 inhabitants). 1981 *Census*.

[5] IWGIA, *Naga Nation*, 124 and parts II and III. See also chapter 14, footnote 28.

[6] Ganguli, *Pilgrimage*, 52.

[8] Singh, *Earth*.

[8] Joshi, 'Pluralism', 155. In what follows I have relied heavily on this unpublished work.

[9] Joshi, 'Pluralism', 94. Cf. also Horam, *Social*, 38.

[10] Cf. Horam, *Social*, 102.

Glossary of terms

Ang: chief, or chiefly clan (Konyak)

apotia: accursed or calamitous death

aren: concept of fertility, potency, prosperity, thought of in material and spiritual senses (Ao)

Ben: commoner clan (Konyak)

dao: all-purpose chopper/axe

dobashi: interpreter

gaonbura government-appointed headman

Gawang: high god (Konyak)

genna: generally, act of worship, religious rite, festival day; has strong association of prohibition, applying to individual or community, similar to 'tabu'. Term used by all Naga groups, though derived from Angami kenna, meaning 'forbidden'

jhuming: slash-and-burn farming (land farmed in this way is *jhum* land)

Job's tears: *coix lachrymae*, a crop

kemovo: religious leader (Western Angami), descendant of village founder; see *tevo*

khel: a residence quarter of a village; and/or an exogamous group

lengta: man's strip of cloth, tied round the waist, ending in a square flap

maiba: shaman

mithan: semi-domesticated Indian bison (Bos frontalis)

morung: young men's/young women's 'dormitory'; also known by the term *dekachang* (Naga-Assamese)

nanu, nanyu: religious rite, incorporating sacrifice and genna prohibition; also used to describe the community of animist (non-Christian) believers (Angami)

pan: a leaf which is chewed with betel nut and lime

panikhet: irrigated rice terrace

panji: hardened bamboo spike, stuck upwards in ground to injure enemies or game

puthi: priest (Lhota)

terhoma: spirit (Angami)

tevo, thevo: religious leader (Eastern Angami)

Thendu: category of social organization stressing autocratic principles (Konyak)

Thenkoh: category of social organization stressing egalitarian principles (Konyak)

Ukepenopfu, Ukepenuophu: high goddess (Angami)

zu: rice beer

Bibliography

This bibliography includes all the works referred to in the text. The abbreviation (author and short title) used in the footnotes is given first, followed by the full reference.

Alemchiba, *Brief Account*. Alemchiba, M., *A Brief Historical Account of Nagaland*, Kohima, 1970.

Archer, *Journey*. Archer, Mildred, *Journey to Nagaland, an account of six months spent in the Naga Hills in 1947*, typescript.

Archer, *Tour Diary* and Archer, *Notes*. *Papers of W.G. Archer*, private collection of Mrs. Mildred Archer.

Assam Administration Reports, Shillong, 1882-1939.

Balfour, *Diary*. Balfour, Henry, *Diary of a Tour in the Naga Hills*, 1922-1923, manuscript, Balfour Ms.B3, Pitt Rivers Museum Archive, Oxford.

Balfour, 'Welfare'. Balfour, Henry, 'Presidental Address: The Welfare of Primitive Peoples', *Folklore*, 1923.

Barnes, 'Iconography'. Barnes, Ruth, 'Iconography and Technology in the Naga Hills: a Historical Collection in the Pitt Rivers Museum, Oxford', typescript, n.d. [1989].

Bellwood, *Conquest*. Bellwood, Peter, *Man's Conquest of the Pacific*, Auckland, London 1978.

Black-Michaud, *Cohesive Force*. Black-Michaud, Jacob, *Cohesive Force: Feud in the Mediterranean and the Far East*, Oxford, 1975.

Blick, 'Genocidal Warfare'. Blick, Jeffrey P., 'Genocidal Warfare in Tribal Societies as a Result of European-induced Culture Conflict'. *Man*, 23:4, 1988.

Bower, 'Cycle-Migration'. Bower, U.V. Graham, 'Cycle-Migration of the Zemi Nagas, North Cachar Hills, Assam', *Man In India*, 1946

Bower, *Naga Path*. Bower, Ursula Graham, *Naga Path*, London, 1950.

Bower, Notes. *Notebooks of Ursula Graham Bower* (later Ursula Betts), private collection of Ms. Katrina Betts.

Bower, *Papers. Papers of Ursula Graham Bower* (later Ursula V.G. Betts), in Archive of Centre for South Asian Studies, University of Cambridge.

Bower, 'Village Organisation'. Bower (Betts), Ursula V. Graham, 'Village Organisation among the Central Zemi Nagas,' Diploma in Anthropology Thesis, University College London, 1950.

Brodie, 'Reports'. 'Reports of Lt. Brodie's dealings with the Nagas on the Sibsagar Frontier, 1841-6', *Selections of Papers regarding the Hill Tracts between Assam and Burmah, and on the Upper Brahmaputra*, Calcutta, 1873, pp. 284-9.

Brown, 'Narrative Report'. Brown, R., 'Narrative Report of the Progress of the Survey Party, Naga Hills, Season 1874', in Elwin (ed.), *Nagas* (original, 1874).

Butler, 'Rough Notes'. Butler, Capt. John, 'Rough Notes on the Angami Nagas', *Journal of the Asiatic Society of Bengal*, I,4, 1875.

Butler, *Sketch*. Butler, Major John, *A Sketch of Assam, with Some Account of the Hill Tribes, By an Officer*, London, 1847.

Butler, *Tour Diary*. Butler, Captain John. *Tour Diary of the Deputy Commissioner, Naga Hills, 1870*, Shillong, 1942.

Butler, *Travels*. Butler, Major John, *Travels and Adventures in the Province of Assam during a Residence of Fourteen Years*, London, 1847.

Census 1931. Census of India, 1931, vol. III, Assam, Shillong, 1932.

Census 1981. Census of India, 1981, Series I, Paper 3 of 1986, Comparative Primary Census Abstract 1971 and 1981.

Dani, *Prehistory*. Dani, A.H., *Prehistory and Protohistory of Eastern India*, Calcutta, 1960.

Das, 'Aspects'. Das, Nava Kishor, 'The Politico-Jural Aspects of the Segmentary Social System of the Zounuo-Keyhonuo Naga', unpublished Ph.D. Thesis, University of Gauhati, 1985.

Eaton, 'Conversion'. Eaton, Richard M., 'Conversion to Christianity among the Nagas of India, 1876-1971', typescript, n.d.

Elwin (ed.), *Myths*. Elwin, Verrier (ed.), *Myths of the North-East Frontier of India*, Shillong, 1958.

Elwin, *Nagaland*. Elwin, Verrier, *Nagaland*, Shillong, 1961.

Elwin (ed.), *Nagas*. Elwin, Verrier (ed.), *The Nagas in the Nineteenth Century*, Bombay, 1969.

Elwin (ed.), *North-East Frontier*. Elwin, Verrier (ed.), *India's North-East Frontier in the Nineteenth Century*, Bombay, 1959.

Friedman, 'Tribes'. Friedman, Jonathan, 'Tribes, States and Transformations', *Marxist Analyses and Social Anthropology*, M. Bloch (ed.), London, 1975.

Fürer-Haimendorf, *Konyak Nagas*. Fürer-Haimendorf, Christoph von, The *Konyak Nagas*, New York, 1969.

Fürer-Haimendorf, 'Morality'. Fürer-Haimendorf, Christoph von, 'Morality and Prestige among the Nagas', *Archaeology and Anthropology, Essays in Commemmoration of Verrier Elwin*, M.C.Pradhan (ed.), Bombay, 1969.

Fürer-Haimendorf, 'Morung System'. Fürer-Haimendorf, Christoph von, 'The Morung System of the Konyak Nagas, Assam', *Journal of the Royal Anthropological Institute*, LXVIII, 1938.

Fürer-Haimendorf, *Notes*. Fürer-Haimendorf, Christoph von, *Field Notebooks*, in Library of School of Oriental and African Studies, London, PPMS 19/1/6-28.

Fürer-Haimendorf, 'Problem'. Fürer-Haimendorf, Christoph von, 'The Problem of Megalithic Cultures in Middle India', *Man In India* XXV, 1945, p74.

Fürer-Haimendorf, *Return*. Fürer-Haimendorf, Christoph von, *Return to the Naked Nagas*, London, 1976 (original, *The Naked Nagas*, London, 1939).

Fürer-Haimendorf, 'Sacred Founder's Kin'. Fürer-Haimendorf, Christoph von, 'The Sacred Founder's Kin among the Eastern Angami Nagas', *Anthropos*, XXXI, 1936.

Fürer-Haimendorf, *Diary*. Fürer-Haimendorf, Christoph von, typescript *Diary*, original in German, Library of School of Oriental and African Studies, London; translated into English by Dr. Ruth Barnes.

Fürer-Haimendorf, *Tribal Populations*. Fürer-Haimendorf, Christoph von, *Tribal Populations and Cultures of the Indian Subcontinent*, Leiden, 1985.

Ganguli, *Pilgrimage*. Ganguli, Milada, *A Pilgrimage to the Nagas*, New Delhi, 1984.

Godden, 'Naga'. Godden, Gertrude M., 'Naga and Other Frontier Tribes of North-East India', *Journal of the Anthropological Institute*, XXVI and XXVII, 1896-1897.

Godwin-Austen, *Journal*. Godwin-Austen, H.H., *Journal of a Tour in Assam, 26th November 1872 to 15th April 1873*, manuscript, Library, Royal Geographical Society, London.

Gray, Structural Transformations. Gray, Andrew, Structural Transformations in Nagaland, M.A. Thesis, University of Edinburgh, 1977.

Green, 'Classified Subjects'. Green, David, 'Classified Subjects: Photography and Anthropology: the Technology of Power', *Ten 8*, no.14, 1984.

Heine-Geldern, 'Ancient Homeland'. Heine-Geldern, Robert, 'Ancient Homeland and Early Wanderings of the Austronesians' (partial translation of 'Urheimat und Früheste Wanderungen der Austronesier', *Anthropos* 27, 1932), in van de Velde, Pieter (ed.), *Prehistoric Indonesia: a Reader*, Dordrecht, 1984.

Heine-Geldern, 'Prehistoric Research'. Heine-Geldern, Robert, 'Prehistoric Research in the Netherlands Indies,' in Honig, Pieter (ed.), *Science and Scientists in the Netherlands Indies', New York, 1945.*

Higgins, 'Kabui'. Higgins, J.C., and others, Kabui file, no. 95165, Papers of J.C. Higgins, 1911-1944, Archive of School of Oriental and African Studies, London.

Hodson, *Naga Tribes*. Hodson, T.C., *The Naga Tribes of Manipur*, London, 1911.

Horam, *Naga Polity*. Horam, M., *Naga Polity*, Delhi, 1975.

Horam, *Social*. Horam, M., *Social and Cultural Life of Nagas (The Tangkhul Nagas)*, Delhi, 1977.

Hutton, *Angami*. Hutton, J.H., *The Angami Nagas*, London, 1921.

Hutton, 'Carved Monoliths'. Hutton, J.H., 'Carved Monoliths at Dimapur and an Angami Naga Ceremony', *Journal of the Royal Anthropological Institute*, 1922.

Hutton, 'Disposal'. Hutton, J.H., 'The Disposal of the Dead at Wakching', *Man*, XXVII, 1927.

Hutton, 'Fijian Game'. Hutton, J.H., 'A Fijian Game in Assam', *Man*, September 1929.

Hutton, 'Meaning'. Hutton, J.H., 'The Meaning and Method of the Erection of Monoliths by the Naga Tribes', *Journal of the Royal Anthropological Institute*, LII, 1922.

Hutton, 'Mixed Culture'. Hutton, J.H., 'The Mixed Culture of the Naga Tribes,' *Journal of the Royal Anthropological Institute*, 1965.

Hutton, *Papers. Papers of J.H. Hutton*, Pitt Rivers Museum Archive, Oxford.

Hutton, *Sema*. Hutton, J.H., *The Sema Nagas*, London, 1921.

Hutton, 'Significance'. Hutton, J.H., 'The Significance of Head-Hunting in Assam', *Journal of the Royal Anthropological Institute*, LVIII, 1928.

Hutton, *Tour Diary. Tour Diaries of J.H. Hutton, District Commissioner, Naga Hills, 1917-1935*, typescript, Hutton MS. Box 2, Pitt Rivers Museum Archive, Oxford.

Hutton, 'Two Tours'. Hutton, J.H., 'Diaries of Two Tours in the Unadministered Area East of the Naga Hills', *Memoirs of the Asiatic Society of Bengal*, XI,1, 1929.

IWGIA, *Naga Nation*. International Work Group for Indigenous Affairs, *The Naga Nation and its Struggle against Genocide*, Copenhagen, 1986.

Janowski, Chiefship. Janowski, Monica Hughes, 'Chiefship among the Naga of N.E. India,' M. Phil. thesis, Dept. of Social Anthropology, University of Cambridge, 1984.

Joshi, 'Pluralism'. Joshi, Vibha, 'Medical Pluralism and Curative Practices in a Village in Nagaland', University of Delhi, Department of Anthropology, M.Sc. dissertation, 1985-6.

Kirsch, *Feasting*. Kirsch, A. Thomas, *Feasting and Social Oscillation*, Ithaca, 1973.

Leach, Political Systems. Leach, E.R., Political Systems of Highland Burma: A Study of Kachin Social Structure, London 1954.

Lintner, War. Lintner, Bertil, 'War in the North, *Far Eastern Economic Review*, 28 May 1987.

McCulloch, 'Account'. McCulloch, Major W., 'Account of the Valley of Munnipore and of the Hill Tribes', in Selections from the Records of the Government of India, No. 27, Calcutta, 1859.

Maitland, *Report*. Maitland, P.J., *Detailed Report of the Naga Hills Expedition of 1879-80*, Simla, 1880.

Marwah and Srivastava, 'Khel Gate'. Marwah, I.S., and Srivastava, Vinay Kumar, 'Khel Gate and Social Structure: A study of their relationship and a note on the place of material culture in anthropology', *Indian Anthropologist*, 17:2, 1987.

Mills, *Ao*. Mills, J.P., *The Ao Nagas*, London 1926.

Mills, 'Aspects'. Mills, J.P., 'Certain Aspects of Naga Culture', *Journal of the Royal Anthropological Institute*, LVI, 1926.

Mills, 'Effect'. Mills, J.P., 'The Effect on the Tribes of the Naga Hills District of Contacts with Civilization', in *Census 1931*, vol.III, Part 1, Appendix A.

Mills, *Lhota*. Mills, J.P., *The Lhota Nagas*, London, 1922.

Mills, *Papers*. Papers and correspondence of J.P. Mills, Pitt Rivers Museum Archive, Oxford.

Mills, Rengma. *Mills, J.P., The Rengma Nagas*, London 1935.

Mills, *Tour Diary (a)*. Mills, J.P., *Tour Diaries and Administrative Notes from the North Cachar Hills, 1928-40*, Unpublished Government Papers, Pam. Assam B. 314349, Library, School of Oriental and African Studies, London.

Mills, *Tour Diary (b)*. Mills, J.P., *Tour Diary, November – December 1936, Mills Papers*, MS. 144764/5, Library, School of Oriental and African Studies, London.

Mills, *Tour Diary (c)*. Mills, J.P., Deputy Commissioner, Cachar, *Tour Diary, March 1927*, with comments by Ursula Graham Bower (1985), in Hutton, *Papers*.

Moffatt Mills, *Report*. Moffatt Mills, A.J., *Report on the Province of Assam, Gauhati, reprinted 1984 (original, 1853)*.

MRG, India. Minority Rights Group, *India, The Nagas and the North-East*, London, 1980.

Mukherjee et al, 'Zeliangrong Movement'. Mukherjee, D.P., Gipta, P., Das, N.K., 'The Zeliangrong or Haomei Movement', *Tribal Movements in India*, vol.1, K.S. Singh (ed.), New Delhi, 1982.

Nagaland '86. Directorate of Information and Public Relations, Kohima, Nagaland '86.

Needham, 'Skulls'. Needham, Rodney, 'Skulls and Causality', *Man*, 11:1, 1976.

Nehru, *Unity*. Nehru, Jawaharlal, *The Unity of India*, London, 1941.

Owen, 'Notes'. Owen, John, 'Notes on the Naga Tribes, in communication with Assam', in Elwin (ed.), *North-East Frontier (original, 1844)*.

Peal, 'Nagas'. Peal, S.E., 'The Nagas and Neighbouring Tribes', in Elwin (ed.), *Nagas* (original, *Journal of the Anthropological Institute*, 1874).

Rosaldo, *Ilongot*. Rosaldo, Renato, *Ilongot Headhunting 1883-1974, a study in society and history*, Stanford, 1980.

Rustomji, *Frontiers*. Rustomji, Nari, *Imperilled Frontiers: India's North-Eastern Borderlands*, Delhi, 1983.

Sahlins, 'Segmentary Lineage'. Sahlins, Marshall D., 'The Segmentary Lineage: an Organisation of Predatory Expansion', *Comparative Political Systems*, New York 1967 (originally published in *American Anthropologist* 63, 1961).

Scott, *Moral Economy*. Scott, James C., *The Moral Economy of the Peasant: rebellion and subsistence in Southeast Asia*, New Haven, 1976.

Sema, *Emergence*. Sema, Hokishe, *Emergence of Nagaland: Socio-Economic and Political Transformation and the Future*, New Delhi, 1986.

Singh, *Earth*. Singh, Malika, *The Earth and the Sky*, typescript, n.d. (1987).

Sollheim, 'Reworking'. Sollheim II, W.G., 'Reworking South East Asian Prehistory', *Social Science Research Institute Reprint no. 34*, University of Hawaii, 1970.

Stevenson, *Economics*. Stevenson, H.N.C., *The Economics of the Central Chin Tribes, Bombay*, 1943.

Stonor, 'Feasts'. Stonor, C.R., 'The Feasts of Merit among the Northern Sangtam Tribe of Assam', *Anthropos*, XLV, 1950.

Thomas, 'Material Culture'. Thomas, Nicholas, 'Material Culture and Colonial Power: ethnological collecting and the establishment of colonial rule in Fiji', *Man* 24,1, 1989.

Vetch, 'Visit'. Vetch, Capt., 'Report of a Visit by Captain Vetch to the Singpho and Naga Frontier of Luckhimpore, 1842', in *Selection of Papers regarding the Hill Tracts between Assam and Burmah, and on the Upper Brahmaputra*, Calcutta, 1873.

Waromung. *Census of India 1961, Vol.I, Monograph Series, part VI, Waromung, An Ao Naga Village*, New Delhi, n.d.

West, 'Costume'. West, Andrew, 'Costume and Status among the Nagas', M.A. Thesis, University of Hull, 1984.

Woodthorpe, 'Notes'. Woodthorpe, Lt.-Col. R.G., 'Notes on the Wild Tribes Inhabiting the So-Called Naga Hills, on our North East Frontier of India', in Elwin (ed.), *Nineteenth Century* (originally in *Journal of the Anthropological Institute*, XI, 1881).

Woodthorpe, *Survey*. Woodthorpe, Lt. R.G., *Report on the Survey Operations in the Naga Hills*, 1875-76, Shillong, 1876.

Yonuo, *Rising Nagas*. Yonuo, A., *The Rising Nagas*, Delhi, 1974.